Mumbai Modern

Mumbai Modern

Vegetarian Recipes Inspired by
Indian Roots and California Cuisine

Amisha Dodhia Gurbani

The Countryman Press
A Division of W. W. Norton & Company
Independent Publishers Since 1923

All photography by the author except for the photographs by Iain Bagwell Photography on
pages 2, 26, 32, 36, 40, 43, 44, 47, 50, 53, 54, 57, 65, 69, 80, 95, 98, 104, 108, 113, 117, 120, 129,
136, 140, 143, 149, 152, 178, 182, 188, 193, 202, 209, 212, 218, 226, 228, 233, 252, 271, 280, 283,
288, 314, 318, 326, 334, 349, 352, 358, 364, 367, 368, 371, 377, 378, 381, and 388.

Decorative Frames © iStock/hpkalyani on pages 30, 62, 114, 176, 238, 310, and 340.

For information about permission to reproduce selections from this book, write to
Permissions, The Countryman Press, 500 Fifth Avenue, New York, NY 10110

 For information about special discounts for bulk purchases, please contact
W. W. Norton Special Sales at specialsales@wwnorton.com or 800-233-4830

Manufacturing by TC Transcontinental
Book design by Allison Chi
Production manager: Devon Zahn

The Countryman Press
www.countrymanpress.com

A division of W. W. Norton & Company, Inc.
500 Fifth Avenue, New York, NY 10110
www.wwnorton.com

978-1-68268-628-7

10 9 8 7 6 5 4 3 2 1

To my mum,
who I always aspired to be,
I miss you and I love you.

To my dad,
for always believing in me and supporting my
dreams,
I love you.

To my dearest husband, Raj, and my kids,
Anishka and Rishan,
for being my biggest fans and for bearing with
the angry baker,
I love you forever and for always.

Contents

CHAPTER 7

Accompaniments and Snacks

Introduction

Food Is Memory, Food Is Communication, Food Is Love

My mum's family, from the United Kingdom, was sharing stories and memories while gathered at my home in Mumbai to cook my mum's favorite meal, undhiyoo.

It is a dish made with winter vegetables like sweet potatoes, potatoes, and eggplant, as well as flat beans, fried fenugreek dumplings, and raw bananas, all cooked in a green paste made with cilantro, green garlic, coconut, green chili, sugar, and salt. It is a feast of the senses, with sweet, salty, sour, tangy, and spicy flavors all in one bite. We ate it with hot puri and shrikhand, a sweetened strained yogurt with saffron, cardamom, pistachios, and almonds.

As we ate this meal together, I was reminded of why we were really gathered here. The food, laughter, and tears were for my mother. She had just passed away. And this meal tasted as if my mum had made it. Tears flooded my eyes as a lifetime of memories, triggered by this food, rushed to my head and heart. Fourteen years ago, I had no way of knowing this was just the start of my food journey.

I am a computer engineer by profession, a mother of two, and a recipe developer and food photographer for my blog, *Jam Lab*. I love sharing Indian flavors I have learned from my mother, my grandmother, and my Gujarati roots.

Indian Food, Gujarati Food, and Its Influence

India is a huge country, consisting of 28 states and eight union territories with a population of 1.3 billion people. Every region of India has its own culture, traditions, and religion that may influence the type of cuisine from that region, and there are more than 30 different types. Neighboring states influence each other with their foods. For example, Maharashtra and Gujarat border each other, so there are some common foods between them, such as vada pav, patra, and bhakri, with similar ingredients and spice levels as well.

Indian food dates back to the Indus Valley Civilization, roughly 2600 to 1700 BC. During archeological excavations, remains of pots, pans, and tawas (an Indian flat pan) were found, which indicated the preparation of grains and rotli (Indian flatbreads). Later, different vegetables, breads, dairy, and spices were introduced that made the food as flavorful as possible. More emphasis on lentils led to the creation of daal, flavored with spices. There are a variety of lentils consumed throughout the country, and each region prepares them with its own signature style.

Gujarat, the state where my grandparents hail from, has influenced my style of cooking. Located on the western coast of India, Gujarat opens to the Arabian Sea and has many major ports, which made it accessible to voyagers over the centuries. Rulers of many kinds, including Mauryan, Muslim, Rajput, or Maratha, have all invaded Gujarat at some point in its history. When the Parsis came over from Persia, they adopted Gujarat's culture, language, and food. Jainism is one of the major religions, and its vegetarian influence is important in Gujarati cuisine as well. Within different regions of Gujarat, the weather spans from cold winters to very hot and humid summers, which explains the variety of many cooking styles and dishes within the state. There are distinct flavors within the regions of Kutch, Kathiawar, Ahmedabad, Surat, and more. People in arid regions incorporate more lentils and potatoes into their dishes while more greens are used in the southern and western parts of Gujarat.

In the hot weather, when temperatures may reach 45°C (113°F), yogurt-based drinks such as mithi (sweet) or kathi (sour/savory) chaas (buttermilk) or shrikhand (sweetened yogurt), flavored with cardamom, saffron, and nuts, as well as tomatoes, lemons, salt, and sugar, help to prevent dehydration. In the cold weather, when temperatures may reach 5 to 10°C (40 to 50°F), Gujaratis tend to eat heavier foods to stay warm: jaggery, whole wheat flour, millet flour, and winter vegetables like yams, sweet potatoes, and bitter melon. Undhiyoo (page 184), Daal Dhokli (page 195), and Bharela Ringan Nu Shaak (page 225) are commonly consumed in the winter months.

The preparation of Gujarati food is mostly vegan. The vegetables are usually stir-fried, and the lentils boiled. Then a vaghar, or tempering, is done, with oil or ghee, along with whole spices, fresh/dried chilis, and fresh aromatics, which are poured into the boiled daal. Gujarati food provides for a well-balanced, healthy diet that is rich in nutrition and conducive to the farmland workers in Gujarat.

The food is popular in India, even outside the state of Gujarat, and the worldwide as well! Sweet, spicy, salty, sour, and bitter all combine to give the perfect harmony of flavors and textures in the different dishes that make up a Gujarati thali. The thali consists of a minimum of five to six dishes, but it can contain more as desired. It has daal (lentils), bhaat (rice or pulao), rotli or bhakri (some form of non-leavened bread), shaak or shaaks (one or more vegetables), farsan (snack such as dhokla), mithai (some form of sweet dish), and condiments such as chutneys, pickle, and papad. Gujarati thali will please everyone, and it is the perfect welcome for any guest that comes to your home. Thali were typically prepared on special occasions by my mum, and there was always so much love, attention to detail, and thought put into it. Thali makes for a meal to remember.

History, Traditions, and Upbringing

History makes us who we are; history builds us. The origins of our families, their upbringing, and what they go through in life shape them and make them who they are, and, in turn, those stories shape us as humans, as people.

My maternal grandparents grew up in Jamnagar, which is part of the Kathiawar area of Gujarat. In 1948, my grandfather married my grandmother, who was 16 at the time, and they left immediately by boat for Kampala in Uganda, Africa, to start a business there.

Due to the expulsion of Indians from Uganda, the whole family fled in the late 1960s to Bombay, now Mumbai. The family settled in Juhu Scheme. After my grandfather (Bapuji) died of a heart attack in 1971, the responsibilities of holding up the family fell to my mother. She had to become a responsible mother figure to her brothers and sisters. She studied home science in college, and

learned a lot of things that she in turn taught me as a kid.

Her knowledge, not only about Indian food but also about Western culture, was vast. She knew how to make shrubs, ketchups, and jams. She also knew how to make all sorts of desserts popular in the 1970s, such as soufflés, cakes, biscuits, puddings, and trifles.

My parents were married in 1975. My mum started her family in Mumbai while her mother and siblings moved to the United Kingdom, where they settled into their lives.

My paternal grandparents were from a small village near Jamnagar called Dhichda. They grew up in the 1930s and moved to Mumbai in 1944. My grandfather was a farmer in his village for a brief period when he was 13. He moved to Mumbai to start his own business, which he gradually developed and took to new heights.

My dad was born in the year of the Indian independence: 1947. He started working with his dad in the business at a young age. He had very low moments in his career. But with his determination, focus, perseverance, and desire to grow and succeed, he also started his own business and grew to the next level.

My mum was a housewife, helping my brother and me with school and homework and making meals—breakfast, lunch, snacks, and finally dinner—every single day of our lives together. In the early days, she held down the fort. We were dependent on her for everything. She was one of those mum bears—protective of her cubs! She was ready to claw anyone who hurt us and lift us up when we fell down.

I came along a couple years after my parents were married. Mumbai is my home city, but you could say I was brought up in the kitchen. One of my earliest memories is holding the end of my mother's saree while watching her cook for the family in the wee hours of the morning. Each day was filled with the sights and smells of home cooking. Mum would wake up at 7 a.m. and start us off with fresh breakfast before we headed out to school.

Lunch was prepped and ready by 10 a.m., and we would get hot lunches at school via the dabbawallas of Mumbai. There would be a homemade snack waiting for us at 4 p.m. With all this eating, did I ever do homework?!

At the young age of 10, I learned how to make a full thali meal. Mum taught me how to roll the rotli. She would always leave a bit of dough every day for me to roll, and perfect the roundness of my rotli. There was flour mess everywhere, but isn't that normal? Whatever the shape, she would still eat it.

She would show me how to make shaaks, or stir-fried masala vegetables. "Put a little bit of the cumin powder, then a little bit of the coriander, then a little bit of the turmeric and red chili powder, and finally a pinch of the garam masala." There were NO measurements whatsoever; it was a taste-and-go, put-more-spices-if-required kind of learning. Everything was an approximation. That is how cooking was taught and passed down generation after generation, and there is really nothing like a simple home-cooked meal made lovingly by grandmothers and mothers.

A visit to the vegetable market every second or third day was the norm. There were no supermarkets back then, where you fill up your carts to the top for the entire week, like here in the United States. I would go with Mum to Vile Parle or Santa Cruz in the rickshaw. She would teach me how to pick the freshest of vegetables and fruits, and what to look for when you are picking them: the color, the smell, the touch. We were lucky to be able to get fresh produce at our beck and call when we needed it. It was our farmers' market, but it was at our disposal on a daily basis. We ate seasonally: lighter vegetables and daals in the summer, and the heartier vegetables that comprise undhiyoo, eggplant, bitter melon, and more in the winter. The Gujarati way of eating is based on Ayurveda, and there is a science to why a certain food is eaten, and which season it is eaten in. It is quite fascinating, if you dig deeper into it.

Mum did not only make Gujarati food for us. There was all sorts of variety because of her curiosity and eagerness to try different cuisines. She loved making North Indian dishes on special occasions, meals that are richer and curry-based called Mughlai food. South Indian food was her favorite—foods such as idlis, dosas, and bisi bele bhath were regulars at home. Apparently, she consumed a lot of South Indian food when she was pregnant with me. She had major food cravings and my dad would indulge her by taking her to street vendors that served South Indian food, which may explain why I love South Indian food! She also loved exploring Western cuisines, and would make pastas, burgers, and pizzas.

Mum was the most generous, kindhearted soul, full of life, and her love and passion for food that knew no bounds. She showed her love for people by feeding them! She was very humble, even as everyone called her a super cook. She could whip up meals for our birthday parties or parties with our friends and family, entertaining crowds of 40 to 50 people. Feeding people filled her heart and soul, and that helped grow her passion and curiosity for creating new, delicious meals. My friends would come over and ask her to prepare their favorite things, and she would oblige with a smile on her face. All she wanted in return was people telling her how good her food was, and there was never a dearth of compliments, because everyone left satisfied, with their hearts and bellies full.

Mumbai Street Food

Our favorite food that Mum would prepare, though, was Mumbai street food. Mumbai street food is a love letter to street food. If you walk on any street in Mumbai, you will run into a food vendor in every nook and corner serving fast food.

Street food has a medley of flavors—sweet, spicy, salty, and sour. People stand by the vendors in the hot and humid weather and patiently wait for their plates to be ready. They eat their chatpata (lip-smacking) dishes, wiping the sweat off their foreheads from the spicy foods and the sweltering heat of cosmopolitan Mumbai.

Mumbai has the best pav bhaji, and nothing really can beat it. I have tried my best to bring that here via my recipe in the Mains section. Mumbai chaats such as bhel puri, pani puri, Dahi Papdi Chaat (page 161), vada pav, and Grilled Bombay Sandwich (page 151) are a few of my favorite things! It is really amazing to watch the street food vendors and consider how many people they serve on a daily basis. This is their bread and butter, and they depend upon school and college students, office workers, and shoppers to come by and grab a snack before heading to their next destination. In fact, my dad arranged for a street food vendor to come to our home for my first birthday. The guy is still there on the streets of Khar, and has been running his business for more than 50 years. My parents had invited around 50 people to my first birthday party, and the guy catered to all of them, making as many dishes as they wanted to eat. It was a chaat bonanza! Definitely something I want to indulge in.

On one winter vacation when I was 10, I picked up a cookbook by Tarla Dalal (India's most famous Gujarati chef) and selected a recipe for each day. I made 10 recipes in 10 days, without my mum's help. I had failures, I cried, and I was upset when things did not turn out well. But there were triumphs too, which I was so happy about! It was a great first experience with trying to cook on my own, following recipes from a cookbook. Little did I know that this would lead to writing my own cookbook one day!

My mum's sisters or masis, Ranju and Chandan, along with my ba (maternal grandmother) have played a huge role in shaping my food journey and my interest in food. We always talked about foods and preparations; it was, and still is, a central topic of conversation during our gatherings, when we would visit the United Kingdom or they would visit us in Mumbai. Our picnics and outings are not complete without taking dabbas and dabbas of foods and a huge thermos of masala chai.

Coming to America

In 1999, with just two bags full of my belongings, I embarked on an 8,000-mile journey to Los Angeles. I was to attend the University of Southern California to work on my master's degree in computer science.

Leaving home was scary and exciting! At 22, I was happy to be on my own, fend for myself, and experience life outside my bubble of a home on Juhu Tara Road. I migrated to Los Angeles without any intention of coming back to Mumbai.

I wanted to make my own money and live by myself, just as my dad had done in his heyday. I was ready to accept the challenge. It was no piece of cake to live in a different country, with very few people I knew nearby, with neither family nor a car, going to classes and doing chores and cooking food by myself. Luckily my mum had taught me well, and trained me for the unexpected. She had given me all her basic recipes, handwritten very neatly in both a book and on pieces of paper, which I still have with me. The notes have so many stains on them! My mother packed the quintessential masala dabba along with a bunch of spices and lentils to start off with in a new country. I cooked for myself, my roommates, and for all my new friends. I made my non-Indian friends try Gujarati food— they enjoyed it and wanted more!

After two years of arduous work, I graduated from my master's program and started working at a tech company in the Bay Area.

My mum was diagnosed with stage three colon cancer in 2005. After surgery, she went through radiation and chemotherapy and was on lots of medication. She recovered and went through remission, but it recurred. In that same period, she had two bone fractures from two falls within a period of six months. It was a really tough time for our family as a whole, and, on a personal level, it was a lot to deal with, being so far away from home.

I made several trips to India to see her and take care of her. She finally passed away in January 2007 from a stroke. Her family from the United Kingdom—her mum and siblings—came to India to pay their respects to her. One never knows what will become a defining moment in one's life. It brought together families from three continents to cook her favorite meal—undhiyoo. We shared stories, ate, and, of course, many tears were shed. It was the day I promised her, looking into the sky, that I would write her the cookbook you are holding now, to pass down her legacy and all that she has taught me. She was the most important person in my life, and as a tribute to her, this book keeps her and her love for food in our hearts forever.

Birth of Jam Lab

We are lucky to live in Northern California, with its vast farmlands and our year-round access to fresh produce. These seasonal vegetables and fruits have become my way of life.

After I had my daughter, and with my intent of providing her with fresh seasonal meals on a daily basis, I started visiting the farmers' market religiously every Sunday. It was my ritual, my Zen moment, my me time to be able to visualize, feel, and taste the produce at the market. "Eat seasonally, eat reasonably" became my motto. I rarely get things out of season beyond the occasional tomatoes because we require them in curries or shaaks. I cannot stress enough the importance of eating in season, though, especially since produce is at its most nutrient-rich at seasonal peak.

Once I had my babies, 22 months apart, I pre-pared fresh vegetable and fruit purees at home for every meal during their baby and toddler years. I can count on my fingers the number of prepackaged bottled foods they must have had—if I cannot eat them, I imagine how bad they must taste for the babies! I would spice the purees with cinnamon, nutmeg, cumin, coriander, and turmeric, depending upon the food that they were eating. All these spices are good for you and have medicinal benefits, so why not give them to my kids in moderation? They were both good eaters as babies and toddlers. At some point around 2 years old, they started eating what we ate, so there were no separate foods being prepared for them, which was a big relief!

Flash forward to my daughter starting preschool, followed by my son two years later. For lunch, we started with the obvious, PB&J. But the available jams were dense and too sweet. I decided to make my own from scratch. Channeling my mother's lessons, I made jams with different spices, herbs, and flavor combinations. That is how my Instagram account was born. My kitchen became a home for experimentation. I created flavors like orange and cardamom marmalade and peach and ginger jam. This was the birth of Jam Lab. I started giving away these batches to friends and family. After receiving positive affirmation, I started selling jams online. My kids and husband are my best taste testers and biggest fans! I ran this business for about two years but, with a full-time job, it was not sustainable to make jams on the side. I stopped selling them.

I started my food blog five years ago as a way to showcase Indian and Gujarati food, along with baking, which has been an integral part of my life. I wanted to have a place where I could store my recipes and share them with my followers. I offered unique flavors, inspired by my heritage and my family. I told stories about my childhood, living in Mumbai at Juhu Beach, because food relates to our background and family and food brings us together in unimaginable ways. I was known by my followers as a "flavor queen," because I would come up with beautiful flavor combinations that would weave together well in my bakes.

Flavor profiles came naturally to me, and became my forte. I started getting a lot of recognition for it, which led to brand partnerships and more acknowledgment in the food space of Instagram. California is the mecca for wine and olive oil companies, so I worked with quite a lot of them for recipe development, food photography, and styling. I worked with renowned food publications like *Sunset*, *Bake from Scratch*, *Wired*, and *Diablo* for my first in-print food articles. It felt good to be recognized for my creative line of work, which I had been pursuing for so long, and to be in a food-related sphere as my side hustle, and be able to express myself through what I loved most—my passion and love for food.

Cooking and baking have been therapeutic for me in all the tough and challenging times I've faced in my adult life and as an immigrant in the United States. It has kept me focused, and given me solace when I needed it the most. I was motivated to cook more traditional foods for my kids because I wanted them to experience the foods I grew up with, which is also part of their culture. Hopefully, they can carry forward the legacy and tradition of the art of cooking Gujarati and Indian food, so that it doesn't become lost in translation.

What to Expect from This Cookbook

I have deep roots in Mumbai, India—the cosmopolitan city that never sleeps, the city that I was born and raised in. This book is about my origins in Mumbai, influenced by my mother's upbringing first in Kampala, Uganda, and then in Mumbai. It is my tribute to my dear mother. It is about my immigrant life and adaptation to life in California, while bringing tradition and culture and keeping them alive for my American-Indian kids, the next generation. This cookbook brings recipes together from three continents—my mother's family in the United Kingdom, from whom I have constantly requested recipes and who have helped me with cooking and baking questions, especially after my mother passed; my upbringing in Mumbai; and my move to California.

This cookbook is a reflection of what I make for my family on a daily basis, the recipes they enjoy cooking and eating with me in our kitchen. The recipes are family-style meals, but can also be made for a party or gathering of 4 to 6 or even 10 to 12, depending upon the recipe. I always make

California produce all around me. It's a journey of Indian cuisine infused with the best kind of Californian flair.

Cooking is a joy, and it is a slow process. It is an experience: The prepping, chopping, tempering, smells, and colors awaken our senses, and can be therapeutic for the mind and soul. I personally love a long recipe, a recipe with steps, because it gives me a chance to feel the recipe and put love into it, making it a meal to enjoy with my loved ones.

My hope is that you will not be intimidated by Indian spices; that, instead, you will learn to explore and appreciate the art of Gujarati and Indian food, and bring flavor, spices, and color into your homes. That you will not depend upon Indian takeout; rather, you will create simple Indian meals yourself at home and experience the diversity and flavor of Indian cuisine, because the best Indian food is homemade.

How to Use This Cookbook

My goal with this cookbook is to have more of you making Indian food in your homes, and for you to not be intimidated by the numerous spices involved in each recipe. The process for many of the recipes is pretty similar: You temper the spices and then add the main ingredient into the tempering to give it flavor and color. Many of the dishes in this cookbook take less than 30 minutes to make, even with the long list of ingredients.

My main pointers for using this cookbook are:

- Always *mise en place*. Mise en place is a French culinary phrase that means to put everything in its place. Gather up your recipe ingredients first, so that you do not forget anything and can go through all the steps efficiently and methodically.
- **Read the recipe thoroughly** before starting. Make sure you have all the ingredients

big meals, because we enjoy leftovers the next day and it helps ease up cooking for a day. Leftovers also mean I can share with family, friends, and coworkers. I keep deli containers at home so that I can transport the food easily!

This book is produce-heavy and relies on seasonal fruits and vegetables to make the dishes. My kitchen and my dishes thrive with what I get from the farmers' market. My goal is to showcase the Gujarati and Indian food that I grew up with in Mumbai while using the best of the required for the recipe. Understand the process and visualize it in your mind. It will make the process of cooking much easier without missing steps and making mistakes.

- Invest in a masala dabba, or a stainless steel dabba to put your dry spices in. It will help to keep everything in one place for your use. I have at least three masala dabbas, one with spice powders and two with whole spices, that help me with my cooking.

- Chapter One, Pantry and Refrigerator Staples (page 30), has many of the staples that I use throughout the book, such as the Date Tamarind Chutney (page 45) and Cilantro Mint Chutney (page 42). They are used in various recipes in the Appetizers and Mains chapters. The Pear and Chai Masala Jam (page 35) is used to make the Pear and Chai Masala Cinnamon Rolls (page 94). Or use the jam to make the Mini Maple Sandwich Cookies with Pear and Spice Buttercream (page 289) to gift to a loved one.

- The book is intertwined so that every recipe can be used with another in the book. This offers creativity, originality, and endless combinations. Your company will enjoy these fabulous dishes for a long time to come.

- Read the Pro Tips at the end of the recipe. I have tried to include as much helpful information as possible to make the process seamless for you.

- For the Indian leavened and unleavened breads, the whole wheat flour I use is from the Indian grocery store. The way different flours absorb the water may vary. So pay attention to the texture of the dough to ensure you get a successful outcome from the Indian breads.

- Indian spices are readily available in Indian grocery stores. They are also available in the international aisles of the bigger grocery stores, or you can source the Indian spices online.

- I would highly recommend you use the metric system (grams) to weigh all your ingredients for maximum accuracy, because the volume of your cups may vary from the ones I have in my home. Weighing your ingredients will lead to a more consistent result every time you make a dish. For the smaller measurements, such as teaspoons and tablespoons, weighing is not necessary.

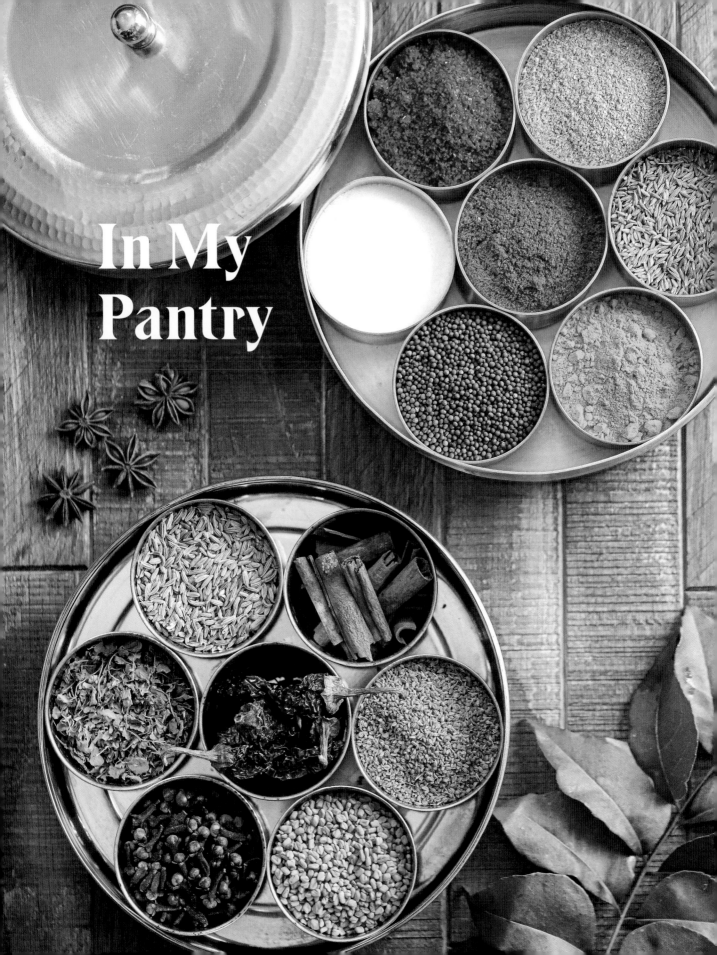

In My
Pantry

In any Indian kitchen, spices are the heart and soul of prepared dishes. For me personally, spices adorn my baked goods as well. Even a simple chocolate chip cookie will have spices, because it makes them extra special.

The quintessential masala dabba is the essence of every Indian Kitchen. Some homes may have one masala dabba, and some may have two or three, to carry the ground spices and whole spices in separate dabbas. Indian food is loved by so many, but people find it intimidating to cook due to the number of ingredients involved in any dish. But it is really not that difficult at all. A little planning and preparation, and you can put together a simple, delicious, home-cooked meal for your family as a weeknight option!

Spices are readily available in all grocery stores. Indian grocery stores carry them in bulk so you can fill up your spice jars. I usually have bulk of the ground and the whole spices in medium-sized jars, and I fill up the masala dabbas as they start to deplete in volume. There is a running joke in my home that my pantry will never run out of any spice, because as soon as I see a bulk jar with only an inch of spice left, I run to the grocery store to fill it up! Spices are available online as well nowadays, and there are many small businesses that carry fair-trade and organic options.

Spices have been used by ancient Indian civilizations for thousands of years. Spices were used for medicinal and healing purposes, and also to preserve food, since there was no refrigeration back then. Because of India's rich soil, climate, heavy rains, and warm weather, these spices grew in abundance. Spices were transported by land initially, until explorers like Vasco da Gama and Christopher Columbus discovered spices in India around 1498, and took the spices back to Europe in bulk for trade. This resulted in the colonization of India by various Europeans such as the Portuguese, Dutch, Spanish, French, and eventually the British, leading to the formation of the British East India Company.

India is one of the largest exporters of spices all around the world. Can you imagine the number of spices generated by farmers in India simply for the sake of export? Spices are good for you, have tons of medicinal benefits, and make food aromatic, tasty, and delicious!

In this chapter, I will highlight the spices that I use throughout the book and some of their benefits and uses that I learned from my grandmother and my mother.

Ground Spices

AMCHUR (DRIED MANGO POWDER): Amchur is dried mango powder. Green mangoes are dried and a powder is made out of them. It has an amazingly tangy and sour taste, which is characteristic of chaat masala—amchur is one of the ingredients in chaat masala. Amchur can be sprinkled over fruits or used in cooked dishes. It has amazing benefits and vitamins such as A, E, and C; is an antioxidant; and aids digestion as well.

ASAFOETIDA: Asafoetida is the dried sap of certain plants in the genus *Ferula*. It is ground into a powder, and a pinch is enough during the tempering phase. It has a strong, pungent smell and flavor as is, but when cooked, it mellows out and boosts the flavor of the dish. It relieves gas and indigestion, and has antibacterial properties as well.

BLACK SALT: Black salt is a type of Himalayan salt that is actually light pink in powder form. It has a sulfurous taste to it. It is used in chaats for a different kind of salty taste. You can find it in my Masala Chaas recipe (page 335). It is all right in trace amounts, but not more than that. It helps aid digestion.

CARDAMOM (GROUND): Cardamom originates from the seeds of wild plants that grow in the ghats of South India. At 4,000 years old (at least), cardamom is one of the oldest spices. There are two types of cardamom: green cardamom (popular for baking and cooking), and black cardamom (typically used to make northern Indian dishes and removed before serving). The fragrant smell of cardamom is soothing and intoxicating. It provides floral notes to savory or sweet dishes, or even wine or any kind of beverage. Cardamom has antibacterial properties, helps relieve asthma, and is a great mouth freshener as well.

CHAAT MASALA: Chaat masala is an essential spice in my pantry. I love using it to flavor fruits, chaats (street foods), and simply adding it to plain yogurt to jazz it up. Chaat masala is basically roasted and ground cumin, coriander, black pepper, and other spices such as amchur, black salt, ground ginger, and asafoetida. I get chaat masala from the Indian grocery store but it is available online as well.

CHAI MASALA: Chai masala is another essential spice in my pantry. I start my morning with Aadhu Masala Chai (page 315), which has my homemade chai masala in it. Chai masala is essentially ground-up whole cinnamon, cardamom, cloves, black pepper, fennel seeds, and dried ginger. See page 41 for the recipe.

CHIPOTLE POWDER: Chipotle powder is ground-up dried chipotle chilis typically grown in Mexico. I use quite a bit in my weekly cooking, and love its smoky, deep flavors in our food. Its beautiful maroon hue provides great color to roasted vegetables as well. A natural anti-inflammatory, it has amazing properties that aid digestion, manage insulin levels, help the respiratory system, and help reduce mucus.

CINNAMON (GROUND): Cinnamon is the dried inner bark of a particular kind of tree. It is largely produced in Sri Lanka and South India. It has a very aromatic fragrance and goes beautifully in savory as well as baked goods. The ground variety is typically used for baking. There are two kinds of cinnamon: Ceylon (more expensive and better) and cassia (commonly found in stores). Cinnamon contains large amounts of highly potent polyphenol antioxidants. It has high anti-inflammatory properties, and also helps fight fungal and bacterial infections.

CLOVES (GROUND): Clove spice is the dried flower bud of a tropical evergreen tree. The black little bud has a very strong, pungent aroma, in a good way. The spice is used in savory dishes and its ground form is used in baked goods. Recipes require only a very small amount because of its pungent taste. Among its many health benefits, it aids in oral health and has antibacterial properties.

CORIANDER (GROUND): Ground coriander is ground-up coriander seeds. Coriander seeds are seeds of the cilantro plant. The seeds are round and brown in color. They smell citrusy, woodsy, and very fragrant. Ground coriander is one of the essential spices of the masala dabba and used in many Indian dishes. Coriander may help to reduce cholesterol, has antibacterial properties, and is good for skin.

CUMIN (GROUND): Ground cumin is ground-up cumin seeds. Cumin seeds are actually dried fruit/seeds of a plant in the carrot family. The seeds are small, brown, and elongated in shape, with an earthy aroma and taste. The fragrance of freshly ground cumin is intoxicating. One of the essential spices of the masala dabba, ground cumin is used in many Indian dishes. Cumin promotes digestion, is very dense in iron, and fights inflammation, to name only a few of its virtues.

GARAM MASALA: Garam masala is another essential spice in the masala dabba that is used extensively in Indian cooking. It contains roasted and ground whole cumin, coriander, cardamom, nutmeg, black pepper, cinnamon, and cloves. Each Indian home has their own recipe. I get garam masala from the Indian grocery store, but it is available online as well.

GARLIC POWDER: Garlic powder is ground-up dried garlic and is used in my home in various dishes, especially in roasted vegetables. It makes them very flavorful. Garlic helps to prevent common colds and flu, and aids in reducing cholesterol and heart diseases as well.

GINGER (GROUND): Gingerroot is the edible rhizome of the ginger plant. This pungent and aromatic root is dried and ground to create ground ginger. Ginger is one of my favorite spices, and I start off my day by including freshly grated ginger in my Aadhu (ginger) Masala Chai (page 315). Ground ginger is mainly used for baking and gives a wonderful flavor and taste to the final product. Ginger has powerful medicinal properties, such as helping with sore throats and common colds, anti-inflammatory issues, nausea, and indigestion.

MASALA MILK MASALA: Masala milk masala is a nut and spice mix that is always in my pantry. It is a ground mixture of almonds, cashews, pistachios, cardamom, nutmeg, and saffron. It is used to make masala doodh, a very warming, cozy drink that my mother used to make for us as kids as a dessert drink. Each home has their own recipe. And it is very easy to make; see page 52. You can create your own desserts with this very potent and fragrant masala.

PAV BHAJI MASALA: Pav bhaji masala is a spice mix that I will always have on hand. It is used to make only one dish—the quintessential Pav Bhaji Sliders (page 189). This dish is really easy to make, so I use this spice mix quite often! The spice mix is made of roasted and ground-up whole cumin, coriander, black cardamom, black pepper, cinnamon, cloves, fennel seeds, dried red chilis, amchur, and turmeric powder. I usually purchase mine from Indian grocery stores, but it is also available online.

RED CHILI POWDER/KASHMIRI RED CHILI POWDER: Spicy dried red chilis from a flowering plant are ground up to form the *lal mirch*, or red chili powder, used in Indian cooking. It is an essential spice of the masala dabba and used in most Indian dishes. Kashmiri red chili powder is ground from a milder dried chili indigenous to the Kashmir region of India. The aromatic dried powder gives a beautiful bright red color to any dish. Red chili powder can help with decongestion, has anti-inflammatory properties, promotes digestive heath, and so much more.

SMOKED PAPRIKA: Smoked paprika is ground-up dried sweet peppers from Mexico. I use it to roast vegetables, which gives the dish a wonderfully sweet aroma without the heat. Paprika imparts a lot of flavor and color to the dish as well. It has tons of benefits, including vitamins and minerals like vitamins A, E, B$_6$, iron, and more. It also helps to reduce cholesterol and aids digestion.

THANDAI MASALA: Thandai masala is perhaps one of my favorite spice mixes, and I always have it in my pantry. Although it consists of more than ten spices, it is very easy to make; see page 38. It is a matter of simply gathering up the ingredients and grinding them in a high-speed blender or spice grinder. The masala is very potent, and makes for some of the best Thandai Shortbread Cookies (page 248)—they make perfect gifts for family and friends! Thandai masala consists of ground-up almonds, pistachios, cashews, cardamom, cinnamon, cloves, nutmeg, saffron, fennel seeds, poppy seeds, edible dried rose petals, black pepper, and star anise.

TURMERIC (GROUND): Turmeric dates back 4,000 years to the Vedic period of India. It was used as medicine as well as for religious purposes. Turmeric is the root of a plant in the ginger family. Orange in color, when dried and ground up, it turns a vibrant yellow associated with turmeric powder. It has an earthy, bitter taste that is slightly peppery. It has become very popular in recent years. Turmeric powder is an essential spice in the masala dabba and is used extensively in Indian cooking. The benefits of turmeric are numerous.

It has antiseptic, anti-inflammatory, and antibacterial properties. To gain the full benefits of this spice, it must be consumed with black pepper. It is used for skin care as well.

Whole Spices

BAY LEAVES: Bay leaves come from the laurel plant and are used in a dried form in Indian cooking. They have an aromatic and sort of minty flavor and are used simply to flavor Indian food, especially biryanis and curries. They are removed from the dish before serving.

CAROM SEEDS: Called ajmo in Gujarati, carom seeds are actually the fruits of an herb. They are smaller than cumin seeds and extremely potent, slightly bitter, and pungent in flavor and smell. They are used in the tempering phase of Indian cooking and are an essential part of my masala dabba. Carom seeds have antibacterial and anti-inflammatory properties. They aid digestion as well, and are especially used in foods that involve frying in order to prevent bloating and gas.

CINNAMON: Whole cinnamon is an essential part of my masala dabba. It is usually used during the tempering phase of Indian cooking to enhance the flavors. Refer to Cinnamon (Ground) on page 22 for more information.

CLOVES: Whole cloves are an essential part of my masala dabba. They are usually used during the tempering phase of Indian cooking to enhance the flavors. Refer to Cloves (Ground) on page 22 for more information.

CORIANDER SEEDS: Refer to Coriander (Ground) on page 22 for more information.

CUMIN SEEDS: Cumin seeds are an essential part of my masala dabba. Refer to Cumin (Ground) on page 22 for more information.

CURRY LEAVES: Curry leaves are aromatic and citrusy in flavor. They are used extensively in Indian cooking, especially at the tempering stage. They give dishes beautiful flavor. The Fried Curry Leaf and Toasted Cumin Aioli (page 370) is one of my favorites!

FENNEL SEEDS: Fennel seeds are derived from the fennel plant. They are in the white and yellow flowers of the plant. They have a mild licorice flavor and are pleasant to chew as is (part of the Indian culture). They are used in savory as well as sweet dishes to flavor the food. Fennel seeds have a myriad of health benefits. They are rich in antioxidants, aid in improving heart health, and are used extensively as a mouth freshener.

FENUGREEK (DRIED): Dried fenugreek is very potent. I always have dried fenugreek in my pantry. It is used as a finishing touch to any curry and to balance out the sweet, spicy flavors with a bit of the bitterness from the fenugreek.

FENUGREEK SEEDS: Fenugreek seeds are brown, tiny, rectangular seeds derived from the pods on the fenugreek plant's white flowers. They are an essential part of my masala dabba. They are used in the tempering phase of Indian cooking. The seeds have numerous benefits that cannot be stressed enough, though they are bitter in taste. They are very effective for lactating mothers, help to reduce cholesterol and diabetes, and have anti-inflammatory properties as well.

GREEN CARDAMOM PODS: Green cardamom pods are an essential part of my masala dabba. Refer to Cardamom (Ground) on page 22 for more information.

JAGGERY: Jaggery is the raw, unrefined part of sugar, made from sugarcane. It has a caramelly, molasses-like flavor. On one of our several vacations to the state of Punjab when I was a teenager, I had the pleasure of witnessing how jaggery is made. There is nothing like freshly made jaggery. It is an essential part of my pantry. Jaggery is sold in blocks at Indian grocery stores and has more nutrients than refined sugar.

MUSTARD SEEDS: Mustard seeds are little round brown or black balls that are an essential part of my masala dabba. The seeds are harvested from the mustard plant. I usually use the black mustard seed variety in my cooking. They are pungent and strong in flavor and used typically at the tempering phase of any Indian dish. Mustard seeds are a rich source for omega-3 fatty acids and an excellent source of zinc, magnesium, and various vitamins. Mustard oil is used in Indian cooking to give good flavor. It is also used for massages and for hair and skin care.

NUTMEG: Nutmeg is a walnut-sized, ball-shaped spice from the seed of an evergreen tropical tree. It can be used for sweet and savory dishes. The ground form is available at grocery stores, but I prefer to have the whole spice and I grate it using a microplane for the most potent flavor. It has a warm, nutty, aromatic flavor. You will always find whole nutmeg in my pantry. It is an antioxidant, aids heart health, helps to improve the mood, and more.

NIGELLA SEEDS: Nigella seeds are tiny, black, oval-shaped seeds from a flowering plant. They give Indian breads like naan and kulcha that extra level of flavor. They have health benefits such as antioxidants and anti-inflammatory properties, to name a few.

SAFFRON: Saffron consists of the dried stigmas and styles of the saffron crocus. It is very labor intensive to harvest, which explains its hefty price tag. Because it is so potent, a little goes a long way. It is used in sweet and savory dishes, and is an essential part of my pantry. Saffron has several benefits. It is a mood booster, powerful antioxidant, and reduces PMS symptoms.

STAR ANISE: Star anise is the dried fruit of an evergreen tree. It has a sweet licorice flavor and is used in sweet and savory dishes. It is an essential part of my masala dabba. It is shaped like a star, and looks woodsy and very pretty. It has good health benefits, including anti-fungal and anti-bacterial properties.

WHOLE DRIED RED CHILIS: Whole dried red chilis are an essential part of my masala dabba. Refer to Red Chili Powder/Kashmiri Red Chili Powder on page 23 for more information.

Aromatics/Alliums

Garlic

Gingerroot

Green chili

Green garlic

Onion

Flours

ALL-PURPOSE FLOUR: All-purpose flour is a refined wheat flour, where the wheat germ and bran have been stripped off along with all the nutrients. The protein content in all-purpose flour is between 9 percent and 11 percent, which explains why it makes for good gluten formation in baked goods. It is definitely a more stable flour than its whole wheat counterpart. I use this flour for almost all my bakes, as well as for naan and kulcha.

ALMOND FLOUR: Almond flour is ground-up almonds. The almonds are initially blanched to remove the skins, then dried and ground into almond flour, which is nutty and has a fine texture. I love using almond flour in my baked goods, as it gives a wonderful chew to the end product. My Chai Masala, Macadamia Nut, and White Chocolate Banana Bread (page 103) and Peacock Macarons (page 291) contain almond flour. It is one of my favorite flours!

Whole Moong Daal (Green Gram)

Channa Daal (Split Bengal Grams)

Tuvar Daal (Pigeon Pea Daal)

Safed Vatana (White Peas)

Split Moong Daal (Split Green Gram)

Urad Daal (Split Black Daal with Skin)

Dalia (Roasted Bengal Daal)

BREAD FLOUR: Bread flour has a higher protein content than all-purpose flour at 13 percent, giving baked goods a chewier texture. This flour is ideal for baking breads and for achieving a chewy texture in cookies as well. My Chocolate Chip and Toasted Almond Cookies (page 279) use bread flour.

CHICKPEA FLOUR: Chickpea flour, called channa no loat in Gujarati, is finely ground split channa daal or chickpeas. This is a dense, earthy, gluten-free flour, and although it cannot really be used for baking, it is a great coating for frying vegetables, which gives them a crispy texture. It has a high protein content, and is nutritious and good for you. While it can lead to bloating and gas, it is always mixed with a bit of carom seeds, or ajwain, to eliminate the bloating. It is always present in any Indian household, and has numerous uses. I have used chickpea flour to make the Vegetable Bhajias (Chickpea and Rice Flour Vegetable Fritters, page 123), also known as pakoras, which turns out really delicious!

OAT FLOUR: Oat flour has been my latest obsession. Oat flour is a grain flour made from ground oats. It gives a wonderful nutty texture and flavor to the final product. I love adding oat flour to my Banana, Walnut, and Chocolate Chip Pancakes (page 97).

RICE FLOUR: Rice flour is made from finely ground rice. The texture is very fine and it gives a good crispy layer to fried foods: only a small amount is required, along with the chickpea flour, to give the perfect crunch to fried foods.

SEMOLINA: Semolina, called sooji in Gujarati, is a flour made from durum wheat. It has a coarse texture and can be yellow or off-white in color. Semolina is used a lot in Indian cooking. Handvo (Savory Rice-Lentil Vegetable Cake, page 166) and Sooji Dhokla (Semolina Savory Spongy Cakes, page 85) are two recipes that contain semolina flour. Semolina also gives the final product a grainy texture as well, making it light and delicious.

WHOLE WHEAT FLOUR: Whole wheat flour, called atta or loat in Gujarati, is essentially ground whole wheat. The texture of this flour is slightly coarser than all-purpose flour due to the wheat germ and bran still being intact. Whole wheat flour has more fiber than all-purpose flour, so it is more nutritious than its counterpart. The color is slightly browner as well. This flour is used for making all the unleavened breads of India, such as rotli, paratha, puri, and more. It is readily available at Indian grocery stores.

Lentils

Channa daal (split bengal grams)
Dalia (roasted bengal daal)
Kala channa daal (brown chickpeas)
Safed vatana (white peas)
Split moong daal (split green gram)
Tuvar daal (pigeon pea daal)
Urad daal (split black lentil with or without skin)
Whole moong daal (green gram)

Equipment/Kitchen Tools

BENCH SCRAPER: My bench scraper is one of my most inexpensive tools that is also one of the most under-appreciated tools in the kitchen. I have used it pretty much every single day in the kitchen since I bought it many years ago. It is really convenient for transferring the chopped vegetables from the cutting board into the pot. It also collects any juices from the chopping board to the pot.

DUTCH OVEN: If you are making any main dishes in a large quantity, I find a Dutch oven very useful. The cast-iron material cooks the food evenly and there is room enough to move the vegetables around, all but ensuring uniform cooking.

FOOD PROCESSOR: I got this appliance years ago, and it has been with me through many cooking adventures. The brand I have is Cuisinart. I have used it to make many tart shells, praline pastes, pesto, and even to chop some vegetables.

HAND BLENDER: I find a hand blender very useful to make a smooth Gujarati Daal (page 179) or to blend any soups into a smooth texture. It saves time, since it is light and easy to store rather than the bulkier Vitamix for the same use.

HIGH-SPEED BLENDER (VITAMIX AND NUTRI-BULLET): High-speed blenders are expensive, but it is an investment worth making. I have used my blender for everything from grinding wet grains to smoothies to making Fajeto (page 208) to grinding spice mixes in bulk and making chutneys in big quantities. The uses are endless. I do love my NutriBullet as well, which is a smaller high-speed blender used for blending small quantities of chutneys or grinding pistachios into a fine powder. It can even be used to grind the spice blends found in Pantry and Refrigerator Staples (page 30). It is light in weight and convenient to store as well.

KITCHEN SCALE: I have been using a kitchen scale for the last three to four years, and I will admit that it has changed my life. When we use measuring cups, the volume of your 1-cup measuring cup may differ from the volume of my 1-cup measuring cup. A kitchen scale in grams and/or pounds helps to avoid this discrepancy, resulting in accurate recipes every single time. It is not as useful to measure smaller quantities such as spices or baking powder and baking soda, but it is much better to use a kitchen scale for bigger measurements. I would highly recommend getting a kitchen scale starting NOW, if you do not already have one.

MINI FOOD PROCESSOR: I find the mini food processor very useful to grind ginger, garlic, and green chili into the coarse paste that I use extensively to make Indian mains. All these aromatics are pungent, and although you can chop them by hand, having a mini food processor helps expedite this process. It is very helpful for making pestos in small quantities as well.

NONSTICK TAWA OR SKILLET: To make good roti, paratha, or thepla (featured in Chapter Seven), it is vital to have a good nonstick tawa, or a medium-sized skillet, to get the best results for these unleavened breads.

OXO HAND GRATER: The OXO hand grater is a tool that I cannot live without. I use it every single day to freshly grate garlic and ginger for dishes. Pre-minced doesn't have half the flavor that freshly grated garlic and ginger do, and grating when needed takes a matter of a few seconds for maximum flavor.

SPICE GRINDER/COFFEE GRINDER: A spice grinder is an inexpensive tool and so useful to grind fresh toasted whole spices and make the food more flavorful. I use it to grind toasted cumin for Dahi Wadas (Lentil Fritters in a Yogurt Sauce; page 133), for example, or to make any of the spice blends in the Pantry Staples chapter.

STAND MIXER: My stand mixer has to be one of my favorite kitchen appliances ever. I got my first one as a wedding gift 16 years ago, and it has been with me through thick and thin. My KitchenAid has made many cookies, and helped celebrate many birthdays with cakes, macarons, pastry fillings, whipped creams, and more. It makes baking a pleasure.

Baking Tools

Baking pan, 9 by 13 inch (23 by 33 cm)
Baking sheets
Cake pans, 8-inch (20 cm) round
Loaf pan
Muffin pan
Parchment paper, set size for baking sheets and cake pans

Pastry bags, 12 and 16 inch (30 and 40 cm)
Pastry brush
Quarter sheet pans
Round piping tip set
Silpat silicone mats, especially for macarons
Small offset spatula
Tart pan, fluted, 9-inch (23 cm) round

Pantry and Refrigerator Staples

Growing up, I always witnessed my mother making fresh spice blends out of whole spices, the aroma of the blended spices filling the kitchen with its fragrance. The chutneys were made from scratch too, probably on a weekly basis. She always had jams, shrubs, and ketchups from scratch. Most of the pantry staples at home were from scratch, with few exceptions. She was a wizard in the kitchen. The kitchen was her temple.

I have carried forward the same tradition in my home, with from-scratch pantry and refrigerator staples. They may have a short shelf life, but we consume them pretty quickly because of how delicious the end product is. This chapter is a building block for the entire book. These are staples that are almost always in my pantry and fridge, so I can whip up any dish or dessert or cocktail with different variations.

Jam making is a therapeutic process. Transforming the seasonal fruits from maceration to the final viscous consistency is pure bliss. Getting those strong fruity and floral or fruity and herbal smells while boiling the fruits and sugars together and letting them rest for just a couple of minutes before pouring and tasting the freshest warm jam is an experience! Jams are very versatile, from simply putting them on toast to using them in breakfast morning buns and cinnamon rolls to using them in desserts like a jammy buttercream for cookies and cakes to using them in cocktails—the uses are endless!

Just like jams, masala blends have many uses in the kitchen. You may need a bunch of ingredients to make a masala blend, but the process takes no time and within minutes you can have a masala blend that can be used in many ways! An additional benefit is the wonderful fragrance that a fresh masala blend imparts—it is simply intoxicating! Thandai Masala (page 38) can be used to transform any dessert into something extraordinary. It can be used to make a Thandai Cocktail (page 336), which serves as a wonderful, delicate dessert cocktail, and is so delicious! Chai Masala (page 41) is a staple used to make morning chai or a splendid dessert creation. Same goes for the Masala Milk Masala (page 52).

Chutneys like the Date Tamarind Chutney (page 45) and the Cilantro Mint Chutney (page 42) are refrigerator staples that are a fantastic accompaniment to various appetizers and snacks. In my opinion, every fridge requires these two condiments at all times! The Peach Chutney (page 60) is a unique condiment on burgers, sandwiches, and even fancy cheese boards. Possibilities are endless! Make these staples and you will be able to tackle many recipes in this book with fun and flair!

Blood Orange and Rosemary Marmalade

Makes about six 8-ounce (250 ml) jars

California has some of the best produce, and wintertime means a ton of citrus. My absolute favorite jam to create with the winter produce is Blood Orange and Rosemary Marmalade. Blood oranges are sweet and slightly tart, and they make one of the best marmalades ever! When I had my jam business going, this flavor was the most popular, and I don't know anyone who did NOT like it. I don't use the entire peel because the white pith is pretty bitter and I'm not a fan of bitter marmalades. So this marmalade simply has the zest of the blood orange, along with the earthy rosemary, which complements the flavor perfectly. Two of my favorite ways to eat this marmalade are slathered with salted butter on sourdough toast and swirled into Greek yogurt! Both ways make for perfect breakfasts.

INGREDIENTS

3½ pounds (about 10) blood oranges
6 cups (1.42 kg) water
2 pounds cane or granulated sugar
1½ ounces (42 g) fruit pectin
½ cup (118 g) freshly squeezed lemon juice
2 sprigs rosemary

METHOD

1. Use a citrus zester to zest all the blood oranges. Collect all the zest and set it aside. Using a sharp knife, peel off the pith (white part of the skin) from the fruit and discard.

2. Cut the fruit in half and then cut each half into six pieces. Using a bench scraper, gather all the fruit and juices into a large pot.

3. Add the zest. Cover all the fruit and zest with the water. Set it on the stove on high heat.

4. Let the mixture come to a boil. Once it boils, set the stove to medium heat and let it cook for about 45 minutes. The fruit will cook and reduce down to half.

5. Keep a small plate with two metal spoons in the freezer. The plate should be level.

To Sterilize the Jars

1. Preheat the oven to 230°F (110°C).

2. Wash the jars with warm water and shake off any excess water. Place them on a baking sheet.

3. Place the tray with the jars in the oven until ready to fill them, or for at least 20 minutes to ensure sterilization.

To Make the Marmalade

1. The cooked fruit should measure about 6 cups. It should be perfectly okay regardless of whether there's more or less.

2. In a large pot, add the cooked fruit, sugar, fruit pectin, lemon juice, and rosemary sprigs. Mix with a rubber spatula.

3. Keep a candy thermometer hooked safely to the pot so you can see the temperature.

4. Over high heat, let the mixture boil for about 30 minutes, or until the temperature on the thermometer shows 220°F (104°C). You will see large bubbles, which will slowly transition

continued ➤

to smaller bubbles. Stir the jam occasionally so it does not stick to the bottom of the pot. Remove from the heat after 30 minutes. Carefully remove the rosemary sprigs from the pot.

To Do the Jam Test

1. Add a teaspoon or two of the jam on each spoon from the freezer, and let it sit in the freezer for 3 minutes. When you remove the plate with the spoons, the jam should slowly come off the spoon but it should NOT be runny. That is when you know that the jam is set. If it is runny, boil the jam for another 2 to 3 minutes, and repeat the procedure until the jam is slightly dense.

2. Another test to determine if your jam is set: Let the jam sit in the pot after you turn off the heat. Use a rubber spatula after 3 to 4 minutes and run it over the top of the jam. If it sets on the spatula and you can run your finger through it, the jam is set. If the layer is still thin, let it boil for another 2 to 3 minutes and do the test again.

3. Remove the tray of jars from the oven, and carefully fill them with a funnel to avoid spillage. Leave about a ¾-inch (2 cm) space from the top of the jar. Put the lids on securely and turn the jars over to mix.

4. Put the tray of jars back into the oven for 15 minutes to sterilize.

5. Remove the jars from the oven and invert them to mix again. Let them cool completely for about 2 hours.

6. Store in a cool, dark place for up to one year or gift them to your family and friends! Remember to refrigerate after opening.

 PRO TIP Always store jam in the fridge after opening.

Pear and Chai Masala Jam

Makes about three 8-ounce (250 ml) jars

Growing up, I loved pears. They were one of my favorite fruits apart from the quintessential Indian mangoes. The pears in India are quite different from the ones you get here in California. I was amazed by how many different varieties of pears there are in California, like the d'Anjou pear (green and red varieties), Bosc, Comice, Bartlett, and Asian pears.

When I started my jam business, one of the flavors I sold was the Pear and Spice Jam. The pears need to be slightly, but not overly, soft and grainy. They need to be the right consistency when making the jam. I used star anise, cinnamon, and clove in the jam—they work beautifully with the pear. It was my second most popular flavor—people loved it. My favorite way to eat this jam is by putting spoonfuls of it on vanilla bean ice cream. Trust me, it is mind-blowingly addictive! Try slathering it on vanilla muffins, too. I changed up the recipe to use Chai Masala (page 41) to give the jam a lovely warmth. The Pear and Chai Masala Jam is used in two recipes in this book that you will surely love: Pear and Chai Masala Cinnamon Rolls (page 94) and Mini Maple Sandwich Cookies with Pear and Spice Buttercream (page 289). Use this jam to make a delicious rustic vanilla cake with a jam buttercream and the jam in the middle. Decorate it with flowers and you have a beautiful cake. The uses are endless! Have fun with it. Grab those pears when they're in season and make this jam, and gift it to your loved ones. Let me know if you get rave reviews!

INGREDIENTS

2 pounds (910 g) d'Anjou pears (slightly soft yet crunchy)

1 pound (454 g) granulated sugar

1½ ounces (42 g) fruit pectin

3 ounces (89 g) lemon juice

2 teaspoons (4 g) Chai Masala (page 41)

METHOD

1. Peel the pears, cut in half, remove the cores (with the seeds), and chop the fruit into small cubes. Place in a large bowl. Add the sugar, fruit pectin, lemon juice, and Chai Masala. Stir, cover, and set it aside for an hour.

2. Keep a small plate with two metal spoons in the freezer. The plate should be level.

To Sterilize the Jars

1. Preheat the oven to 230°F (110°C).

2. Wash the jars with warm water and shake off any excess water. Place them on a baking sheet.

3. Place the tray with the jars in the oven until ready to fill them, or for at least 20 minutes to ensure sterilization.

To Make the Jam

1. In a large copper saucepan or nonstick saucepan, on medium to high heat, add the bowl ingredients and stir to incorporate.

2. Keep a candy thermometer hooked safely to the pot so you can see the temperature.

continued ➤

3. Let the mixture come to a boil. It takes about 5 minutes. Let it boil until it starts foaming, about 10 minutes. Stir occasionally with a rubber spatula, so as not to let the jam get stuck at the bottom of the pan. Let it bubble for another 10 minutes; the foam will gently subside. Remove any excess foam with a spoon and keep a cup handy to discard it into.

4. Reduce the temperature to medium as the jam continues bubbling. The bubbles will be smaller as the jam reduces. Keep stirring to ensure that it does not stick to the bottom of the pan at this stage, and also that the jam does not bubble vigorously. Let it boil for another 5 minutes. Total time is around 30 minutes. The temperature on the thermometer should reach 220°F (105°C). The jam consistency will be thick.

To Do the Jam Test

1. Add a teaspoon or two of the jam on each spoon from the freezer, and let it sit in the freezer for 3 minutes. When you remove the plate with the spoons, the jam should slowly come down off the spoon but it should NOT be runny. That is when you know that the jam is set. If it is runny, boil the jam for another 2 to 3 minutes, and repeat the procedure until the jam is slightly dense.

2. Another test to determine if your jam is set: Let the jam sit in the pot after you turn off the heat. Use a rubber spatula after 3 to 4 minutes and run it over the top of the jam. If it sets on the spatula and you can run your finger through it, the jam is set. If the layer is still thin, let it boil for another 2 to 3 minutes and do the test again.

3. Remove the tray of jars from the oven, and carefully fill them with a funnel to avoid spillage. Make sure the funnel spout is large enough to fit the chunks of pear. Leave about a ¾-inch (2 cm) space from the top of the jar. Put the lids on securely and turn the jars over to mix.

4. Put the tray of jars back into the oven for 15 minutes to sterilize.

5. Remove the jars from the oven and invert them to mix again. Let them cool completely for about 2 hours.

6. Store in a cool, dark place for up to one year or gift them to your family and friends!

PRO TIP Always store jam in the fridge after opening.

Thandai Masala

Makes about 1⅔ cups (185 g)

Let me explain Thandai. Thandai, a.k.a. thand, means cold in Hindi. Thandai is a spiced, boozy, cold milk drink served during the Holi festival in India signifying the onset of spring. It is made with a mix of nuts, spices, and dried rose petals steeped in warm milk, and then made cold before serving. The drink is luxurious, rich, and very delicious. My mum would make this drink for us as kids, without the booze of course, and, to date, it is my absolute favorite drink! The powder is made with almonds, cashews, pistachios, and spices such as star anise, fennel, cardamom, cinnamon, nutmeg, poppy seeds, cloves, and black pepper. This powder is really versatile and imparts a wonderful aroma to the dish. I have two recipes in this book using the Thandai Masala—Thandai Shortbread Cookies Dipped in White Chocolate with Pistachios and Rose Petals (page 248) and Thandai Cocktail (page 336). It can also be used in white hot chocolate, adding wintry, warming spices.

INGREDIENTS

⅓ cup (45 g) almonds

¼ cup (36 g) pistachios

¼ cup (36 g) cashews

¼ cup (36 g) poppy seeds

¼ cup (3 g) edible dried rose petals or 20 dried rosebuds (remove the stem)

20 black peppercorns

20 cardamom pods

1 cinnamon stick (5 g), crushed

8 cloves

2 tablespoons (14 g) fennel seeds

2 star anise (3 g)

1 teaspoon (2 g) freshly ground nutmeg

½ teaspoon saffron

METHOD

1. In a small bowl, roughly stir together all the ingredients. Working in batches, add mixture to a coffee or spice grinder and blend until finely ground. Or you could use a high-speed blender to grind all the ingredients at once into a fine powder.

2. Store in an airtight container in a cool, dark place for up to 6 months.

Chai Masala

Makes about 1 cup (90 g)

Growing up in an Indian and Gujarati family, masala chai, or spiced tea, is ingrained in our routine. We drink it first thing in the morning, and the intoxicating smells of the spices wake us up and get us ready to start our day!

Masala chai is made of ginger, cinnamon, cloves, cardamom, and black pepper. I love adding fennel to the mix because it adds freshness to the ground masala and its licorice notes take it to the next level. All these spices are so good for us, especially from an Ayurvedic perspective, where each spice imparts some benefit to our body, such as stimulating our appetite, helping with acidity, providing antioxidant and antibacterial properties, and improving our digestion.

I have seen versions of masala chai where whole spices are put in the black tea. This is not necessary—a little bit of the Chai Masala goes a long way. If you have the Chai Masala powder, only half a teaspoon is required per cup of chai, which is easier on the pocket and an efficient use of the spices. The recipe is really easy. I love making the ground masala at home, because it comes together within minutes, stores well, makes an amazing masala chai, and is an impressive addition to desserts.

INGREDIENTS

6 cinnamon sticks (24 g)
1½ tablespoons (15 g) black peppercorns
1 tablespoon (7 g) cloves
2 tablespoons (16 g) fennel seeds
3 tablespoons (21 g) cardamom pods
¼ cup + 1 tablespoon (32 g) ground ginger

METHOD

1. Grind all the whole spices except the ground ginger in a high-speed blender for 2 minutes. The mixture should form a fine powder.

2. Pour the ground mixture into a glass jar using a funnel (to prevent spills). Add the ground ginger, and mix it well with a spoon or simply close the jar and shake it to combine.

3. Store in an airtight container in a cool dark place for up to 6 months.

PRO TIPS

1. The Chai Masala can be used to make the Aadhu Masala Chai (page 315) or the Chai Masala Crème Brûlée (page 263). You can also add it to a shortbread dough to make Chai Masala shortbread cookies.

2. The Chai Masala will make an excellent cold vanilla masala chai latte as well!

Cilantro Mint Chutney

Makes about one 8-ounce (250 ml) jar

Cilantro Mint Chutney, a very essential part of Indian cuisine, is served with many appetizers, and is always on the table during lunches and dinners, especially in western and northern India. There are a million uses for Cilantro Mint Chutney, from appetizers like paneer tikka and samosas to chutney sandwiches to serving it as a side accompaniment to main meals. No Indian meal is complete without this chutney.

I love how easy it is to make. You simply put all the ingredients in a high-speed blender and the chutney is ready within minutes! It can be stored in the freezer for a couple months (if it lasts that long) or you can simply keep it in the fridge for a week or so. The chutney is tangy, spicy, salty, and bright, and the freshness comes from the cilantro and mint.

Without this chutney, you cannot make the very famous Dahi Papdi Chaat (page 161) or the recipes in the Snacks/Appetizers chapter, which are lip-smackingly delicious! Mumbai is known for its street food, which encompasses chaat. Chaat is derived from the Indian word "chatpata," which means lip-smacking, and that is exactly what it is! We grew up eating a lot of chaat from street vendors. Cilantro Mint Chutney is an essential component of any chaat, and is a MUST in your refrigerator!

INGREDIENTS

2½ cups (62 g) packed cilantro (including stems)
½ cup (13 g) packed fresh mint leaves
¼ cup (60 g) water
2 tablespoons (30 g) lemon juice
2 tablespoons (18 g) roasted unsalted peanuts
2 teaspoons (8 g) granulated sugar
1 teaspoon (2 g) cumin seeds
1 teaspoon (6 g) table salt
2 garlic cloves
1 serrano pepper or 2 small chilis
(remove seeds for less heat)

METHOD

1. In a blender, whirl all ingredients together until very smooth, scraping down the sides of the container a couple of times.

2. Pour the chutney in an 8-ounce (250 ml) glass jar and keep refrigerated.

 PRO TIP You can also freeze this chutney in an ice cube tray for easy use and it will keep for up to 2 months.

PRO TIP

Thin the chutney out by adding ½ cup (120 g) water to the entire mixture. Do not over dilute.

Date Tamarind Chutney

Makes about three 8-ounce (250 ml) jars

Date Tamarind Chutney perfectly accompanies the Cilantro Mint Chutney (page 42). It is the ying to its yang, the butter to its bread, the jelly to its peanut butter. They complement each other and are served together for most appetizers, making both essential parts of the pantry! This chutney is key to making any kind of Mumbai street food (chaat); it adds beautiful, delicate, sweet, and tangy notes.

The best part is it can be stored in the freezer for up to 6 months and it will still retain its freshness. I usually make a big batch and store it in the freezer, so whenever my family wants to eat chaat, such as sev puri or bhel puri, I always have this chutney on hand. It is made with clean and healthy ingredients, which is a big plus!

My mum would have this chutney, along with the Cilantro Mint Chutney, in her fridge all the time. I would watch her make them on a biweekly basis because of how quickly we consumed chaat in our home. My brother and I would come back from school around 4 p.m., and Mum would have chaat ready for us to devour. We were really lucky to get fresh, homemade snacks from Mum every single day of our lives when we lived in Mumbai.

So if you make the Cilantro Mint Chutney, you should also make the Date Tamarind Chutney. That way, you can have chaat anytime, just like we did growing up—my kids enjoy chaat too now! See the recipe for Dahi Papdi Chaat on page 161.

INGREDIENTS

2½ cups (340 g) Medjool pitted dates

1⅓ cups (110 g) dried tamarind (deseeded)

80 grams jaggery or ⅓ cup (70 g) brown sugar

1 teaspoon (6 g) table salt

1 teaspoon (2 g) red chili powder

5 cups (1.2 kg) water

METHOD

1. In a medium saucepan, on medium to high heat, combine all the ingredients except 1 cup (240 g) of the water. Let the mixture boil and cook for 20 to 22 minutes. The dates and tamarind will soften and the jaggery will dissolve into the water with the heat. After 20 minutes, turn off the heat and let it sit for 5 minutes.

2. Put the cooked ingredients into a high-speed blender and blend until smooth, about 2 minutes.

3. Keep a medium-sized bowl with a medium sieve ready. Add the ingredients through the sieve, using a rubber spatula; clean up the bottom of the sieve with the spatula. The chutney will be thick.

4. Add the remaining 1 cup (240 g) of water to loosen the consistency of the chutney. Stir to combine.

5. Ladle the Date Tamarind Chutney into clean, sterilized jars (see To Sterilize the Jars steps in Blood Orange and Rosemary Marmalade recipe on page 33), and close the lids tightly.

6. The jars can be kept in the fridge for up to 3 weeks.

Strawberry and Hibiscus Jam

Makes four 8-ounce (250 ml) jars

Strawberry season is a joyous time in California. We yearn for strawberry season because it screams the onset of spring, and then summer. It also means a lot of things like strawberry cakes, muffins, milkshakes, and, of course, jam! My kids love strawberry jam. When I first started my jam business, the first flavor I developed was Strawberry and Chocolate. PB&J was the predominant school lunch when my kids were toddlers, so I developed this jam recipe because I didn't like the commercial jams on the market. It became an instant hit with my bambinos, and my friends' bambinos too! My brother only eats jam made by me—now that is special, isn't it?

We are lucky to get beautiful produce in California, and to have berry farms within 50 miles of where we live. We go berry picking every year in Watsonville, California, where there are miles and miles of gorgeous berries—strawberries, blackberries, raspberries, and boysenberries. I have pictures of my kids eating off the vines while picking when they were little, and it is so cute to see their red-stained mouths from eating all those gorgeous berries! I always pick quite the haul and make a lot of jam to last us through the winter until next season, and to give to family and friends. Jam makes for a special gift, as it is home-made with love.

Hibiscus is one of my favorite florals next to rose. It was also my mum's favorite. I grew up with hibiscus around us in our gardens in Mumbai. They are so pretty to look at, but I only discovered eating them after I got married, during a trip to Mexico, where hibiscus is widely used to make cocktails, lemonades, and desserts. I love using fruit and flowers together to create magic, and strawberry and hibiscus is one of those combinations that really pairs well. Hibiscus brings out the best in this strawberry jam and takes it to the next level. I hope you enjoy it as much we do!

INGREDIENTS

2 pounds (910 g) strawberries, hulled and cut into small pieces

1 pound 2 ounces (510 g) granulated sugar

⅓ cup (13 g) dried hibiscus

3 ounces (89 g) fresh lemon juice

1 ounce (28 g) fruit pectin

METHOD

1. In a large bowl, add all the ingredients and, using a rubber spatula, stir the mixture until well combined. Cover with plastic wrap and set it aside for 2 hours. This process is called macerating, and is used for releasing all the liquid from the strawberries, with the help of the sugar.

2. Keep a small plate with two metal spoons in the freezer. The plate should be level.

continued ➡

To Sterilize the Jars

1. Preheat the oven to 230°F (110°C).

2. Wash the jars with warm water and shake off any excess water. Place them on a baking sheet.

3. Place the tray with the jars in the oven until ready to fill them, or for at least 20 minutes to ensure sterilization.

To Make the Jam

1. In a large saucepan, on medium to high heat, add the bowl ingredients and stir to incorporate.

2. Keep a candy thermometer hooked safely to the pot so you can see the temperature.

3. Let the mixture come to a boil. It takes about 5 minutes. It will foam for about 10 minutes. Stir occasionally with a rubber spatula, so that the jam does not get stuck at the bottom of the pan. The foam will gently subside. Remove any excess foam with a spoon, and keep a cup handy to discard it into.

4. The jam will start bubbling. Keep stirring to ensure that it does not stick to the bottom of the pan at this stage, and also that it does not bubble vigorously. Let it boil for another 5 minutes. The temperature on the thermometer should reach 220°F (105°C).

To Do the Jam Test

1. Add a teaspoon or two of the jam on each spoon from the freezer, and let it sit in the freezer for 3 minutes. When you remove the plate with the spoons, the jam should slowly come off the spoon, but it should NOT be runny. That is when you know that the jam is set. If it is runny, boil the jam for another 2 to 3 minutes, and repeat the procedure until the jam is slightly dense.

2. Another test to determine if your jam is set: Let the jam sit in the pot after you turn off the heat. Use a rubber spatula after 3 to 4 minutes and run it over the top of the jam. If it sets on the spatula and you can run your finger through it, the jam is set. If the layer is still thin, let it boil for another 2 to 3 minutes and do the test again.

3. Remove the tray of jars from the oven, and carefully fill each with a funnel to avoid spillage. Leave about a ¾-inch (2 cm) space from the top of the jar. Put the lids on securely and turn the jars over to mix.

4. Put the tray of jars back into the oven for 15 minutes to sterilize.

5. Remove the jars from the oven and invert them to mix again. Let them cool completely for about 2 hours.

6. Store in a cool, dark place for up to one year or gift them to your family and friends! Remember to refrigerate after opening.

PRO TIP Substitute the dried hibiscus with edible dried rose petals to make Strawberry and Rose Petal Jam. Once the jam is done, add a tablespoon of rose water for extra flavor!

Apricot and Saffron Jam

Makes about four 8-ounce (250 ml) jars

Come summer with all its gorgeous summer fruits, I squeal in excitement and become like a child in a candy store when I visit the farmers' market! The best way to start my Sunday morning is observing all the different colors and textures of fruit, like the berries glistening in the sun or the pretty stone fruits that grab my attention immediately. I think about all the jams that I can make—some with herbs, some with dried florals, all to be taken to the next level. Jam making has been an integral part of my food journey and one that gives me limitless joy. The summer is when I start preparing for jams to give as presents during the holidays.

Apricot jam is really versatile—it can be eaten with toast and butter or as a savory component with good quality cheese and crackers. I love pairing apricot with saffron, as it takes me right back to my childhood flavors of dried apricot and mithai—Indian desserts with saffron. It reminds me of when guests would visit our home for Diwali to wish us Happy Diwali and enjoy plates full of flavor offered to them. Our Diwali plate consisted of dried fruits and nuts, some savory snacks, and mithai, which is where my inspiration came from for this jam flavor. You can see how I use it to create the Peacock Macarons (page 291), plus it goes perfectly with some cheese and Chorafali Crackers (page 391).

INGREDIENTS

2¼ pounds (1.02 kg) apricots, washed, cut in half, pitted, and diced into 1-inch (2½ cm) cubes

1 pound 3 ounces (540 g) granulated sugar

1½ ounces (45 g) fresh lemon juice

1 ounce (28 g) fruit pectin

1 teaspoon saffron

METHOD

1. In a large bowl, add all the ingredients except the saffron and, using a rubber spatula, stir the mixture until well combined. Cover with plastic wrap and set it aside for 2 hours. This process is called macerating and is used for releasing all the liquid from the apricots with the help of the sugar.

2. Keep a small plate with 2 metal spoons in the freezer. The plate should be level.

To Sterilize the Jars

1. Preheat the oven to 230°F (110°C).

2. Wash the jars with warm water and shake off any excess water. Place them on a baking sheet.

3. Place the tray with the jars in the oven until ready to fill them, or for at least 20 minutes to ensure sterilization.

To Make the Jam

1. In a large saucepan, on medium to high heat, add the bowl ingredients and stir to incorporate. Stir in the saffron at this stage.

2. Keep a candy thermometer hooked safely to the pot so you can see the temperature.

3. Let the mixture come to a boil. It takes about 5 minutes. You will see it foaming for about 10 minutes. Stir occasionally with a rubber spat-

continued ➡

ula, so as not to let the jam get stuck at the bottom of the pan. The foam will gently subside. Remove any excess foam with a spoon, and keep a cup handy to discard it into.

4. When the jam starts bubbling, you will see tiny bubbles on the surface of the jam. You have to keep stirring to ensure that it does not stick to the bottom of the pan at this stage, and also that the jam does not bubble vigorously. Let it boil for another 5 minutes. The temperature on the thermometer should reach 220°F (105°C).

To Do the Jam Test

1. Add a teaspoon or two of the jam on each spoon from the freezer, and let it sit in the freezer for 3 minutes. When you remove the plate with the spoons, the jam should slowly come off the spoon, but it should NOT be runny. That is when you know that the jam is set. If it is runny, boil the jam for another 2 to 3 minutes, and repeat the procedure until the jam is slightly dense.

2. Another test to determine if your jam is set: Let the jam sit in the pot after you turn off the heat. Use a rubber spatula after 3 to 4 minutes and run it over the top of the jam. If it sets on the spatula and you can run your finger through it, the jam is set. If the layer is still thin, let it boil for another 2 to 3 minutes and do the test again.

3. Remove the tray of jars from the oven, and carefully fill them with a funnel to avoid spillage. Leave about a ¾-inch (2 cm) space from the top of the jar. Put the lids on securely and turn the jars over to mix.

4. Put the tray of jars back into the oven for 15 minutes to sterilize.

5. Remove the jars from the oven and invert them to mix again. Let them cool completely for about 2 hours.

6. Store in a cool, dark place for up to one year or gift them to your family and friends! Remember to refrigerate after opening.

PRO TIP Substitute the saffron with rosemary to make Apricot and Rosemary Jam. The apricot jam is fantastic on a cheese board with some good cheese and crackers!

Masala Milk Masala

Makes about 1½ cups (180 g)

Masala Milk powder. So few ingredients and so much flavor! This powder is made in most Indian households, where it is mixed with sugar in milk. The drink is boiled and given to kids. The idea is that milk, a.k.a. calcium, and nuts, a.k.a. protein, are good for brain development and help make kids healthy and strong. Picky kids are given this milk to put some sort of nutrition in their bodies, which provides them with the energy they need!

In Gujarati, this drink is called badam pista doodh (almond pista milk). My mum would make it warm for us in the winter months. (There was really not much winter in Mumbai, especially when I think about it now, compared to Northern California!) In the summer, she served it cold to cool us off, especially at night. Mumbai gets very hot and reaches 100% humidity in the summer and monsoon seasons. The masala doodh was made with full-fat milk and I remember the layer of cream, or *tarr*, on the top, which I hated and would remove. But it was so delicious and I loved getting the bits of nuts in my milk, along with some coarse bits of cardamom too. You could taste the saffron, nutmeg, and cardamom in it and, because it was sweet, it made for a wonderful dessert to end the day!

This powder is full of flavor and super easy to make. It can be used to make shortbread cookies, ice cream, or the Masala Milk Popsicles (page 254), which are a favorite with my kids in the summer!

INGREDIENTS

½ cup (70 g) raw unsalted almonds
½ cup (70 g) raw unsalted cashews
¼ cup (35 g) raw unsalted pistachios
8 cardamom pods
1 teaspoon freshly grated nutmeg
1 heaped teaspoon saffron

METHOD

1. Grind all the ingredients in a high-speed blender until fine.

2. Store in an airtight container in a cool dark place for up to 3 months.

PRO TIPS

1. Double or triple the quantity to make jars of Masala Milk Masala to give as gifts for the holidays! It is a fantastic treat to make warm masala milk during the cold winter months.

2. To make masala milk: Add about 1½ tablespoons (20 g) powder to 1 cup (240 g) of milk, along with a sweetener of your choice. Warm it on a stove at medium heat for 5 minutes until it comes to a boil. Let it boil for a minute and remove from the heat. Let it steep, covered, for 3 to 4 minutes. Strain, garnish with a few chopped almonds and pistachios, and enjoy!

PRO TIPS

1. Substitute jalapeño pepper or pasilla chili instead of the poblano pepper. Deseed it, if you do not want it spicy.

2. The dressing can be used for sweet potato fries or the Masala Potato Chips (page 375), Squash Blossom Tacos (page 214), Summer California Salad (page 141), or simply as a dip for tortilla chips!

Avocado, Cilantro, and Poblano Pepper Dressing

Makes 1½ to 2 cups (350 to 500 ml)

My family loves Mexican food. Mexican cuisine is very similar to Indian cuisine. Both have bold flavors, lots of spices and chilis, varied spice levels, wonderful colors, and an abundance of fresh produce. The proximity of California to Mexico influences the cuisine of California by amping up the flavor profile and making it produce-rich and generally tasty!

We are huge fans of a wonderful Mexican restaurant in the Bay Area called Tacolicious. I could probably drink all the different sauces and salsas that they carry. They change up their menu depending on the seasonal produce, and their sauces change as well. One of their outstanding sauces on rotation is their avocado sauce, and I wanted to recreate something similar at home for our weekly taco night. I came up with this avocado sauce/dressing that has fresh ingredients, including one of my favorite peppers, poblanos. When poblano peppers are charred, it brings out an amazing depth of flavor. These charred peppers are added to the sauce, along with other ingredients, to make a smooth, silky sauce perfect for my Squash Blossom Tacos (page 214). I love this dressing even on my Summer California Salad (page 214). It is pretty low calorie, since it has no oil like typical dressings do. It is light, full of freshness, and absolutely delicious!

INGREDIENTS

½ poblano pepper, deseeded

½ ripe avocado

½ cup cilantro

½ teaspoon (3 g) Maldon salt

½ teaspoon black pepper

¼ cup (57 g) Greek yogurt

¼ cup (60 g) water

1 garlic clove

Juice of 1 lime

2 tablespoons (15 g) raw pepitas or raw pumpkin seeds

METHOD

1. To char the poblano pepper: Roast the poblano pepper directly on the stove top, over medium-high heat, using tongs to turn the pepper. It should take 20 seconds to char one side of the pepper. Keep turning to char the pepper on all the sides. In total, this process should take about 3 to 4 minutes. Wrap the completely charred pepper in aluminum foil. Set it aside for 10 minutes.

2. Remove the foil. The pepper should have cooled and will be wrinkled. Using a spoon, gently spoon off the char from all sides and discard.

3. Add all the ingredients, including the charred poblano pepper, into a high-speed blender. Start slow and then increase the speed to make a smooth mixture. If the mixture is too thick, incrementally add a tablespoon of water until you reach a dressing-like consistency.

4. Store in a squeeze bottle in the refrigerator for up to a week.

Cilantro, Peanut, and Toasted Coriander Seed Pesto

Makes about 1 cup (230 g)

Basil pine nut pesto is an Italian sauce consisting of fresh basil, pine nuts, parmesan cheese, garlic, extra virgin olive oil, salt, and pepper. Pesto makes a fantastic base for pizzas, is great for making a wonderful summery pasta, and can be used as a spread for delicious sandwiches.

Here is an Indian-inspired pesto, with tons of fresh cilantro, roasted peanuts, toasted coriander seeds, garlic, parmesan cheese, and extra virgin olive oil, along with salt and pepper. It makes for a very tasty pesto. The toasted coriander seeds provide the earthiness to this pesto, and add to the fragrance from all the fresh summer cilantro leaves. I am very fond of this pesto, and love using it for my Summer California Pizza (page 221) and also to drizzle on the Summer Hariyali (Green) Paneer Skewers (page 145). It has become one of our favorite condiments to use for many more dishes and is a constant in our fridge!

INGREDIENTS

3 cups washed and tightly packed cilantro

¼ cup roasted, unsalted peanuts

3 garlic cloves

¾ teaspoon (5 g) table salt

½ teaspoon (1.2 g) black pepper

1 teaspoon (2 g) toasted coriander seeds (see Pro Tip below)

¼ cup (15 g) finely grated parmesan cheese

⅓ cup (43 g) extra virgin olive oil, plus 2 or 3 tablespoons for garnish

METHOD

1. In a food processor, add all the ingredients except the parmesan cheese and olive oil, and process the contents until paste-like. Use a small rubber spatula to clean up the sides and push the mixture down into the processor.

2. Add the parmesan cheese and ⅓ cup (43 g) olive oil and pulse to mix until well blended.

3. Using the rubber spatula, transfer the pesto into an airtight container, cover with the additional olive oil, and store in the fridge for up to 2 weeks for maximum freshness.

PRO TIP Toast the coriander seeds in a small skillet on medium heat. Let them toast for 1 minute. Stir occasionally and toast for another minute. Remove from the heat. Let them cool completely.

PRO TIPS

1. Best eaten with plain rice and Gujarati Daal (page 179) or plain rice and Kala Chana Daal (page 232).

2. For a sweet and spicy flavor, add 1 teaspoon of Kashmiri red chili powder and 2 teaspoons of granulated sugar during Step 3.

Lemon Pickle

Makes one 32-ounce (1 L) jar

Lemon Pickle, or preserved lemon, is a favorite pickle in our household. With the sultry heat and humidity in the Mumbai air, Mum would get loads of lemons from the vegetable stand in Parle West. She would make a gallon of Lemon Pickle, filling the whole jar with lemons cut into a cross, stuffed with salt, turmeric, and whole black peppercorns. She let the lemons do their magic, using age-old preservation techniques passed down through generations. She would forget about the huge glass jar for 6 to 8 weeks. The lemons would soften, the peel ever so slightly sweet, tangy, and sour, with a slight fermented taste that was oh so good! I found out that my mum's brother, my favorite uncle, LOVES Lemon Pickle. My 90-year-old grandma still makes it for him!

I planted a lemon tree about six years ago, and it has really given me a lot of bounty in the last three years. I use these fresh, organic lemons to make Mum's Lemon Pickle. Anishka loves lemons, so I made her try this with Gujarati Daal (page 179) and plain rice. The combination marries together beautifully, and the pickle really gives a lot of flavor to the daal and rice. Lemon Pickle also makes a great gift. Preserved lemon is a popular condiment in North African cuisine as well, and is used in Moroccan stews. Preserved lemon is also popular in Greek food.

This is my ba's (grandma's) recipe. Mum learned from her, so I called Ba last summer to ask her how to make it. She was sure to ask me 2 months later how the pickles turned out. When I told her that the recipe was going in the book, her face lit up with her beautiful smile—she was so pleased!

INGREDIENTS

5 small lemons, washed
¾ cup (165 g) sea salt or good-quality salt
1 tablespoon (9.5 g) ground turmeric
2 teaspoons (6 g) whole black peppercorns

METHOD

1. Cut the lemons in half, to the ends but not all the way through. Repeat with a cross section to form a cross cut, but all the way through to the end of the lemon. You want the lemon to stay intact.

2. Mix the sea salt and turmeric together. Add a bit with your hands into each crevice of the lemon.

3. In a clean, sterilized jar (see page 33), add the stuffed lemons, along with the remaining sea salt-turmeric mixture and the peppercorns, and seal the jar.

4. Let it sit in a cool place for 6 weeks. Shake it every 3 to 4 days to mix everything. The lemon juice from the lemons will release and blend in with the salt, turmeric, and black pepper. Over a period of 6 weeks, the lemon peel softens and it becomes really fragrant and delicious to eat!

Peach Chutney

Makes about three 8-ounce (250 ml) jars

California is bursting with stone fruits in the summer months, and it gives me a ton of inspiration to make fruity things. Stone fruits consist of peaches, nectarines, pluots, plums, plumcots, apricots, cherries, and more. With all the beautiful stone fruit in season, I end up making varieties of chutneys, jams, shrubs, and compotes—and yes, we eat them all. Our favorite family activity is to go stone fruit picking and berry picking in the summer months. We live an hour away from Brentwood to the northeast, where all the stone fruit farms are, and an hour away from Watsonville to the south, where all the berry farms are. I have several pictures of my kids when they were toddlers, picking the fruits and immediately eating them as they were picked. Those are fond memories, to see the joy on their faces, eating nature's candy right off a tree!

Inspired by the beautiful summer produce and my Indian heritage, I make a peach chutney every year. The touch of garam masala, freshly ground cardamom, and cinnamon gives this Peach Chutney a beautiful depth of flavor, from the sweetness of the fruit to the bold flavors of garam masala and the earthy and floral sweetness of cinnamon and cardamom. We love this chutney and use it in many different ways, such as on the Ultimate Mumbai-California Veggie Burger (page 217) or simply as a dip on our cheese plates. It will become your favorite condiment too!

INGREDIENTS

2 tablespoons (29 g) vegetable oil

1 teaspoon (3 g) mustard seeds

1 medium (90 g) white onion, diced

1 Kashmiri dried red chili or 2 small dried red chilis

1 cup (230 g) apple cider vinegar

1 cup (200 g) packed light brown sugar

1 inch (2½ cm) ginger, freshly grated

1 teaspoon (2 g) freshly ground cardamom powder

1 teaspoon (2.6 g) ground cinnamon

1 teaspoon (3 g) garam masala

½ teaspoon (3 g) table salt

2 pounds fresh yellow peaches, washed, pitted, and cut into small pieces

METHOD

1. In a large saucepan on medium heat, add the vegetable oil. After 30 seconds, when the oil has heated, add the mustard seeds, and wait 20 to 30 seconds for it to splatter. Add the onion and sauté until onions are translucent, 3 to 5 minutes. Add the dried red chilis and sauté for 20 seconds.

2. Add the apple cider vinegar, brown sugar, ginger, cardamom, cinnamon, garam masala, and salt. Raise the heat to medium-high and bring to a boil. Add the peaches and stir to mix. Reduce the heat to medium and simmer, stirring occasionally until the mixture looks jammy, 35 to 40 minutes. The mixture will reduce to about 2¾ cups (650 ml).

3. Carefully pour the chutney into a pourable jar, and fill about three 8-ounce (250 ml) jars with the chutney. Seal airtight and chill in the fridge. It can be stored for up to 1 month.

Sandwich Masala

Makes about ⅓ cup (52 g)

The iconic Grilled Bombay Sandwich (page 151), one of the most popular street foods of Mumbai, is really incomplete without the Sandwich Masala. Sandwich Masala is the masala sprinkled on each layer when building the layers of the Grilled Bombay Sandwich. The vegetables impart the overall flavor to the sandwich, but it is the Sandwich Masala that really ties the whole sandwich together and takes it to the next level to give you an experience like none other! On the roadside, the sandwich vendors have a few stainless steel dabbas with a handle and small holes on the top. They fill them with the Sandwich Masala. It is a really fun experience to watch how quickly the vendor builds this sandwich to give you one of the fastest and tastiest street foods ever.

Although my mum used to buy Sandwich Masala from one vendor that we used to go to regularly in Santa Cruz (in Mumbai), I started making my own in California to bring a taste of Mumbai to my family, and have my kids share the same ethereal experience that I had growing up. The masala comes together easily. Toast, grind, store—that's it! If you plan to make the Grilled Bombay Sandwich (which you MUST!), then you have to make this Sandwich Masala, because the Grilled Bombay Sandwich is incomplete without its partner in crime!

INGREDIENTS

2 teaspoons (4 g) cumin seeds

16 cloves

1 cinnamon stick, broken into small pieces

1 teaspoon black peppercorns

2 tablespoons (14 g) fennel seeds

2 teaspoons (6 g) amchur (dried mango powder)

3 teaspoons (16 g) rock salt (sanchar)

METHOD

1. In a small skillet on medium heat, add the cumin seeds, cloves, cinnamon stick, black peppercorns, and fennel seeds. Sauté, stirring occasionally, for 3 minutes, until you get the fragrance of the spices. Remove from the heat and let it cool completely.

2. In a coffee or spice grinder or a high-speed blender, add the spices and grind until you have a fine powder.

3. Using a fine sieve, sieve the powder to catch any coarse bits.

4. Mix in the amchur and rock salt until combined. Store in a small, airtight jar in a cool, dark place for up to a year.

PRO TIP Use the Sandwich Masala on any kind of sandwich or sprinkle on fruits for a savory kick!

Breakfast

"When you wake up in the morning, Pooh," said Piglet at last, "what's the first thing you say to yourself?"

"What's for breakfast?" said Pooh.

"What do *you* say, Piglet?"

"I say, I wonder what's going to happen exciting *today*?" said Piglet.

Pooh nodded thoughtfully.

"It's the same thing," he said.

—A. A. Milne, *Winnie-the-Pooh*

Breakfast is the most important meal of the day, the meal that sets the day's mood. As a kid in Mumbai, in a Gujarati household, savory breakfasts were the norm. There was no mention of sweet breakfasts. Savory breakfasts consisted of simply toast with butter, with masala chai, or any of the Gujarati breakfast options like dhokla, thepla, or any savory leftover snacks. Pudla (page 110) are high in protein and were fantastic quick options on weekdays before going to school. Masala chai was a must. The fragrance of brewing spices along with the Assam CTC black tea leaves really woke me up as a teenager. That tradition has continued into adulthood too, and now I have passed it on to my son. Breakfast and chai go hand in hand. Like two peas in a pod, they are inseparable.

When I migrated to the United States, I discovered a whole new world of sweet breakfasts. Pancakes, waffles, toaster pastries, muffins, Danish, and so on. It definitely expanded my breakfast repertoire. After having kids, it became even more important to make sure to provide them with good breakfast options, especially once they started going to school. I have never been a fan of sugary cereals or store-bought Pop-Tarts and pancake/waffle mixes. From scratch was what my mother taught us as kids, with a homemade, you-can-control-what-goes-in-it mentality. Homemade is the best. With that always in the back of my mind and with my mother's voice faintly whispering in my ear, I have made things from scratch, which included the use of seasonal fruits and vegetables as part of our breakfast meals, even for the occasional sweet breakfast. Apple, Fennel, and Cardamom Tarts (page 64) on the weekend make for a great breakfast option for on-the-go mornings. My Banana, Walnut, and Chocolate Chip Pancakes with Caramelized Bananas (page 97) are wholesome, and leftover pancakes can be eaten for a couple days. Waffles are made in bulk and frozen so they can be toasted quickly in the toaster oven and served up with some fruit. My granola recipes make great options with Greek yogurt and extra fruit. For savory breakfast, the Sooji Dhokla (Semolina Savory Spongy Cakes, page 85) and the Pudla (Chickpea Flour Crêpes) with Carrot and Purple Cabbage Salad (page 110) come together pretty quickly for a healthy, savory breakfast. Breakfast Naan Pizza (page 81) forms a great savory option with any leftover Butter Garlic Naan (page 357).

For leisurely weekend mornings, the Pear and Chai Masala Cinnamon Rolls (page 94) are a favorite, second only next to the savory Huevos Rancheros Waffles (page 88). My Chocolate Cardamom Pastry Cream, Halvah, and Pistachio Danish (page 73) is a hit for slow Sunday mornings. I use Saturdays to prepare the pastries and have them ready for Sunday mornings.

There are a lot of good breakfast options in this book, and I hope you can make them and enjoy them with your families and loved ones, because the best ideas sometimes germinate over a good breakfast, and a good breakfast sets the right tone for the day.

Apple, Fennel, and Cardamom Tarts

Makes 10 to 12 tarts

I came to this country a little over 20 years ago. I was fascinated by the grocery store then, seeing how big the store was and the many different products on the shelves. We had smaller stores with specific items in Mumbai. There would be a grain and spice store, or a snack store, or a spice store by itself. Fresh produce was from the vendors sitting by the markets, like an open farmers' market concept, which is the way of life in India. There are small bakeries with only baked goods or fresh bread available. Each vendor has their own specialty that they sell, similar to the European culture.

I wanted to try a lot of things from the grocery stores here, and I did. They were all processed with a ton of preservatives, though, which led to some unhealthy choices and, in turn, becoming unhealthy myself. Growing up in Mumbai, we never ate sweet breakfasts. It was always something savory, so having a sweet breakfast like Pop-Tarts for breakfast, was completely new and fascinating to me and, of course, addictive! I had to stop my processed, sweet indulgences as soon as I realized how bad the processed foods are. Fast forward a few years, and now I have two kids who have grown up in the United States. They do love a good breakfast in the mornings, but being the make-from-scratch mom that I am, I prepare and bake a lot of things that they like so that they do not have to eat processed foods.

These homemade tarts are not hard to make at all. They use the same dough that I have used to make pies, and it is the flakiest, most delicious dough ever! The tarts are filled with sweet spices like ground fennel, which gives it a wonderful, mild licorice flavor, and ground cardamom, which gives it an amazingly sweet aroma. Give it a pop of color and make it fun for your kids by adding some sprinkles. My kids love these little breakfast treats and cannot get enough of them. I promise yours will feel the same way!

PRO TIPS

1. Do not overwork the dough when mixing and rolling it out. Overworking the dough will prevent the tarts from being flaky.

2. You can substitute the fennel and the cardamom in the filling with 2 teaspoons of the Chai Masala (page 41) to make Apple and Chai Masala Tarts. They are sublime!

3. The tarts will stay fresh for a week in an airtight container at room temperature.

continued ➞

INGREDIENTS

PIE DOUGH

3 cups (360 g) all-purpose flour,
   plus extra for rolling the dough

1 teaspoon (3 g) ground cinnamon

1 teaspoon (6 g) table salt

1½ tablespoons (18 g) granulated sugar

1 cup (2 sticks; 226 g) unsalted cold butter,
   cut into small cubes

¾ cup (180 g) ice-cold water

½ cup (75 g) ice cubes

1 tablespoon (14 g) apple cider vinegar

APPLE, FENNEL, AND CARDAMOM FILLING

2 large apples or 3 small apples (360 g),
   peeled, cut into small cubes
   (about ⅓ inch; 1 cm)

⅓ cup (65 g) light brown sugar

1 tablespoon (15 g) lemon juice

1 tablespoon (8 g) cornstarch

1 teaspoon (2 g) fennel seeds,
   ground into a fine powder

1 teaspoon (6 g) table salt

1 teaspoon (2 g) ground cardamom

2 tablespoons (28 g) unsalted butter

EGG WASH

1 egg

2 teaspoons water

1 teaspoon granulated sugar

CARDAMOM ICING

1 cup (120 g) powdered sugar

½ teaspoon (1 g) ground cardamom

½ teaspoon vanilla extract

2 tablespoons (30 g) whole milk or
   more if required

DECORATIONS

Sprinkles

METHOD

To Make the Pie Dough

1. In a large bowl, whisk together the flour, cinnamon, salt, and sugar. Add the cold butter and, with a pastry blender or your fingers, cut through the butter so that the flour coats all the pieces and the butter is pea sized.

2. In a medium bowl, mix the water, ice, and apple cider vinegar. Add 2 tablespoons of cold water at a time to the pastry dough and, using the pastry blender or your hands, mix so that the water absorbs into the dough. Add up to 8 tablespoons of water to combine, until the dough just starts to come together. You should still see the butter pieces, which will make the dough flaky.

3. If you need to add a tad bit more water, add in 1-tablespoon increments until the dough comes together. Do not add more water, or the dough will become soggy.

4. Divide the dough into two equal parts. The total dough weighs approximately 730 g, so about 365 grams each.

5. Wrap each portion in plastic wrap, and shape them into rectangles. Keep patting and shaping the dough to form neat rectangles, about 5 inches by 6 inches in size.

6. Refrigerate for an hour.

To Make the Filling

1. In a medium bowl, combine the cut apples, brown sugar, lemon juice, cornstarch, fennel, salt, and cardamom and mix with a spatula to combine. Let it sit for 15 minutes.

2. In a large saucepan, on medium heat, add the butter. Once melted, add the apple mixture and sauté for a total of 7 to 8 minutes, until the apples soften. Remove from the heat.

3. Use a mesh strainer over a medium bowl to strain out the juices. Let the filling cool.

To Roll Out the Dough

1. Line three baking sheets with parchment paper.

2. Take one rectangle of dough out of the fridge. Dust a work surface with flour. Unwrap the dough and roll it out into a roughly 10-by-15-inch (25-by-40 cm) rectangle. Make sure to keep sprinkling the surface and the rolling pin with additional flour to ensure that it does not stick. The thickness of the rolled dough should be between 1/8 to 1/4 inch (1/4 to 1/2 cm) thick.

3. Using a steel ruler and a sharp knife, trim the rough edges to form a smooth rectangle.

4. The tarts will be 3½ by 3 inches (7½ by 9 cm). Using a pastry cutter and a ruler, cut the dough lengthwise in 3-inch (7½ cm) sections. Then cut it across widthwise in 3½-inch (9 cm) sections. Alternatively, you can use a sharp knife to cut the rectangles. You will get eight rectangles.

5. Use a flat spatula to place the rectangles on a parchment-lined baking sheet and put the sheet in the freezer for 10 minutes.

6. Meanwhile, repeat for the second rectangle of dough, place the rectangles on the second baking sheet, and freeze for 10 minutes.

7. Collect all the scrap pieces of dough and place them in plastic wrap. Form a rectangle and refrigerate for 30 minutes. These scraps should form four to six rectangles for two to three more tarts.

8. Roll out the scrap dough to a thickness between 1/8 and 1/4 inches (3 and 5 mm), form four rectangles, and freeze them on a baking sheet for 10 minutes.

To Assemble

1. Remove the first baking sheet from the freezer.

2. In a small bowl, prepare the egg wash by using a fork to whisk together the egg, water, and sugar until well combined.

3. Use a pastry brush to brush each rectangle with the egg wash.

4. Spoon about 1 heaping tablespoon of the filling in the center of each tart, leaving a ½- to ¾-inch (1¼ to 2 cm) gap around the filling.

5. Remove the second baking sheet from the freezer, and place each rectangle gently on top of a rectangle with filling. Use your fingertips to gently press around the filling to seal the tarts. Using a fork, press the edges of the tarts to seal and make a pattern. Cut an X with a sharp knife in the middle of the tarts so that the steam can escape while they bake.

6. Brush each tart with egg wash.

7. Freeze the tarts for 10 minutes.

To Bake

1. Preheat the oven to 375°F (190°C).

2. Give the tarts one more egg wash after they are removed from the freezer. Pop them in the oven for 25 minutes or until golden brown in color.

3. Remove from the oven, transfer to a wire rack, and let them cool completely.

To Ice and Decorate

1. In a medium bowl, whisk together the powdered sugar and cardamom. Add the vanilla extract and milk and whisk until it is a thick yet spreadable consistency. If it is too thin it will not form a thick enough layer of icing on top of the tart.

2. Spread about 2 teaspoons of the icing on each tart and decorate with some sprinkles. Let them rest for about 30 minutes to set the icing.

Strawberry and Hibiscus Morning Buns

Makes 24

Raj and Rishan have a deep love for breakfast pastries. Anishka and I prefer our savory breakfasts. My only exception to the rule is sweet waffles, especially stacked with a bunch of berries on them. I do like breakfast pastries, but I prefer them as a snack rather than for breakfast. Is that weird? They are a labor of love, but they are so rewarding. The fragrance that fills the kitchen when they're baking, especially when they come out of the oven, and the look of anticipation and joy on my not-so-little-one's face is pure bliss!

The first time I was looking to make morning buns, I found *Bon Appétit*'s recipe. I adjusted it to make it my own, and added Calamansi Curd to the morning buns. Calamansi is a tart fruit, which comes from the lovely country of the Philippines. It is found in the Bay Area too, and I have obtained the fruit from the farmers' market. With all the spices and the addition of the tart curd, the buns are pure perfection! I have tried this recipe with different fillings, and my favorite thus far has to be the Strawberry and Hibiscus Jam (page 46). I love the combination of fruit and floral together. It really elevates any dish to next-level deliciousness. Using this jam in the buns and covering them with strawberry sugar (freeze-dried strawberries and powdered sugar together) makes them the perfect morning buns to share. They are best when eaten the same day, so make the whole batch and share with your neighbors, friends, and family!

INGREDIENTS

YEASTED DOUGH

1¼ ounces (7 g; about 2¼ teaspoons) active dry yeast

1¼ cups (300 g) whole milk, warmed

¼ cup (50 g) + 1 teaspoon (4 g) granulated sugar

4 large eggs

2 teaspoons (9 g) vanilla extract

Zest of a whole lemon

3½ cups (445 g) bread flour, plus extra for rolling

1 cup (120 g) whole wheat flour

1½ teaspoons (9 g) table salt

1 cup (2 sticks; 226 g) unsalted butter, room temperature, cut into cubes

FILLING

½ cup (1 stick; 113 g) unsalted butter, room temperature

¾ cup (150 g) light brown sugar, packed

½ cup (100 g) granulated sugar

1 tablespoon (8 g) ground cinnamon

2 teaspoons (4 g) ground cardamom

1 teaspoon (2 g) ground star anise

½ teaspoon (3 g) table salt

8 ounces (227 g) Strawberry and Hibiscus Jam (page 46)

continued →

FOR BRUSHING THE MUFFIN PAN
AND THE BAKED BUNS

½ cup (1 stick; 113 g) unsalted butter,
    room temperature

¼ cup (50 g) granulated sugar, for sprinkling the
    muffin pan

STRAWBERRY-SUGAR MIXTURE

1½ cups (300 g) granulated sugar

1 ounce (28 g) freeze-dried strawberries, finely
    ground in a high-speed blender

METHOD

To Make the Yeasted Dough

1. In the bowl of an electric stand mixer fitted with a paddle attachment, combine the yeast with 1 cup of warm milk (should not be hot or else it will kill the yeast) and 1 teaspoon of sugar. Let it sit until it turns foamy after 5 minutes.

2. Add the eggs and whisk until well blended, about 1 minute. Add the granulated sugar, vanilla extract, and lemon zest and whisk for a few seconds.

3. In a separate bowl, add the bread flour, whole wheat flour, and salt and whisk.

4. Remove the paddle, fit with a dough hook attachment, and add the dry mixture to the wet mixture. Start the mixture on slow speed so as not to spread all the flour. Increase the speed to medium-high as the flour mixture comes together. Let the dough mix for about 8 minutes total. The dough will start climbing onto the hook slowly, and will be sort of firm so that it can clean the sides of the bowl as it turns, although the bottom may still be sticky.

5. Add ¼ cup (60 g) of milk and whisk again at medium speed for 2 minutes.

6. Reduce the speed to medium-low and add the butter one cube at a time, only adding the next cube when the dough completely absorbs the butter. This part requires patience. Continue until all the butter is absorbed and you get a smooth, soft dough.

7. Cover the mixing bowl with plastic wrap and chill in the fridge overnight for at least 8 hours. It will double in size.

To Make the Filling

In a small to medium saucepan, add the butter, brown sugar, granulated sugar, cinnamon, cardamom, star anise, and salt. Cook over low heat, stirring constantly to form a smooth mixture. Let it cool.

To Assemble

1. Punch down the dough. Transfer the dough to a lightly floured surface. Divide the dough in half, putting the second half back in the fridge. Roll out the dough evenly, using flour as needed, to make a 16-by-12-inch (40-by-30 cm) rectangle.

2. Evenly spread half of the filling mixture on the dough with a pastry brush, leaving a 1-inch (2½ cm) border all around.

3. Using a small offset spatula, spread the Strawberry and Hibiscus Jam onto the mixture, very lightly so as not to disrupt the sugar mixture filling.

4. Using the long side closest to you, start rolling the dough tightly all the way to the end. Transfer the rolled dough onto a baking sheet. Chill the dough for 15 minutes in the freezer.

5. Repeat the process with the remaining dough and put it in the freezer. Remove the first one from the freezer.

6. Preheat the oven to 350°F (175°C).

7. Melt the stick of butter in a small saucepan. Using a pastry brush, brush a 12-cup muffin

pan with the butter. Sprinkle each cup generously with sugar.

8. Trim the ends of the chilled dough log by ½ inch (1¼ cm). Cut the remaining log into 12 equal pieces, at a slight diagonal. Put each piece into each muffin cup. Cover with plastic wrap and let it sit at room temperature for 40 minutes. The pieces will expand to the width of the muffin cups.

9. Bake the buns in the oven until golden brown, 25 to 30 minutes. Keep a watch in the last 5 minutes, because some oven temperatures are hotter than others.

10. Place 1½ cups (300 g) of granulated sugar and the strawberry powder in a medium bowl, and whisk to combine. Remove the buns from the oven. Brush them with the melted butter and roll each bun generously in the sugar. Let cool on a wire rack. They are ready to serve!

11. Repeat Steps 7 to 10 with the second half of the dough.

12. The buns are best eaten the day of baking.

PRO TIPS

1. Follow the steps exactly to be able to get your morning buns right.

2. Substitute the Strawberry and Hibiscus Jam with a jam or curd flavor of your choice.

3. When rolling out the dough, use a bench scraper to straighten the sides of the dough. Work fast, as the dough gets soft.

4. The rectangle will be wobbly in the sense that it will NOT be an exact rectangle, and that is OK. This dough is forgiving when you roll and cut it, so do not worry about getting an exact rectangle.

Chocolate Cardamom Pastry Cream, Halvah, and Pistachio Danish

Makes about 14 to 16 square Danish, plus extra dough to make smaller pastries

When I was in engineering college in Mumbai, my friends and I were frequent visitors of this place nearby called Candies. Candies had a range of sweet Danish with simple fillings like cream cheese and jam. They also had a range of savory Danish and croissants, filled with Indian-spiced fillings such as spiced potato and pea, different meats, and paneer tikka. I have fond memories of eating all the sweet and savory offerings with my dear friends.

I love French and Danish pastries, but I was always intimidated to make them. So I decided to learn the proper, authentic method of making pastry. I took a weeklong class of extensive lamination at the San Francisco Cooking School and I loved the experience! The amount I learned in that one week was immeasurable. I started thinking of all the possibilities of making croissants and puff pastries with the rough puff, and using these skills to create my own Indian-inspired Danish.

I wanted to create a sweet pastry that could be enjoyed for breakfast and show you, my dear readers, the detailed process of making Danish. It is not hard at all, trust me! It is a bit tedious but, let me tell you, lamination is therapeutic. The whole process of rolling the dough and seeing the lamination layers is soulfully satisfying. For a detailed timeline of the lamination process, please see page 159. And ultimately, when you bake the pastries and see the puffy layers and the golden-brown color, it is almost hard to believe that you created this Danish right from your own kitchen. The chocolate cardamom pastry cream here, along with the halvah, pistachios, and dried raspberries form an absolutely delicious treat to enjoy with your morning tea or coffee!

INGREDIENTS

PASTRY CREAM

2 ounces (60 g) semisweet chocolate, coarsely chopped

1¼ cups (300 g) whole milk

½ teaspoon (1 g) ground cardamom

3 egg yolks

¼ cup (50 g) granulated sugar

3 tablespoons (21 g) cornstarch

2 tablespoons (15 g) cocoa powder

½ teaspoon (3 g) table salt

2 tablespoons (28 g) unsalted butter

1 tablespoon (13 g) vanilla extract

BUTTER BLOCK

2 cups + 1½ tablespoons (470 g) cold, unsalted, European-style butter

DANISH BRIOCHE DOUGH

6 cups minus 4 teaspoons (720 g) bread flour

⅓ cup (65 g) granulated sugar

4 teaspoons (12 g) instant yeast

2 teaspoons (4 g) ground cardamom

2 teaspoons (12 g) table salt

1 cup + 3 tablespoons (280 g) whole milk, room temperature

3 eggs

5 tablespoons (72 g) European-style butter, melted and cooled

continued ➡

SUGAR SYRUP

¼ **cup (60 g) water**

¼ **cup (50 g) granulated sugar**

FILLINGS AND TOPPINGS

⅓ **cup (130 g) halvah**

4 **tablespoons freeze-dried raspberries,
finely crushed between your fingers**

¼ **cup (25 g) finely chopped pistachios**

EGG WASH

1 **egg**

1 **teaspoon water**

1 **teaspoon granulated sugar**

EQUIPMENT

Wide rolling pin

Parchment paper

Half-sheet baking sheets

Bench scraper

2–foot stainless steel ruler

Pastry brush

Wide-haired brush to brush off excess flour

**5-wheel stainless steel pastry cutter
(a sharp knife will do)**

METHOD

DAY 1

To Make the Pastry Cream

1. Set a small saucepan filled with water ⅓ way up over medium heat, and bring to a simmer. In a medium bowl add the chocolate and set it over the saucepan to melt, making sure that the bowl does not touch the water. Stir with a small rubber spatula until it melts, 3 to 4 minutes. Remove from the heat and set the bowl and saucepan aside.

2. In a medium saucepan over medium heat, add the milk, cardamom, and melted chocolate, and let it simmer for 3 to 4 minutes until it is hot.

3. Set aside a medium bowl with a fine-mesh sieve.

4. Meanwhile, in a medium bowl, add the egg yolks and sugar, and whisk vigorously for 2 to 3 minutes until the mixture is frothy and pale yellow. When you lift the whisk, the mixture should look smooth and have a ribbon-like consistency. Whisk in the cornstarch, cocoa powder, and salt. The mixture will form a thick paste.

5. Slowly add half the milk mixture, whisking until smooth, making sure there are no lumps.

6. Pour the mixture back into the saucepan with the remaining milk and whisk. Turn the heat on medium and continue to whisk, so that it does not stick to the bottom of the pan, until the mixture thickens within 5 minutes. It happens pretty quickly so do not leave the stove at this time.

7. Strain the mixture through the sieve into the bowl. Whisk in the butter and vanilla until smooth.

8. Place plastic wrap onto the pastry cream, so that it touches the pastry cream and does not form a skin.

9. Refrigerate overnight.

To Make the Butter Block

1. Cut the chilled butter into rectangular blocks to form an even square on the center of a sheet of parchment paper. It is almost like playing Tetris with the butter on the parchment to form a square.

2. Cover with another piece of parchment paper and start pounding the butter block with a rolling pin until the layer evens out. The goal is to smooth out the butter into an even layer of an 8-inch (20 cm) square butter block.

3. Keep measuring after a few poundings to see if it is reaching an 8-inch (20 cm) square butter block. You can use a bench scraper to even out the edges and smooth out the top. You can even flip the parchment paper upside down, since the bottom will be smoother, and then use a rolling pin to smooth the butter. Keep pushing the sides to be straight and form a square.

4. The whole process takes anywhere from 5 to 10 minutes. The goal is for the butter to remain chilled during the entire time and not soften. If you feel the butter is too soft, put it in the fridge for 30 minutes and try forming it into a square again.

5. Once the square is formed, tuck the parchment paper overhang around the butter block and set it in the fridge overnight.

To Make the Danish Brioche Dough

1. In the bowl of a stand mixer with a dough hook attachment, add all the dry ingredients—bread flour, sugar, yeast, ground cardamom, and salt and whisk to combine.

2. Add the milk, eggs, and butter to the mixture. Start the stand mixer at low speed for a minute so the dough can mix together. Increase to medium speed for 3 minutes until the dough is smooth and the bowl is clean.

3. Mix for another 2 to 3 minutes for the dough to develop gluten and become sturdy.

4. Do the windowpane test: Take a small piece of dough, and, using your first three fingers and thumb on both hands, gently smooth and stretch the dough until thin. If you can stretch the dough without breaking it, the dough has been sufficiently kneaded and the gluten is well developed. If it breaks, knead the dough in the mixer for another 1 to 2 minutes and do the windowpane test again.

5. Place the dough onto a clean surface. Shape into a rectangle, place it on a piece of parchment paper on a baking sheet, cover with plastic wrap, and refrigerate overnight.

DAY 2

To Laminate the Dough

1. Keep the stainless steel ruler, bench scraper, wide-haired brush, extra flour, and rolling pin handy. See photographs of the lamination process on page 76.

2. Remove the dough from the fridge. Using extra flour sprinkled on a clean surface and extra flour on the rolling pin, roll out the dough to an 8-by-18-inch (20-by-45 cm) rectangle. You have to keep straightening the sides of the rolled-out dough with the bench scraper and rolling pin to ensure that the rectangular shape is maintained at all times, while at the same time maintaining the thickness of the dough throughout. Use extra flour as needed to ensure that the dough does not stick to the surface.

3. Remove the butter block from the fridge and place in the middle of the dough. Remove the excess flour from the dough using the wide-haired brush. Wrap the left side over half the butter block, then wrap the right side over the other half of the block. Secure it from the top, bottom, and the middle by pinching the dough together. This is called a classic enclosure. Square out the entire block by using the bench scraper to align all the sides in parallel.

4. We will do three turns to the dough to laminate it.

continued ➤

5. Sprinkle flour on the work surface. With an open side of the dough-enclosed butter block toward you, roll lengthwise, up and down, to lengthen the dough. Make sure that the edges are straightened by using the bench scraper and rolling pin and keeping the thickness the same throughout the length of the dough.

6. Make sure that you spread flour beneath the dough by lifting it with one hand and sprinkling flour with the other. Always be sure to sprinkle flour on the top as well. You want to ensure your dough does not stick underneath or on your rolling pin.

7. Roll until you have an 8-by-18-inch (20-by-45 cm) rectangle. Make sure the corners are even and squared off. You can roll out to 8 by 19 inches (20 by 40 cm) and, using a pastry cutter, cut off half an inch (1½ cm) from the width of the rectangle to even out the sides. Use the wide-haired brush to gently remove any excess flour.

8. With a long side of the rectangle parallel to you, wrap the dough by folding the left side of the dough two-thirds of the way in. Brush off the excess flour using the wide brush and then wrap the right side of the dough over the left side. Again, brush off the excess flour. Straighten out the dough with a bench scraper and the rolling pin to an exact 8-by-18-inch (20-by-45 cm) rectangle. Place it on the baking sheet, wrap it with plastic wrap, and put it in the fridge for an hour.

Second Turn

9. With an open edge of the dough toward you, roll lengthwise, up and down, to lengthen the dough. Make sure that the edges are straightened by using the bench scraper and rolling pin to maintain an even thickness throughout the length of the dough.

10. Repeat Steps 6, 7, and 8.

Third Turn

11. With an open edge of the dough toward you, roll lengthwise, up and down, to lengthen the dough. Make sure that the edges are straightened by using the bench scraper and rolling pin to maintain an even thickness throughout the length of the dough.

12. Repeat Steps 6, 7, and 8.

To Cut the Laminated Dough

1. With an open edge of the dough toward you, roll lengthwise, up and down, to lengthen the dough. Make sure that the edges are straightened by using the bench scraper and rolling pin to maintain an even thickness throughout the length of the dough.

2. Make sure that you spread flour beneath the dough by lifting it with one hand and sprinkling flour with the other. Always be sure to sprinkle flour on the top as well. You want to ensure your dough does not stick underneath or on your rolling pin.

3. The desired size is 9 by 26 inches (23 by 66 cm) and about ¼ inch (5 mm) thick. You want an even rectangle. Cut off half an inch from the width and the length of the rectangle to even out the sides, using a sharp knife and the stainless steel ruler. Use the wide-haired brush to brush off the excess flour.

4. Using the stainless steel pastry cutter set to 3½ inches (9 cm) wide, cut strips from the rolled-out dough, lengthwise first. When using the pastry cutter, cut at a 60-degree angle, putting even pressure across the entire cutter to make neat, consistent squares. Using the same 3½-inch (9 cm) setting, cut widthwise to form the squares. You will get 14 exact squares, with additional scraps of dough to play with or to make cylinder pastries with. You can also use a knife and ruler to cut the squares if you do not have a cutter.

5. Place the squares 2 inches (5 cm) apart on a parchment paper-lined baking sheet, cover with plastic wrap, and put it in the fridge for 30 to 40 minutes.

To Shape, Proof, Fill, and Bake the Danish

1. **To shape the Danish:** Remove four squares at a time. Roll them out slightly larger to about 4-inch (10 cm) square. Using a sharp knife, cut about 1½-inch (4 cm) L-shapes on each of the corners, keeping ¼-inch (½ cm) distance from the edge of the square. Take each corner and bring it to the center and press gently to seal. You will see a flower shape (see the photo below).

2. Place the squares on the baking sheet 2 inches (5 cm) apart and proof the Danish.

3. **To proof the Danish:** To proof, you can choose two different methods. The first option is to put a large plastic bag or an unscented garbage bag over the baking sheet, sealing the tray. Make sure that the bag does not touch the Danish by putting inverted glasses on the four corners of the tray inside the bag to hold it up. Repeat for the other trays. Leave the trays in a warm place, around 75°F (25°C). The second option is to place the baking sheets in the oven with a pot of warm water (around 75°F [25°C]) to create the warm environment required for proofing. Proof for 2½ to 3 hours.

4. **To make the simple syrup:** In a small saucepan, combine the water and sugar. On medium heat, let the sugar dissolve for 2 minutes. Remove from the heat and let the syrup cool.

5. **To fill the Danish:** Whisk the Chocolate Cardamom Pastry Cream to make a smooth mixture. Make sure the center of the Danish square is sealed. Scoop about 1 heaped tablespoon of the pastry cream onto the middle of the Danish. Add about 1 heaped teaspoon of the halvah on top.

6. **To make the egg wash:** Combine the ingredients in a small bowl and whisk for 2 minutes until the mixture is smooth.

7. **To bake the Danish:** Preheat the oven to 415°F (210°C). Dip the pastry brush into the egg wash, removing excess, and lightly brush on the border and sides of each Danish. Place the baking sheet on the center rack of the oven. Bake for 5 minutes, then reduce the temperature to 375°F (190°C) and bake for about 20 to 25 minutes until golden brown, rotating the trays after about 15 minutes for an even bake.

8. **To decorate the Danish:** When the Danish come out of the oven, use a pastry brush to apply the simple syrup over the pastries to give them a nice shine and crunch after cooling. Sprinkle generously with the dried raspberries and chopped pistachios and more halvah if you're fancy! Enjoy with some tea or coffee.

PRO TIPS

1. You can make the Chocolate Cardamom Pastry Cream a week in advance.

2. The butter block can be made 3 to 4 days in advance. Keep it refrigerated.

3. If the butter starts seeping out while making the turns, you can cover it up with the dough, or add some flour on it to cover it.

4. If the butter/dough gets too soft during lamination, put it in the fridge for 30 minutes.

5. If you want to make these Danish in the summer, make sure the AC is on in your home. The butter tends to melt fast, and the butter and dough have to be chilled constantly throughout the lamination process.

6. You have to work fast through the lamination process and the shaping process so as not to melt the butter between the layers; otherwise, the dough will not be easy to handle. When the laminated dough is chilled, it is easier to handle to make the desired shapes.

7. You can use any fillings you want, like sweetened cream cheese and the jam of your choice, or simply vanilla pastry cream and jam, or be creative and add your own sweetened fillings to make a delicious pastry to enjoy for breakfast.

8. These Danish can be enjoyed for up to 2 days. Simply toast them in the toaster oven for 2 minutes before eating.

9. I usually remove the number of Danish squares that we plan to eat within the day and go through the shaping/proofing/filling/baking process while the rest of the squares stay wrapped in plastic wrap and frozen. The day before shaping/proofing/filling/baking, etc., I put them in the fridge so that they are not rock hard to roll out.

PRO TIPS

1. If you do not have Oaxaca cheese or cannot find it, substitute with pepper Jack or Monterey Jack cheese.

2. You could add anything that is seasonal, such as fresh corn, squash blossoms, cherry tomatoes, and more.

Breakfast Naan Pizza

Serves 2

While my family loves their sweet breakfasts like waffles, pancakes, and Pop Tarts, once in a while they do appreciate a Breakfast Naan Pizza. I make from leftover naan. On weekends, especially when we tend to skip breakfast and go for brunch, this is a great, hearty option. Use the leftover naan and top it with your favorite cheese. I love using Oaxaca cheese, which has the taste of Monterey Jack and the string-like stretchy texture of mozzarella. Top it with vegetables—I add spiced potatoes, bell peppers, and onions. And finally, top it off with an egg or two. I would use small eggs so that they do not spill over the edge of the naan. The Breakfast Naan Pizza is quite versatile and would be perfect for lunch or dinner too. Hope you love it as much as we do in our home!

INGREDIENTS

3 small potatoes, scrubbed

1 tablespoon olive oil

¼ teaspoon red chili powder

¼ teaspoon ground turmeric

¼ teaspoon ground coriander

¼ teaspoon salt

2 Butter Garlic Naan (page 357)

½ cup (60 g) thinly sliced or grated Oaxaca cheese

½ small red onion, sliced thin

½ small green bell pepper, sliced thin

2 to 4 small eggs

GARNISH

Cilantro leaves

Finely chopped chives

Maldon flaky salt

Kashmiri red chili powder

METHOD

1. Preheat the oven to 400°F (200°C).

2. Slice the potatoes thin with a mandoline, or with a sharp knife, about ¼ inch (½ cm) thick. Place them on a plate not overlapping each other and microwave for 1 minute to soften.

3. In a medium bowl, whisk together the olive oil, spices, and salt. Add the potatoes and gently toss to coat them evenly with the oil and spices.

4. Place the naan on a parchment paper–lined baking sheet.

5. Equally distribute the cheese on each naan.

6. Top each naan with a few slices of spiced potatoes, red onion, and green bell pepper.

7. Make one or two small indentations in the fillings with a spoon, depending upon how many eggs you want to use.

8. Break an egg into a small bowl, and carefully pour the egg into an indentation. Repeat for all the eggs. Place the baking sheet in the oven for 10 minutes, until the eggs are just set.

9. Remove from the oven and garnish with the cilantro leaves and chopped chives. Sprinkle with a bit of Maldon salt and Kashmiri red chili powder for the final touch!

Strawberry and Rose Petal Granola

Makes about one 32-ounce (1 L) jar

Strawberry and edible dried rose petal has always been my all-time favorite combination. One of my favorite jams to make during strawberry season is a Strawberry and Rose Petal Jam (see Pro Tip on Strawberry and Hibiscus Jam on page 48) because of its fruity and floral notes. A quick sourdough toast, doused with some good-quality salted butter and a smidge of the jam, and my morning is made! Roses remind me of my mum. She loved them. She would grow them on our veranda along with hibiscus and bougainvillea. She wore roses and jasmines in her hair bun too, especially when we would go to a wedding or a special occasion. It looked so elegant on her. As with everything she did, she carried it off beautifully.

With this combination in mind, and my love for a good nourishing breakfast, here is my take on a lovely Strawberry and Rose Petal Granola with freeze-dried strawberries and edible dried rose petals. The best part is that you can make it even in the winter because freeze-dried strawberries are available all year round. My mother-in-law enjoys this granola a lot so I like to make a double batch to give her half. That way, she can eat it with her morning Greek yogurt parfait.

INGREDIENTS

2 cups (180 g) rolled oats

1 cup (130 g) coarsely chopped cashews

½ teaspoon (1 g) ground cardamom

½ teaspoon (1 g) nutmeg

½ teaspoon (1 g) black pepper

½ to 1 teaspoon (3 to 6 g) Maldon sea salt

¼ cup (50 g) coconut oil

¼ cup (50 g) light brown sugar

¼ cup (80 g) honey

1½ teaspoons (6 g) rose water

1 teaspoon (4 g) vanilla extract

¼ cup edible dried rose petals or 10 edible dried rosebuds

½ cup freeze-dried strawberries, broken into coarse pieces

½ cup (70 g) finely chopped dried apricots

METHOD

1. Preheat the oven to 300°F (150°C). Line a baking sheet with parchment paper.

2. In a large bowl, mix the oats, cashews, cardamom, nutmeg, black pepper, and sea salt.

3. In a small saucepan on medium heat, add the coconut oil, brown sugar, and honey, and whisk until the brown sugar blends into the mixture, about 3 minutes. Turn off the heat. Add the rose water and vanilla extract and whisk to blend.

4. Add the wet ingredients to the dry ingredients and mix well. Spread the granola onto the baking sheet and press it flat with the rubber spatula.

5. Bake the granola in the oven for 40 minutes, stirring it around, and flattening it with a rubber spatula every 15 minutes to make sure that the granola bakes evenly.

continued →

6. In the last 5 minutes of baking, add the rose petals and freeze-dried strawberries to the granola, stir around with the spatula, and flatten it again.

7. Once out of the oven, add the apricots, and press them gently into the granola, without stirring or disturbing it. Let it cool for an hour.

8. Once completely cooled, fill up small glass jars as gifts or store in an airtight glass jar for up to 2 weeks.

PRO TIPS

1. Granola is very forgiving. You can switch up the nuts, the freeze-dried fruit, and the dried fruit to your liking. I just happen to love the flavor combination of strawberries, rose petals, and cashews!

2. This makes for a fantastic breakfast with Greek yogurt: Swirl in some floral honey, add the granola, and top with seasonal fruit. Enjoy a healthy and filling breakfast.

Sooji Dhokla
(Semolina Savory Spongy Cakes)

Makes about 12 to 14 pieces

What is dhokla? Dhokla is a soft and spongy savory cake that originated from Gujarat. It makes the best healthy and delicious breakfast, or it can be served as a treat, an after-school snack, or an appetizer. It is so versatile. There are many varieties of dhokla, such as white or yellow, made with different lentils and rice, gram flour, or, in this case, semolina. My favorite dhokla is the khatta dhokla or sour dhokla made with rice and lentils and fermented for a day. Fermentation gives the batter the typical sour taste, which is absolutely delicious! I can still remember how wonderful Mum's dhoklas were and how my friends would specifically ask Mum to make the dhoklas when they would visit my home.

These Sooji Dhoklas are made with fine semolina. They are mixed with Greek yogurt for that sour tangy taste. The tempering, after the dhoklas are steamed, is essential to the overall taste of the dhokla. They are very easy to make and come together pretty quickly. They are best eaten with the Cilantro Mint Chutney (page 42); however, my kids love them with the Date Tamarind Chutney (page 45) too!

INGREDIENTS

1 green chili
½ inch (1¼ cm) ginger
¾ cup (135 g) fine sooji or semolina
½ cup (113 g) Greek yogurt
⅔ cup (160 g) water
1¼ teaspoons (7.5 g) table salt
1 teaspoon (4 g) granulated sugar
2 tablespoons (14 g) vegetable oil
¾ teaspoon fruit salt, such as Eno Fruit Salt
1 teaspoon lemon juice
Pinch of red chili powder
Pinch of black pepper

TEMPERING

1 tablespoon (14 g) vegetable oil
Pinch of asafoetida
6 to 8 curry leaves
1 teaspoon (4 g) mustard seeds
1 teaspoon (3 g) sesame seeds
1 green chili, split into two lengthwise

GARNISH

2 tablespoons finely chopped fresh cilantro
Cilantro Mint Chutney (page 42)

METHOD

1. In a small food processor, mince the green chili and ginger to form a paste.

2. In a medium bowl, add the semolina, yogurt, water, salt, sugar, 1 tablespoon vegetable oil, and ginger-green chili paste, and whisk well to combine. Set it aside for 20 to 30 minutes.

3. Meanwhile, prepare a steamer or a large pot with a lid, on medium to high heat, with a metal ring at least 2 inches high in the center. Put 3 to 4 cups (720 to 960 g) of water in the pot, and let it come to a boil.

continued ➡

4. Prepare an 8-inch (20 cm) cake pan by applying 1 tablespoon vegetable oil all over the inside of the pan.

5. After the batter has rested, add the fruit salt and lemon juice and whisk in one direction continuously for 30 to 40 seconds. The batter should rise and become light. Quickly add this whipped batter into the cake pan and tap the pan a few times to level the batter.

6. Sprinkle the red chili powder and black pepper evenly over the batter. Put the cake pan immediately into the steamer or large pot and close the lid. Let the dhoklas steam for 15 minutes.

7. After 30 minutes, turn off the heat and poke a knife in the center to check for doneness. If the knife comes out clean, the dhoklas are done. Remove the pan from the steamer and let it rest for 10 minutes. After 10 minutes, run a sharp knife around the edge to loosen the dhoklas from the tin. Cut the dhoklas vertically and horizontally to form squares. Remove them with an offset spatula onto a platter.

8. Meanwhile, prepare the tempering. In a small saucepan on medium heat, add the vegetable oil. After a minute, add the asafoetida, curry leaves, mustard seeds, sesame seeds, and green chili. Once the seeds start splattering, the mixture is ready. Pour this mixture all over the dhoklas. Sprinkle with the chopped cilantro. The dhoklas are ready to be eaten with the Cilantro Mint Chutney (page 42).

PRO TIPS

1. Eno Fruit Salt is available in retail online stores or at any Indian grocery store.

2. If you do not have access to Eno Fruit Salt, you can substitute ½ teaspoon baking soda and 1 extra teaspoon lemon juice.

3. Omit the green chili and red chili powder if you do not like it spicy.

4. Dhoklas can be made a day ahead and kept in the fridge. Simply heat them up in a microwave for 30 to 40 seconds.

Almond Cinnamon Waffles
WITH SUMMER BERRIES

Makes about 8 waffles (depending on the waffle maker)

Perhaps the first recipe I posted when I started my Instagram account was for Belgian-style waffles. I have been making waffles since my kids were little and they could eat the same breakfast as us. I have made so many variations of this base waffle recipe, with fruits, nuts, and chocolate, and it always turns out fantastic. When I have visitors from out of town, I make waffles for them. It is our happy breakfast, one that fuels us and brings a smile to our faces. I make the entire batch and freeze the leftovers, which makes for quick 5-minute weekday school breakfasts. We love our waffles with whatever in-season fruit there is, thus ensuring that the fruit food group is covered for breakfast. Waffles have become our Sunday breakfast tradition, so much so that when my father-in-law visits us from Los Angeles, his one and only ask is for Sunday morning waffles.

I love the texture that almond flour brings to these waffles, along with the sliced almonds and the almond extract. Our absolute favorite way to eat this breakfast is with summer berries. In the summer, when the California berries are in full swing, I put together a platter of mixed berries, like strawberries, raspberries, blackberries, and blueberries. I have an assembly line of all the toppings and let the family help themselves to whatever they fancy on their waffle. It makes for a fun way to enjoy our breakfast and start our Sunday on a sweet and fruity note.

INGREDIENTS

1¾ cups (210 g) all-purpose flour

½ cup (62 g) almond flour

½ cup (100 g) granulated sugar

3½ teaspoons (14 g) baking powder

1 teaspoon (2.6 g) cinnamon powder

½ teaspoon (3 g) table salt

½ cup (1 stick; 113 g) unsalted butter, melted

1 cup (240 g) whole milk, room temperature

2 large eggs, at room temperature, yolk and white separated

1 tablespoon (13 g) vanilla extract

1 teaspoon (5 g) almond extract

¾ cup to 1 cup (130 g to 175 g) dark chocolate chips (60% cacao)

½ cup (55 g) toasted sliced almonds

SUGGESTED TOPPINGS

Good-quality maple syrup

Whipped cream

Summer berries such as strawberries, raspberries, blueberries, and blackberries

Powdered sugar

Sliced almonds

Sprigs of mint

METHOD

1. In a large bowl, add the flour, almond flour, sugar, baking powder, ground cinnamon, and salt, and whisk to combine.

2. In a medium bowl, add the melted butter, whole milk, egg yolks, vanilla extract, and almond extract, and whisk well to combine.

continued ➤

3. Make a well in the dry ingredients bowl, and add the wet ingredients. Using a balloon whisk, slowly incorporate the dry ingredients into the well and keep whisking until the entire mixture is homogeneous and well combined.

4. In a medium bowl with a hand mixer, whisk the egg whites for 1 to 2 minutes, until the egg whites are fluffy and cloud-like.

5. Using a rubber spatula, gently fold the whipped egg whites into the mixture until incorporated. Do not overmix. The batter will be light and airy.

6. Add the chocolate chips and sliced almonds, using a rubber spatula to incorporate them into the batter.

7. Warm up your waffle iron and cook the waffles per the waffle iron manufacturer's instructions, until brown in color. Let them cool a bit so that they crisp up.

8. Plate the waffles and add the toppings, such as maple syrup, whipped cream, fruits, a sprinkling of powdered sugar, sliced almonds, and a sprig of mint. Enjoy.

PRO TIPS

1. To bring the whole milk to room temperature, warm it in the microwave for 40 seconds.

2. To bring the eggs to room temperature, you can submerge the eggs in warm water for about 10 minutes.

3. The waffles can be made in advance, and frozen for up to a week. They make for a fantastic breakfast option for weekday school mornings. Pop a waffle into the toaster oven for a minute or two and breakfast is ready within 5 minutes.

Huevos Rancheros Waffles
WITH ROASTED CHIPOTLE POTATOES

Makes about 10 waffles

What is huevos rancheros? It is essentially fried eggs on a corn tortilla, with a spicy tomato salsa. My first experience with huevos rancheros was when Raj and I were on our first trip to Cancun as a married couple, eons ago. I fell in love with this dish. I would alternate between huevos rancheros and chilaquiles. It became my go-to dish when we brunched on weekends at any Mexican restaurant. Because of the close proximity of California to Mexico, and the abundance of fresh seasonal produce, we are lucky to have some really good Mexican restaurants with some of the best Mexican food—a cuisine that my whole family is very fond of. The taste of that rancheros sauce on top of a fried egg, black beans, and the freshly made corn tortilla, along with the toppings—and let's not forget the oodles of hot sauce on top—is simply sublime.

I created this recipe a few years ago. My family LOVES waffles, any kind. Sweet or savory, they are all in. Waffles are something that they look forward to on weekends. I usually make brunch out of these waffles. It's my take on huevos rancheros. I love the freshness of the summer sweet corn, jalapeños, and red bell peppers, along with the bold and beautiful spices and the corn masa in these waffles. Corn masa harina is flour made out of dried corn and is readily available at grocery stores. You can even make fresh homemade corn tortillas using the masa harina. I make a Roasted Tomato and Dried Pasilla Chili Salsa (page 373) that pairs perfectly with these waffles, along with Roasted Chipotle Potatoes, a classic side dish for our Sunday brunch. The waffles, along with some seasonal alcoholic and virgin margaritas, hit the spot, and make for very satisfied bellies in our home.

INGREDIENTS

BUTTERMILK CORN, JALAPEÑO,
RED BELL PEPPER WAFFLES

1 cup (120 g) all-purpose flour

½ cup (67 g) masa harina flour

2½ teaspoons (10 g) baking powder

2 teaspoons (12 g) salt

2 teaspoons (4.6 g) black pepper

1 teaspoon (2 g) smoked paprika

1 teaspoon (3 g) ancho chili powder

½ teaspoon (1 g) garlic powder

1½ cups (360 g) buttermilk

½ cup (1 stick; 113 g) unsalted butter, melted and cooled

2 large eggs

1 cup (110 g) grated cheddar cheese

1 ear corn, boiled for 4 minutes or microwaved for 2 minutes in plastic wrap and kernels cut off

½ red bell pepper, diced small

½ medium red onion, finely chopped

½ jalapeño, finely chopped (remove the seeds if you do not want it spicy)

¼ cup finely chopped cilantro

2 tablespoons (42 g) green Hatch chilis from a can (optional)

½ cup (120 g) water, if needed

continued ➡

PRO TIPS

1. Use frozen corn instead of fresh; simply boil it for 2 to 3 minutes to cook it.

2. Waffle batter can be made a day in advance. Make sure to thin it out slightly before making the waffles.

3. Waffles can be made all at once and stored in the fridge in an airtight container for up to a week. Pop in the toaster oven for 2 to 3 minutes. They make for a great filling breakfast that can be prepared quickly in no time.

ROASTED CHIPOTLE POTATOES

6 medium (500 g) Yukon Gold potatoes, chopped

¼ (30 g) small red onion, finely diced

2 tablespoons (27 g) vegetable oil

1 tablespoon chipotle in adobo sauce

1 teaspoon (6 g) table salt

1 teaspoon (2 g) black pepper

1 teaspoon (2 g) smoked paprika

½ teaspoon (1.5 g) ancho chili powder

1 teaspoon (2 g) garlic powder

BLACK BEANS

1 tablespoon (13.6 g) olive oil

One 15-ounce can black beans

1 teaspoon (6 g) table salt

1 teaspoon (2 g) black pepper

GARNISH

Fried egg for each waffle

Roasted Tomato and Dried Pasilla Chili Salsa
   (page 373)

2 avocados, thinly sliced

Cotija cheese

¼ (30 g) small red onion, finely diced

¼ cup finely chopped cilantro

3 to 4 radishes, thinly sliced

METHOD

To Make the Waffles

1. In a large bowl, whisk to combine the flour, masa harina, baking powder, salt, pepper, smoked paprika, ancho chili powder, and garlic powder.

2. In a small bowl, whisk together the buttermilk, melted butter, and eggs. Mix the wet ingredients into the dry ingredients until well combined.

3. Add cheese, corn, red bell pepper, onion, jalapeño, cilantro, and green Hatch chilis (if using). Use a rubber spatula to mix it well. If the mixture is TOO thick, you can add water a few tablespoons at a time, up to ½ cup (120 grams), and stir to combine.

To Make the Potatoes

1. Preheat the oven to 420°F (215°C) and place a rack on the lowest level. In a large bowl with a rubber spatula, combine all the potato ingredients and mix well.

2. In a jelly roll pan, spread the mixture evenly. Place the jelly roll pan on the lowest oven rack. Roast for about 30 to 35 minutes until everything is caramelized and charred with a crust on the potatoes. Insert a knife into a few of the potatoes to make sure they are cooked through.

3. Remove the pan from the oven and let the potatoes cool slightly before serving.

To Make the Black Beans

In a small saucepan on medium heat, add the oil and wait for it to become hot, about 1 minute. Add the black beans, salt, and pepper, and, using a wooden spatula, mix to combine for 2 minutes. Turn off the stove.

To Assemble

1. Make the waffles per the waffle iron manufacturer's instructions. Keep warm in a 275°F (135°C) oven on a baking sheet.

2. Cook the fried eggs one at a time in an oiled pan; try not to break the yolk.

3. Place a waffle on a plate, spoon on a bit of the black beans, and then top with the fried egg.

4. Drizzle 1 to 2 tablespoons of Roasted Tomato and Dried Pasilla Chili Salsa om the waffle. Place some roasted potatoes and avocado on the side. Top the plate with a sprinkle of Cotija cheese, red onion, cilantro, and radishes.

Pear and Chai Masala Cinnamon Rolls

Makes 12 rolls

The Bay Area gets pretty cold in the winters. I love the foggy and misty mornings, cuddled up in warm pajamas and socks with the family, and having a lovely, warm breakfast. My family loves cinnamon rolls. I mean, what is not to love, right?. Warm, gooey, fluffy, melt-in-your-mouth goodness. Best enjoyed with a warm beverage like coffee or masala chai, there is a reason they are so popular, with kids and adults alike.

The Pear and Chai Masala Cinnamon Rolls recipe is a fun one. You can even make the rolls, let them sit overnight in the fridge, and bake them off in the morning, after an hour or so of the dough resting and rising. That way, you can enjoy fresh cinnamon rolls, first thing in the morning. I use bread flour in this recipe, because bread flour's higher protein content enhances the development of gluten. It also makes the final product very fluffy and light. Bread flour is easily available online and in grocery stores. You can use all-purpose flour as a replacement. For the filling, I use warming spices, such as cinnamon (of course), cardamom, ginger, and nutmeg. I also use my Pear and Chai Masala Jam (page 35), which is one of my favorite winter jams. The rolls—filled with the jam and pear pieces and topped with the delicious vanilla bean icing—are special, and a wonderful way to spend the weekend with your loved ones.

INGREDIENTS

CINNAMON ROLL DOUGH

1 cup (240 g) whole milk, warmed, about 110°F (45°C)

One ¼-ounce packet (about 2¼ teaspoons; 7 g) active dry yeast

¼ cup (50 g) + 1 teaspoon (4 g) granulated sugar

½ cup (1 stick; 113 g) unsalted butter, melted

4½ cups (540 g) bread flour, plus extra for rolling out the dough

2 teaspoons (4 g) ground ginger

1 teaspoon (6 g) table salt

2 large eggs

2 teaspoons (9 g) vanilla extract

FILLING

½ cup (100 g) light brown sugar, packed

2 teaspoons (6 g) ground cinnamon

1½ teaspoons (3 g) ground ginger

1 teaspoon (2 g) ground cardamom

½ teaspoon to 1 teaspoon (1 to 2 g) freshly ground nutmeg

4 tablespoons (½ stick; 56 g) unsalted butter, melted

6 ounces Pear and Chai Masala Jam (page 35)

2 small pears (any kind you prefer), halved, cored, and cut into small cubes (about ⅓ inch; 1 cm; you can keep the skin on)

VANILLA BEAN ICING

2 cups (256 g) confectioners' sugar

4 tablespoons to 5 tablespoons (61 to 77 g) whole milk, room temperature

1½ teaspoons vanilla bean paste

continued ➞

METHOD

To Make the Cinnamon Roll Dough

1. Warm the milk to about 110°F (45°C). Add the yeast and 1 teaspoon granulated sugar to it, stir, and let sit for 10 minutes. You will see it foam up, and you know that the yeast is active.

2. Add the melted butter to the warm milk mixture.

3. Mix the bread flour, ginger, salt, and ¼ cup (50 g) sugar in a large bowl.

4. In the bowl of a stand mixer with a dough paddle attachment, add the milk mixture. Add the eggs and vanilla extract and mix to combine. Alternatively, you could do this in a large mixing bowl, if you do not have a stand mixer. Add the dry mixture to the wet, at slow speed, increasing the speed gradually and mix for about 8 minutes until well combined. The dough starts off very sticky, and as the gluten develops, you will see the dough leaving the sides of the bowl and a ball forming. The dough will still be slightly sticky but it will have structure.

5. If you are using a mixing bowl, then knead the just-combined dough on a lightly floured surface for about 10 minutes until it forms a nice ball.

6. Lightly oil a large bowl, add the dough ball, and cover with plastic wrap. Cover with a kitchen towel and let it sit for at least 1½ to 2 hours until it doubles in size.

To Make the Filling

Meanwhile, make the filling by mixing all the filling ingredients, except the butter, jam, and pear, in a small bowl. Set it aside.

To Assemble and Bake

1. Turn the dough out onto a lightly floured surface. Form it into a rectangle shape first and start rolling it evenly into a 12-by-20-inch (30-by-50 cm) rectangle. Brush the dough with the melted butter. Sprinkle the filling mixture evenly all over the dough, leaving a 1-inch (2½ cm) border all around the dough. Evenly dollop the jam all over the dough. Using a small offset spatula, gently spread the jam all over, leaving a 1-inch (2½ cm) border around the dough. Finally, sprinkle the pear evenly all over the dough. Starting from the long edge, roll the dough tightly until it forms a log shape. You have to nudge the dough all along the length of it to roll it up evenly and tightly. Trim the sides. Measure the log and cut it evenly into 12 rolls. Each roll will be about 1½ inches (4 cm) wide.

2. Place them evenly spaced in a buttered 9-by-13-inch (23-by-33 cm) baking pan and cover with plastic wrap. Cover with a kitchen towel and place in a cool place for at least 2 hours. The rolls will rise and double in size.

3. Preheat the oven to 350°F (175°C). Place the pan on the center rack of the oven and bake for about 40 minutes or until golden brown. The inside temperature should be about 190°F (90°C).

To Make the Icing

1. While the buns are baking, make the icing. Combine all the ingredients and whisk until smooth. The consistency should not be too thick, so it can drip on the sides of the bun. I leave extra frosting, to put on each bun as served. Spread the frosting 10 minutes or so after the buns are out of the oven.

2. Serve immediately with some hot coffee. Enjoy.

Banana, Walnut, and Chocolate Chip Pancakes
WITH CARAMELIZED BANANAS

Makes about 14 pancakes, serves 6 to 8

Pancakes are one of the easiest breakfasts to make from scratch. I could care less for pancakes, but my kids LOVE pancakes. I make a whole batch over the weekend and the leftovers carry over as breakfast for the next couple of days. My favorite are these Banana, Walnut, and Chocolate Chip Pancakes. I add oat flour and oat milk, which provide a wonderful texture and oat flavor to them.

Growing up, my mum would make caramelized bananas in ghee and cardamom on almost a daily basis as a treat to have with our lunch. When babies are able to eat solid foods, this is one of the first foods that Indian parents love giving them. The ghee, natural sugar in the bananas, and floral cardamom make for a very nourishing meal for babies. Well, that transitioned into my adulthood as well, and I still love this heavenly combination. It pairs really well with the pancakes and makes for a filling breakfast.

INGREDIENTS

PANCAKES

1½ cups (180 g) all-purpose flour

½ cup (60 g) oat flour

4 teaspoons (16 g) baking powder

½ teaspoon (2.5 g) baking soda

1 teaspoon (6 g) salt

¼ cup (50 g) granulated sugar

1 teaspoon (2 g) ground cardamom

1 teaspoon (2.6 g) ground cinnamon

1 teaspoon (2 g) ground ginger

2 overripe mashed bananas (230 g)

1 cup (240 g) oat milk

½ cup (113 g) Greek yogurt

1 tablespoon vanilla extract

4 tablespoons (½ stick; 56 g) unsalted butter, melted and cooled, plus 6 to 8 tablespoons (¾ to 1 stick; 85 to 113 g) for making the pancakes

2 large eggs

¾ cup (75 g) coarsely chopped toasted walnuts

1 cup (170 g) chocolate chips

CARAMELIZED BANANAS

3 tablespoons (45 g) ghee

3 firm bananas, sliced into ¾-inch-thick pieces

1 teaspoon (2 g) freshly ground cardamom

GARNISH

Bananas in ghee and cardamom

¾ cup (75 g) coarsely chopped toasted walnuts

Maple syrup

Confectioners' sugar

continued ➤

METHOD

To Make the Pancakes

1. In a large bowl, add the all-purpose flour, oat flour, baking powder, baking soda, salt, granulated sugar, cardamom, cinnamon, and ginger, and whisk to combine.

2. In a separate medium bowl, add the mashed bananas (make sure they're completely mashed), oat milk, Greek yogurt, vanilla extract, melted and cooled butter, and eggs. Whisk to combine.

3. Add the wet ingredients to the dry ingredients. Whisk to combine. Fold in the walnuts and chocolate chips.

4. Let the batter sit for 10 minutes.

5. Meanwhile, on low to medium heat, warm up the griddle or a large nonstick pan. Wait 3 to 4 minutes for it to heat up properly.

6. Add a teaspoon of butter on the heated pan. Once it melts, use a ¼-cup (60 ml) ice cream scoop to add the pancake batter to the greased griddle, to form a circle about 4 to 5 inches (10 to 12 cm) in diameter. Wait 2 to 3 minutes. When you can see bubbles and holes on the top of the pancake, flip it onto the other side. Cook for about 30 seconds to a minute or until the bottom side is browned.

7. Remove the pancake onto a plate. Repeat with the other pancakes.

To Make the Caramelized Bananas

1. In a large nonstick skillet on medium heat, add the ghee. Wait for it to heat up for a minute. Add the bananas flat on the skillet, and sprinkle the cardamom on the top of the bananas.

2. Let the bottom of the banana slices heat up for 2 minutes, so that they brown well. Flip each banana slice to brown the other side for 2 minutes.

3. Remove from the skillet and set aside.

To Assemble

Stack up to three pancakes on a plate. Garnish with bananas in ghee and cardamom, walnuts, maple syrup, and a sprinkle of confectioners' sugar.

PRO TIPS

1. If you do not have ghee, you can caramelize the bananas in butter.

2. Replace the oat flour and oat milk with regular all-purpose flour and whole milk. I personally love oat and bananas together.

Dried Fig, Walnut, and Chocolate Chunk Granola

Makes about one 32-ounce (1 L) jar

My dad has always been an advocate for Ayurveda and eating good, nourishing foods for your body. If there is anyone I can take healthy-eating inspiration from, it is my dad. He has asthma issues, and, with the pollution in Mumbai, the asthma can become aggravated if he is out and about. He knows how to control his asthma. He will go on a liquid diet to remove the toxins from his body, and take his medication too, but removing toxins makes him feel better instantly. Now that is self-control!

My dad eats breakfast like a king. He starts off with a hot savory breakfast like upma, which is made with semolina and spices. His breakfast also includes dried figs, raisins, and walnuts every single day, along with some seasonal fruit. When he comes to visit me in California, his hot breakfast will consist of cooked oatmeal, but the dried figs and walnuts with seasonal fruit are a constant. He ends the day with a small piece of dark chocolate. That is his only sweet or dessert in the entire day. He doesn't even have sugar in his tea. This inspired me to make a fall-inspired granola, with dried figs, walnuts, and chocolate chunks, with a hint of orange zest and spices like cardamom, star anise, and cinnamon. This granola is sweetened with brown sugar and maple syrup and a hint of vanilla as well. I know my dad would love this granola, as it has all his favorite things in one jar. Dad, this one's for you!

INGREDIENTS

2 cups (180 g) rolled oats

1 cup (150 g) coarsely chopped walnuts

2 tablespoons (15 g) white sesame seeds

½ teaspoon (1 g) ground star anise

½ teaspoon (1 g) ground cardamom

1 teaspoon (2.4 g) ground cinnamon

1 teaspoon (6 g) Maldon sea salt

¼ cup (50 g) coconut oil

¼ cup (50 g) light brown sugar

¼ cup (85 g) maple syrup

1 tablespoon orange zest

1 teaspoon (4 g) vanilla extract

¾ cup (105 g) coarsely chopped bittersweet chocolate (60% cacao)

¾ cup (105 g) finely chopped dried figs

METHOD

1. Preheat the oven to 300°F (150°C). Line a baking sheet with parchment paper.

2. In a large bowl, mix the oats, walnuts, white sesame seeds, star anise, cardamom, cinnamon, and sea salt.

3. In a small saucepan on medium heat, add the coconut oil, brown sugar, maple syrup, and orange zest, and whisk until the brown sugar blends into the mixture, about 4 minutes. Turn off the heat. Add the vanilla extract and whisk to blend.

continued ➤

4. Add the wet ingredients to the dry ingredients and mix well. Spread the granola onto the baking sheet and press it flat with the rubber spatula.

5. Bake the granola in the oven for 40 minutes, stirring it around and flattening it with a rubber spatula every 15 minutes so that the granola bakes evenly.

6. Remove from the oven and add the dried figs and chocolate chunks on top and press them gently into the granola, without stirring or disturbing it. Let it cool for an hour.

7. Once completely cooled, fill up small glass jars as gifts or store in an airtight glass jar for up to a month.

PRO TIPS

1. Granola is very forgiving. Switch up the nuts and the dried fruit to your liking. I love the flavor combination of figs, walnuts, and chocolate.

2. This makes for a fantastic breakfast with Greek yogurt: Swirl in a good floral honey or honeycomb, add the granola on the top, along with seasonal fruit. Enjoy a healthy and filling breakfast.

3. Add it over a creamy oat porridge, along with fresh seasonal fruit and a drizzle of honey for a warm breakfast.

Chai Masala, Macadamia Nut, and White Chocolate Banana Bread
WITH PASSION FRUIT AND VANILLA BEAN BUTTER

Makes 1 loaf

Bananas are a staple in our home. Not a day goes by without bananas on the kitchen counter. We come back from a vacation and the first groceries we get are milk, bread, and bananas. And if there are ripe bananas, they almost always get converted into some form of banana bread. I make many variations of banana bread, always with dark chocolate chips.

When I was creating this recipe, I had my kids—and Hawaii—as inspiration. If you ask my kids what their absolute favorite vacation is, they mention three places: Jaipur, London, and Hawaii. The vibrant and calm vibes from the people and islands of Hawaii have always been such a blessing—to be whisked away from our hectic schedules and immerse ourselves in nature to enjoy serenity and peacefulness. The banana macadamia nut pancakes that we have had on our trips to Hawaii inspired me to put them in this loaf along with white chocolate chips. I also pair it with a passion fruit and vanilla bean butter. This recipe has become a favorite in our household, and Raj, who is a fan of neither bananas nor banana bread, loves it too! The Chai Masala (page 41) adds that extra touch of warm spice that elevates the bread.

INGREDIENTS

PASSION FRUIT AND VANILLA BEAN BUTTER
¼ cup passion fruit juice (from 4 to 5 passion fruits)
2 tablespoons (30 g) lemon juice
½ cup (100 g) granulated sugar
2 egg yolks
3 tablespoons (42 g) unsalted butter
½ teaspoon vanilla bean paste

CHAI MASALA, MACADAMIA NUT, AND WHITE CHOCOLATE BANANA BREAD
1¼ cups (150 g) all-purpose flour
⅓ cup (48 g) almond flour
1 teaspoon Chai Masala (page 41)
1 teaspoon (6 g) table salt
2 teaspoons (8 g) baking powder
2 ripe bananas (230 g)

¼ cup (57 g) Greek yogurt
1 tablespoon (13 g) vanilla extract
½ cup (1 stick; 113 g) unsalted butter, room temperature
¾ cup (150 g) light brown sugar
¼ cup (50 g) granulated sugar
2 eggs
¾ cup (90 g) coarsely chopped macadamia nuts
¾ cup (105 g) mini white chocolate chips

TOPPING
2 tablespoons (25 g) sparkling or turbinado sugar

continued ➤

METHOD

To Make the Butter

1. Remove the pulp/seeds and juice from all the passion fruit into a strainer that has been fixed over a bowl. Using a rubber spatula, press on the seeds continuously to extract as much juice as possible from the passion fruit pulp. Scrape underneath the strainer with the spatula to get all the pulp from the bottom of the strainer into the bowl.

2. Add the lemon juice into the passion fruit juice, along with ¼ cup (50 g) of the sugar.

3. Fill a small saucepan with a few inches of water and place over medium heat. Pour the passion fruit–lemon juice into a heat-safe glass bowl. Once the water starts boiling, carefully set the glass bowl on top of the saucepan. (The glass bowl should be slightly bigger than the saucepan. Allow the juice to heat up.)

4. Meanwhile, in a medium bowl, whisk the egg yolks and the remaining sugar, beating vigorously in one direction, until the color is pale yellow and the mixture is ribbon-like in consistency and flow.

5. While the juice mixture is still warm, add about ¼ cup (60 ml) to the egg yolk mixture and whisk to temper the yolks. Add the entire yolk mixture into the juice over the saucepan, and keep stirring continuously.

6. Using a rubber spatula, stir the mixture continuously for 8 to 10 minutes. It will thicken as you keep stirring. Remove from the heat. Remove the glass bowl from the saucepan.

7. Add the unsalted butter and whisk until combined and the mixture is smooth and silky.

8. Add the vanilla bean paste, stir to combine. Cover with plastic wrap touching the surface of the butter, so the butter does not form a skin. Store the Passion Fruit and Vanilla Bean Butter in the fridge to cool.

9. Once cooled after 3 to 4 hours, it will be firm in consistency. Using a rubber spatula, pour it into a glass jar, seal, and store in the fridge for up to 2 weeks.

To Make the Bread

1. Preheat the oven to 350°F (175°C). Prepare a 9-by-5-inch (23-by-13 cm) loaf pan by spraying it with cooking spray. Using parchment paper, cut to the size of the pan, place the paper into the pan across the length with a bit of overhang so it is easy to lift the loaf out when the banana bread is ready. Spray the parchment paper with the cooking spray as well.

2. In a medium bowl, add the all-purpose flour, almond flour, Chai Masala, salt, and baking powder, and whisk to combine.

3. In another medium bowl, add the bananas and, using a fork, mash the bananas completely. Add the Greek yogurt and vanilla extract and mix to combine.

4. In the bowl of a stand mixer with a paddle attachment, add the butter, brown sugar, and granulated sugar. Start with low speed and gradually increase the speed to medium-high. Beat the mixture for 2 minutes, until light, fluffy, and pale in color.

5. Add the eggs, one at a time, and beat to combine.

6. Add the banana mixture and beat to combine.

7. Add the flour mixture, and starting on slow speed, beat until the flour mixture is incorporated. Do not overmix.

8. Remove the bowl from the stand mixer. Add the chopped macadamia nuts and white chocolate chips. Fold them into the batter with a rubber spatula until the nuts and chips are evenly distributed.

continued ➡

9. Add the batter into the loaf pan and evenly distribute it using a small offset spatula. Sprinkle the sparkling or turbinado sugar on top, evenly distributed. Place the pan on the middle rack of the oven and bake for 1 hour to 1 hour 10 minutes, or until a cake tester comes out clean.

10. Take the bread out of the oven and let it cool outside for an hour. Once it has cooled completely, remove it from the pan using the overhangs and place gently onto a cutting board. Cut 1-inch (2½ cm) slices and serve with the Passion Fruit and Vanilla Bean Butter. Enjoy with a cup of tea or coffee..

PRO TIPS

1. The banana bread will keep up to 4 or 5 days at room temperature in an airtight container.

2. The Passion Fruit and Vanilla Bean Butter will keep up to 2 weeks in the fridge.

Carrot, Pineapple, and Candied Ginger Muffins

Makes 12 muffins

Come winter in the Bay Area, when the mornings are cold and nippy and the sun is not yet shining through, there is frost on the roofs of the homes outside our window. Stepping outside in the garden, misty fog blowing out of your mouth, a warm cuppa Masala Chai and these delicious muffins are all that I need to start off my day.

With the onset of winter, the carrots at the market are much sweeter and deep orange in color. Candied ginger hits the grocery stores because all the holiday baked goods need a whiff of warm ginger in them. These muffins also have sweet pineapple because it complements the carrots and candied ginger really well, which I simply love. I finely chop the candied ginger so that you get tiny bites of it in the muffin for that slight kick. The spices that I use in these muffins are ground ginger, ground cinnamon, and nutmeg—bring on all the winter spices in one delicious morning treat. These muffins are a hit with my kids and they love them for breakfast with a warm glass of milk before they start their school day.

There is nothing Indian-inspired about these muffins, but living in the United States, this recipe has become a part of our lives, part of our routine, and one of several breakfasts that I make for my kids. We have roots in one place, and carry the foods, culture, and tradition from our roots to wherever we end up. We adapt to the place we settle in as adults. We evolve with the culture and the foods from that place while also trying to maintain our original culture and traditions. In the process of building new traditions for our kids, they can experience both and embrace them as their own.

INGREDIENTS

2 cups (240 g) all-purpose flour

½ cup (56 g) almond flour

½ teaspoon (2.5 g) baking soda

2 teaspoons (8 g) baking powder

1 teaspoon (6 g) table salt

2 teaspoons (4 g) ground ginger

1 teaspoon (2 g) ground cinnamon

½ teaspoon (2 g) freshly grated nutmeg

½ cup (100 g) granulated sugar

⅔ cup (135 g) light brown sugar

¾ cup (145 g) vegetable oil

3 large eggs, room temperature

½ cup (114 g) Greek yogurt

1 tablespoon (13 g) vanilla extract

1 cup (100 g) tightly packed grated carrots

1 cup (175 g; about 5 rings) finely chopped canned pineapple

½ cup (68 g) finely chopped candied ginger

6 to 8 teaspoons coarse sparkling sugar or turbinado sugar

continued ➤

METHOD

1. Preheat the oven to 400°F (200°C).

2. In a medium bowl, add the all-purpose flour, almond flour, baking soda, baking powder, salt, ground ginger, ground cinnamon, and nutmeg, and whisk until combined.

3. In a large bowl, add the granulated sugar and light brown sugar. Add the vegetable oil and, using a balloon whisk, whisk for a minute to combine. Add the eggs, one at a time, and whisk vigorously after the addition of each egg. Add the Greek yogurt and vanilla extract and whisk to combine.

4. Add the dry ingredients to the wet ingredients, and, using a rubber spatula, fold in the wet with the dry, just until you see specks of flour throughout. Do not overmix.

5. Add the grated carrots, pineapple, and candied ginger, and mix gently to fold them into the batter. Do not overmix.

6. Add cupcake liners to the cupcake pan. Using an ice cream scoop, scoop out a heap of the batter into each liner, leaving a ⅓-inch (1 cm) gap from the top of the liner. Distribute the b ͏ ͏ong the liners. Sprinkle the ͏ally ͏spoon ͏y crispy

7. Put the pan ͏dle rack of the oven to bake for 10 minutes. Lower the temperature to 375°F (190°C), and bake for another 20 to 22 minutes or until a tester comes out clean and the tops are golden brown and shiny in color.

8. Remove the muffins from the oven and let them rest for 30 minutes. They are ready to eat.

PRO TIPS

1. If you do not like candied ginger, you can substitute it with ¾ cup (105 g) of toasted and coarsely chopped walnuts or pecans.

2. For maximum freshness, muffins should be consumed within 2 to 3 days. Store them in an airtight container.

Pudla (Chickpea Flour Crêpes)
WITH CARROT AND PURPLE CABBAGE SALAD

Makes around 6 to 8 crêpes

Pudla, or chickpea flour crêpes, are a very common breakfast dish for Gujaratis. My mother would often make this as breakfast for us, before we went to school. The batter is simple, and it comes together very quickly. Since this is made with chickpea flour, which is high in protein content, it gives a much-needed protein boost. Carom seeds are added to chickpea flour dishes, because although chickpeas are high in protein and very good for you, chickpea flour can be hard to digest—carom seeds help with the digestion of the pudla.

Growing up, my mother was a huge advocate of us eating a lot of fruits and vegetables, and a very balanced diet. But now as an adult, I realize that she tricked us! She would eat less of the vegetables herself, and indulge in sodas, which we were not allowed at all! Because of the light dinners, she would get hungry at 10 p.m. and make herself pudla as a snack. Well, at least it was healthy.

I make these for my kids sometimes, and they enjoy them with ketchup. I love them with my Cilantro Mint Chutney (page 42), yogurt, and a side salad consisting of grated carrots and purple cabbage, seasoned lightly with salt, sugar, and lemon juice. The salad is so tasty by itself that I could eat a bowlful of it. I love a light meal like this as breakfast—it fuels me up so I can tackle the rest of my day.

INGREDIENTS

CARROT AND PURPLE CABBAGE SALAD

2 medium (100 g) carrots, grated

1 cup (100 g) purple cabbage, grated

2 tablespoons finely sliced red onion

1 tablespoon cilantro

¼ to ½ teaspoon salt

¼ to ½ teaspoon granulated sugar

½ teaspoon lemon juice

PUDLA

2 cups (190 g) chickpea flour

1 teaspoon (2 g) ground turmeric

½ teaspoon (1 g) red chili powder

1¼ teaspoon (7.5 g) table salt

1 teaspoon (2 g) carom seeds or ajwain

1 green chili, finely chopped

1 inch (2½ cm) ginger, freshly grated

¼ small red onion, finely chopped

2 tablespoons finely chopped cilantro

1¼ cups (300 g) warm water

¼ cup (60 g) vegetable oil

Cilantro Mint Chutney (page 42), for serving

METHOD

To Make the Carrot and Purple Cabbage Salad

In a medium bowl, gently combine the carrots, purple cabbage, red onion slices, and cilantro. Add the salt, sugar, and lemon juice, tossing gently to combine. By tossing it lightly you will maintain its crunchiness.

continued ➤

To Make the Pudlas

1. In a medium bowl, sift the chickpea flour. Add the turmeric, red chili powder, salt, carom seeds, green chili, grated ginger, red onion, and cilantro. Add the water slowly and whisk with a balloon whisk to combine the ingredients. Keep whisking vigorously for about 2 to 3 minutes, until smooth and well combined. Set it aside for 10 minutes.

2. Meanwhile, heat up a medium skillet on medium to high heat for 2 to 3 minutes. Splash some water on top of the hot skillet. When the water sizzles and evaporates, you know the skillet is hot enough. Wipe a wet paper towel (water squeezed out) on the skillet, to lower the temperature.

3. Using about ¼ cup (60 ml) of the batter, pour it in the middle of the skillet, and using the back of a rounded ladle, immediately start spreading the batter in an outward spiral fashion, forming a circle about 7 inches (18 cm) in diameter.

4. Drizzle 1 teaspoon oil around the pudla or crêpe. Let it cook for about 2 minutes. Using a flat spatula, invert the pudla to cook on the other side. The cooked side should be slightly brown in color. Cook for 30 seconds. Invert again, fold, and plate it.

5. Repeat for the remaining pudla.

6. Serve with Cilantro Mint Chutney, ketchup, or yogurt. Enjoy.

PRO TIPS

1. To make the pudlas even healthier, you could add about ½ cup finely chopped fenugreek or spinach.

2. You can store the batter in an airtight container for a day.

Appetizers
and Salads

"The appetizer is an excuse for an extra meal."

—Jim Gaffigan

What whets one's appetite? An appetizer! Appetizers have always been one of my favorite parts of any meal. My family loves small plates too, because it means an array of different kinds of foods to sample as we get ready for the main meal. Appetizers also make a great option for community sharing. Sometimes a bunch of appetizers can be made into the main meal too. My mother would do that on days when she didn't want to make a proper meal. Appetizers or Mumbai street food prepared at home became our main meal, and to be honest, those were the best dinners! I like to do this too—I'll make a few appetizers for just the four of us or set them out on the table for guests to help themselves. It becomes fun and interactive for them to pick and choose what they want to enjoy with wine or cocktails. You can fit the appetizers on a small plate and walk around, having fun conversations as you nibble away.

In this chapter, there are a variety of appetizers, from fried foods to salads, from authentic Gujarati recipes to Mumbai street foods and fusion foods that make me happy! All the appetizers range across the seasons, using the best California seasonal fruits and vegetables in each of the dishes. Cruciferous vegetables are highlighted in Sambhaaro (Cabbage and Carrot Salad, page 127), a very special recipe that I grew up with. Carrots and savoy and purple cabbage give this dish its color and texture, along with a very simple preparation of mustard seeds and curry leaves.

The salads include the Winter Citrus and Roasted Beet Salad with Paneer Nuggets (page 119) with a wonderful orange-fennel seed vinaigrette that complements the flavors beautifully. Deconstructed Kachumber (Indian Salad, page 138) is my favorite. It is a salad I grew up eating and this deconstructed version is fun and pretty! My Summer California Salad (page 141) celebrates quintessential California produce featured in the avocado dressing.

Some of the traditional appetizers celebrate Mumbai street food, like the Dahi Papdi Chaat (page 161) or Vegetable Bhajias (page 123), which your loved ones won't be able to get enough of. The infamous Grilled Bombay Sandwich (page 151) is probably one of the tastiest, easiest appetizers out there. The other traditional recipes are based on my Gujarati roots. Handvo (page 166), which is a rice and lentil cake, is really one of my favorite traditional dishes of all time, and the Dahi Wadas (page 133) have a melt-in-your-mouth goodness that my husband has an endless appetite for.

My fusion twists are ones that I am really fond of, like the Spring Masala Matar (Green Peas) Galette (page 128). It reminds me of the matar kachoris that my mum would make. The Corn Mushroom Tomato Chili Cheese Danish (page 154) require a bit of work and prep time, but they are so worth it! We love these Danish for dinner with a side salad and a glass of wine. The Caramelized Onion, Fontina, and Samosa Tart (page 172) will be a showstopper at your next party, I guarantee you. These dishes have delighted a lot of people, and I hope they leave you pleased and satisfied too!

Masala Smashed Potatoes

Serves 4

Potatoes, any kind, and flavored any way, are extremely popular in India. Gujaratis like to put potatoes in all the vegetable dishes we cook. When potatoes are cooked dry with spices and a bit of oil in a pan, they crisp up beautifully and make for a very delicious meal, either as is or with any kind of daal and some cumin white rice.

Smashed potatoes are a popular appetizer, so I decided to make them with an Indian twist. Make the smashed potatoes with a brushing of the spiced oil, laden with spices such as ground turmeric, red chili, coriander, and chaat masala. Chaat masala is essential and available at any Indian grocery store or online. The chaat masala has a key component called amchur, which is ground dried mango, which makes the dish flavorful. The powder enhances the taste by giving the potatoes a sour tang. You can find more information on chaat masala on page 22.

INGREDIENTS

CILANTRO GARLIC YOGURT SAUCE

1½ cups (345 g) Greek yogurt

½ cup (12 g) packed cilantro

2 tablespoons (5 g) finely chopped mint

1 tablespoon (15 g) fresh lemon juice

2 garlic cloves

1 teaspoon (6 g) table salt

MASALA SMASHED POTATOES

1½ pounds (680 g) baby potatoes, washed well

2 teaspoons (12 g) table salt

½ cup (65 g) olive oil

1 teaspoon (2 g) ground turmeric

1 teaspoon (2 g) red chili powder

1 teaspoon (2 g) ground coriander

1 teaspoon (6 g) table salt

1 teaspoon (2 g) chaat masala

1 teaspoon (3 g) garlic powder

GARNISH

½ cup (12 g) finely chopped cilantro leaves

METHOD

To Make the Cilantro Garlic Yogurt Sauce

In a high-speed blender, add all the ingredients and blitz until smooth. It should be a thick sauce that can be drizzled. If needed, add water a tablespoon at a time to get it to a drizzle consistency.

To Make the Masala Smashed Potatoes

1. In a medium to large pot, add all the potatoes. Add water to a level about 1 inch (2½ cm) higher than the potatoes. Add the salt. On high heat, let the potatoes cook for 20 minutes, until they are fork-tender.

2. Turn off the heat and drain the water. Let the potatoes cool for about 10 minutes until you can handle them.

3. Preheat the oven to 400°F (200°C).

4. Meanwhile, in a small bowl, combine the olive oil and the spices, and whisk to combine. Set it aside.

continued ➞

5. Generously coat a large baking sheet with cooking/baking spray. Place the potatoes on the tray. Using a flat-bottomed glass, gently press each potato to flatten them slightly, but not more than ½ inch (1¼ cm) thick.

6. Using a pastry brush, take a generous serving of the spice-oil mixture and coat each potato with it, until all the potatoes are evenly coated.

7. Place the sheet in the oven on the middle rack, and cook for about 25 minutes. For the last 10 minutes, let it cook on the bottommost rack to crisp up the bottom.

8. Remove and let cool for 5 minutes.

9. Serve on a platter with the Cilantro Garlic Yogurt Sauce or drizzle the sauce over the potatoes using a squirt bottle or a spoon. Garnish with cilantro and serve.

PRO TIPS

1. Use smoked paprika or Kashmiri red chili powder instead of the red chili powder to reduce the spice levels.

2. Make the Cilantro Garlic Yogurt Sauce a day ahead and store in the refrigerator.

3. The Masala Smashed Potatoes should be eaten the same day to preserve the desired freshness and crispness of the potatoes.

Winter Citrus and Roasted Beet Salad
WITH PANEER NUGGETS AND
ORANGE-FENNEL SEED VINAIGRETTE

Serves 4

Although winter spells cold months and you would think not much produce grows at that time of year, we are lucky to have an abundance of gorgeous winter bounty in California. The leafy greens are in full bloom—the kales, romaine, fenugreek, cilantro, butter lettuce. They look fresh and vibrant, plus they are very good for you with vitamins A, C, K, and a lot of iron and calcium too. The variety of beets at the local farmers' market brings so much joy, with all the different varieties and colors.

I love to support our local farmers' market and my Sundays always feel incomplete if I miss it. They open at 9 a.m. and I am there first thing in the morning to get all my fresh fruits and vegetables for the week. You can literally taste the difference in the produce as compared to the grocery stores. If you can and have the ability, please support your local farmers' market. It helps them provide us with beautiful produce that has not traveled far, and in turn we support them and give them business.

I love the different winter citrus varieties, such as blood oranges, cara cara, navel, satsuma, mandarins, kumquats, and more. I get these varieties and use them for different purposes in my cooking and baking. Citrus and beets make a classic combination. I gave them a twist using a wonderful orange and toasted fennel seed vinaigrette, which is fantastic on this salad, along with paneer nuggets. This makes for an easy salad to prepare for a close gathering with friends and family.

INGREDIENTS

SALAD

2 small red beets or 1 medium to large beet

2 small yellow beets

1 bunch leafy lettuce such as romaine or butter lettuce, washed and patted dry

2 cara cara oranges

1 navel orange

2 small blood oranges

20 pistachios, chopped coarsely

PANEER NUGGETS (MAKES 12 TO 14)

1 cup (130 g) paneer

1 teaspoon (6 g) table salt

1 teaspoon (2 g) black pepper

1 teaspoon (3 g) garam masala

1 tablespoon (2 g) chopped cilantro

1 teaspoon (2 g) cumin seeds

2 teaspoons (18 g) sour cream

Vegetable oil for shallow frying

½ cup (20 g) panko bread crumbs

ORANGE-FENNEL SEED VINAIGRETTE

½ teaspoon (1 g) toasted fennel seeds

¼ cup (50 g) orange juice

1 tablespoon (14 g) white wine vinegar

2 teaspoons (10 g) Dijon mustard

1 tablespoon (18 g) honey

1 teaspoon (6 g) table salt

1 teaspoon (2 g) black pepper

¾ cup (160 g) olive oil

continued ➝

METHOD

To Roast the Beets

1. Preheat the oven to 400°F (200°C).

2. Trim the leafy greens and the roots off the beets. Scrub the beets well with warm water. Pat them dry.

3. Wrap the red and the yellow beets separately and loosely into aluminum foil to create two pouches.

4. Place the beets in the oven for about 45 to 50 minutes until you can pierce them with a knife without effort. Be careful as the foil will be hot.

5. Remove the beets from the oven and let them cool in the enclosed foil for 15 minutes.

6. Using a paring knife, remove the beet skins and cut each beet into eight slices. Set aside.

To Make the Paneer Nuggets

1. In a medium bowl, grate the paneer. Add the remaining ingredients, except the panko bread crumbs and oil, and mix with a small rubber spatula until combined.

2. Make small nuggets ¾ to 1 inch (1 to 2½ cm) in diameter, by rolling each nugget between the palms of your hands in a counterclockwise direction to make a round ball. You should get about 12 to 14 balls out of the mixture. Set them aside on a plate.

3. In a small frying pan on medium heat, add vegetable oil to about ½ inch (1¼ cm) in height and wait for the oil to get hot.

4. In a small bowl, add the panko bread crumbs. Take each nugget and cover it with the panko thoroughly.

5. Add three to four nuggets to the frying pan and lightly fry them until golden brown, about 2 minutes. Keep moving them to brown them evenly on all sides. Repeat with the remaning nuggets.

6. Remove and place them on a plate.

To Make the Orange-Fennel Seed Vinaigrette

1. Lightly crush the fennel seeds to a coarse consistency, using a mortar and pestle.

2. Add the orange juice, white wine vinegar, Dijon mustard, honey, salt, pepper, and crushed fennel seeds in a small bowl, whisking to combine.

3. Slowly drizzle in the olive oil and whisk until well combined. Set it aside.

To Assemble the Salad

1. On a large platter, assemble the greens.

2. Using a paring knife, remove the skin of the oranges, including the white pith (the bitter part).

3. Slice the oranges about ¼ inch (½ cm) thick to get about five to six slices per orange. Layer them on the lettuce.

4. Keep the sliced red and yellow beets in separate bowls so as not to stain them. Add about 1 tablespoon of the dressing into each bowl to coat the beets. Place the beets throughout the salad platter on the sliced oranges.

5. Place the paneer nuggets all over the platter.

6. Sprinkle with the chopped pistachios.

7. Serve with the dressing.

PRO TIPS

1. Use whatever oranges you like! I love the cara caras, blood oranges, and navel varieties, which are available at our local farmers' markets.

2. The beets can be made a couple days ahead of time.

3. The vinaigrette can be made a week in advance and stored in the fridge in an airtight glass jar.

Vegetable Bhajias (Chickpea and Rice Flour Vegetable Fritters)

Serves 6

Call them bhajias or pakoras or fritters—fried food is popular everywhere in the world! Bhajias are synonymous with the rains. Come monsoon season, the extremely desirable snack in India is bhajias/fritters and masala chai. There is something blissful about eating those fried chickpea and rice flour fritters with a spicy cilantro and mint chutney alongside sweet and gingery masala chai, especially as the rain pours down and you can smell the whiff of the fresh mud. In these moments, you can close your eyes and breathe a sigh of relief that the summer humidity is behind you.

Bhajias and chai are popular street foods, seen at every nook and corner on the streets of Mumbai. They are a quick snack on the go for when you're leaving work and have a long journey ahead of you. Or after all those grueling college classes when you need a quick bite to enjoy with your friends, before heading home. Bhajias are best eaten when hot. They make an absolutely delicious snack, sandwiched in a pav (a soft bun), slathered with some Cilantro Mint Chutney (page 42) or Date Tamarind Chutney (page 45), maybe a bit of ketchup too, along with chaat masala.

Mum made these bhajias very often, especially in the monsoon season, or when we had guests over. My family loves them too, and the first time I made these, they asked me, "Mummy, why have you not made these before?" The bhajias are quick to whip up, and are loved by young and old. I guarantee you, you will NOT stop at a few.

INGREDIENTS

KAANDA BHAJIA (ONION FRITTERS)
1 cup (90 g) chickpea flour
¼ cup (40 g) rice flour
½ teaspoon (1 g) carom seeds or ajwain
½ teaspoon (1 g) red chili powder
1 teaspoon (6 g) table salt
1 teaspoon (2 g) ground turmeric
Pinch of asafoetida

2 tablespoons (4 g) finely chopped fresh fenugreek (optional)
2 tablespoons (4 g) finely chopped cilantro
2 tablespoons (30 g) fresh lemon juice
¼ cup (60 g) warm water
⅔ cup (150 g) thinly sliced red onion—separate all the onion slices
Vegetable oil, for frying

continued ➤

VEGETABLE BHAJIA

2½ cups (225 g) chickpea flour

½ cup (80 g) rice flour

1 teaspoon (2 g) carom seeds or ajwain

1½ teaspoons (3 g) red chili powder

2 teaspoons (12 g) table salt

1½ teaspoons (3 g) ground turmeric

Pinch of asafoetida

3 tablespoons (6 g) finely chopped cilantro

4 tablespoons (60 g) fresh lemon juice

1¼ to 1½ cups (300 to 360 g) warm water, depending on the thickness of the batter

⅔ cup (150 g) eggplant, cut into ½-inch (1¼ cm) slices

5 to 6 small (225 g) potatoes, cut thinly into slices, about ¼ inch (5 mm) thick

⅔ cup (150 g) cauliflower florets

1 firm banana, cut into ½-inch (1 cm) slices

Vegetable oil, for frying

FOR SERVING

Chaat masala

Chopped cilantro

Cilantro Mint Chutney (page 42)

Aadhu Masala Chai (page 315)

Ketchup

METHOD

To Make the Batter for the Onion Fritters

1. In a large bowl, add all the dry ingredients, and whisk to combine.

2. Add the optional fenugreek, cilantro, lemon juice, and warm water and whisk until the batter is smooth. The batter consistency has to be thick, so that it can stick to the vegetable for frying.

3. Add the red onion slices and mix with your hand so that every onion slice is coated. Set the bowl aside.

4. Fry the other vegetable fritters before the onion fritters.

To Make the Batter for the Vegetable Fritters

1. In a large bowl, add all the dry ingredients and whisk to combine.

2. Add the cilantro, lemon juice, and 1¼ cups (300 g) warm water initially and whisk until the batter is smooth. If the batter is too thick, add ¼ cup (60 g) water, a tablespoon at a time, and whisk again to smooth it out. The batter consistency has to be thick, but not too thick—it should be thick enough to stick to the vegetable for frying.

To Fry the Fritters

1. Heat up the vegetable oil in a large pot at medium to high heat. It takes about 5 minutes for the oil to heat. It should reach a frying temperature of 350°F (175°C), if you want to test the temperature. Another way to test it is to put a drop of the batter into the oil. If it comes up immediately with tiny bubbles, then you know the oil is ready to fry. If the batter drop stays down and takes its time to come up, you know the oil is not yet ready to fry.

2. Keep a large plate lined with parchment paper on the side to drain off the excess oil.

3. Take one vegetable at a time to coat in the batter, and then fry it in the pot. Start with the eggplants. Dip the sliced eggplants into the batter and coat them well. Take each slice, shake off the excess by slapping it gently against the sides of the batter bowl, and carefully put it into the oil for frying. You can fry four slices at a time; no more or else it will bring the temperature of the oil down and not fry the bhajias properly.

4. Fry for about a minute on each side, until golden brown in color. Using a spider skimmer, remove the fritters onto the plate.

5. Next add the sliced potatoes to the batter and coat them evenly. Take each slice, shake off the excess by slapping it gently against the sides

of the batter bowl, and carefully put it into the oil for frying. You can fry four to five slices at a time; no more or else it will bring the temperature of the oil down and not fry the bhajias properly.

6. Repeat Step 4.

7. Next add the cauliflower florets to the batter and coat them evenly. Take each floret, shake off the excess by slapping it gently against the sides of the batter bowl, and carefully put it into the oil for frying. You can fry four florets at a time; no more or else it will bring the temperature of the oil down and not fry the bhajias properly.

8. Repeat Step 4.

9. Next add the sliced bananas to the batter and coat them evenly. Take each slice, shake off the excess by slapping it gently against the sides of the batter bowl, and put it into the oil for frying. You can fry four to five slices at a time; no more or else it will bring the temperature of the oil down and not fry the bhajias properly.

10. Repeat Step 4.

11. Take about ¼ cup (60 ml) of the onion batter, or use your hands to carefully put small mounds of the batter in the oil to fry them.

12. Repeat Step 4, and ensure that the onion fritters are golden brown all around before removing them from the hot oil.

13. Sprinkle with a generous amount of chaat masala to give additional flavor. Garnish with chopped cilantro on the top. Serve warm with ketchup, Cilantro Mint Chutney, and very hot Aadhu Masala Chai.

PRO TIPS

1. Use any vegetables that you fancy to dip into the chickpea and rice flour batter. The vegetables mentioned above are what we enjoyed in our family growing up.

2. Banana in this batter is really delicious and I hope you try it!

3. These are best eaten when they are freshly fried and slightly warm.

4. Onion fritters have a separate batter because they release some water, and they do not require as much batter as the other vegetables to coat them.

Sambhaaro
(Cabbage and Carrot Salad)

Serves 10

I have fond memories of eating Sambhaaro, or this slightly cooked cabbage and carrot salad. This salad is a Gujarati specialty, and is served as a side in a typical Gujarati thali. It can sometimes have shredded raw green papaya too.

My brother and I would wake up late on Sundays. Mum would always ask Dad on Sunday, "Are you going to get jalebi-fafda from Modern?" We had the biggest smiles and gleaming eyes! Dad would go in the early morning to get this breakfast from a famous place called Modern in Santa Cruz, Mumbai. The vendor would pack jalebis—fried yellow fritters dipped in a saffron-cardamom sugar syrup—and fafda—long and 2-inch (5 cm) wide fried chickpea flat crisps—wrapped in Gujarati newspapers along with a side of the delicious Sambhaaro—cabbage, carrot, papaya salad. The fragrance would wake us up. This was a Sunday breakfast we cherished. The combination of sweet and salty with the spicy Sambhaaro is absolutely divine!

I love eating this salad as is, with some yogurt on the side as a light lunch, or with our meals. Cabbage is a cruciferous vegetable, and quite underrated in my opinion. We are lucky to get amazing varieties of cabbage in California like savoy, Napa, and purple cabbage, and I love to take advantage of it via this delicious salad.

INGREDIENTS

3 tablespoons (40 g) olive oil

1½ teaspoons (3 g) mustard seeds

10 to 12 curry leaves

1 to 2 green chilis, split in half and seeds removed

1 cup (200 g) finely shredded savoy cabbage

1 cup (200 g) finely shredded purple cabbage

½ cup (100 g) finely shredded carrots (preferably long shreds)

¾ teaspoon (2 g) ground turmeric

1½ to 2 teaspoons (9 to 12 g) kosher salt

1½ teaspoons (6 g) granulated sugar

1 tablespoon (15 g) fresh lemon juice

METHOD

1. In a large wok or large deep saucepan on medium heat, add the olive oil. Let it heat up for a minute. Add the mustard seeds, curry leaves, and green chilis and sauté for 30 seconds until the mustard seeds splatter. This process is called tempering.

2. Add all the shredded vegetables, and toss for a minute with tongs or two wooden spatulas to gently coat the tempering on the vegetables.

3. Add the turmeric, salt, sugar, and lemon juice, and toss again for another minute to gently coat all the vegetables.

4. Turn off the heat and plate the salad onto a platter. It is ready to serve.

Spring Masala Matar (Green Pea) Galette

Makes 7 or 8 galettes

Matar kachori or peas kachori is a very famous Gujarati snack, typically served at weddings. As a kid, I hated going to weddings. Mum would try really hard to drag me to every wedding, and I would try to avoid them as much as possible. The only way she could perhaps persuade me was with the buffet served at the weddings. The food was simply phenomenal. I cannot rave enough about it. You get a thali filled with different varieties of vegetables, lentils, flatbreads, appetizers, and dessert. And then you go for seconds and thirds. Gujarati thali are really something! The variety of dishes showcase sweet, salty, sour, and spicy in their own special way. One dish that I loved eating was matar kachori. It is an appetizer of fried dough stuffed with a mixture of fresh green peas spiced with cumin, fennel seeds, garam masala, and fresh ingredients like coconut, green chili, ginger. It is sweetened with sugar and a bit of tang with lemon juice. It is sublime and I used to love it with ketchup. My grandma, or ba, makes it too, and we used to love it when she would make it for us.

I am very fond of savory galettes and, come summer, savory galettes are usually dinner for us. We sit outside in our yard on balmy summer evenings and eat galettes, usually with a simple arugula salad and a glass of wine. I decided to combine my love for savory galettes and these kachoris into a spring green pea galette. Spring season starts with the freshest of green peas at the market and the peak season is in May and June. I have my kids remove the peas from the pods—fun activity for them, eh? This recipe uses the green pea stuffing used in kachoris as the filling in this savory galette. The galette dough is extremely flaky and, with the green pea mixture, it makes for the perfect appetizer for entertaining. My family loves this galette. I typically serve it with the Date Tamarind Chutney (page 45), but they love it with ketchup, just like me.

INGREDIENTS

SAVORY GALETTE DOUGH

4 cups (600 g) all-purpose flour, plus extra for rolling out the dough

2 teaspoons (12 g) table salt

2 teaspoons (4.5 g) freshly cracked pepper

1 teaspoon (2 g) carom seeds or ajwan

1½ cups (3 sticks; 340 g) unsalted butter, chilled and cut into small cubes

1 tablespoon (15 g) apple cider vinegar

1 cup (240 g) iced water

continued ➡

MASALA PEA FILLING

2 cups + 1 tablespoon (500 g) green peas, fresh or frozen

1 inch (2½ cm) ginger

1 green chili

4 tablespoons (52 g) vegetable oil

1 teaspoon (2 g) cumin seeds

Pinch of asafoetida (optional)

2 teaspoons (6 g) garam masala

1 teaspoon (6 g) table salt

1 tablespoon (12.5 g) granulated sugar

1½ teaspoons (3 g) toasted fennel seeds, coarsely crushed

2 tablespoons (10 g) green garlic

3 tablespoons (45 g) lemon juice

½ cup (60 g) fresh or frozen coconut

¼ cup (32 g) coarsely chopped cashews

¼ cup (85 g) heavy cream, for coating

2 teaspoons good olive oil per galette

GARNISH

Date Tamarind Chutney (page 45)

¼ cup finely chopped cilantro

¼ cup (30 g) coconut, fresh or frozen

METHOD

To Make the Savory Galette Dough

1. Mix together the flour, salt, cracked pepper, and carom seeds, and whisk until blended.

2. Add the butter using a pastry blender and mix until the butter is partially broken up but still chunky and pea sized. You can mix with your hands as well and rub the butter between your fingertips. When you hold the dough together it should stay together.

3. Add the apple cider vinegar to the iced water and stir to combine. Add ¾ cup (180 g) of the liquid to the dough, tossing until the dough is uniformly moist and holds together when pinched. If it seems too dry, add 2 more tablespoons of the liquid and mix again with your

hands to form a dough. Do not overmix. You want bits of butter throughout the dough for a flaky galette.

4. Gather the dough with your hands and shape into two discs. Wrap each piece in plastic and shape it with your hands into a disc again, by gently pressing the sides of the dough.

5. Refrigerate for at least 30 minutes or until ready to roll out.

To Make the Masala Matar (Pea) Filling

1. Add the green peas, ginger, and green chili in a food processor and make a coarse mixture. You want some texture, so do not grind it all the way to make a paste.

2. In a large skillet on medium heat, add the vegetable oil. Let the oil heat up for 30 seconds. Then add the cumin seeds and optional asafoetida and let it crackle, about 20 seconds.

3. Add the green pea mixture into the pan and sauté for 2 minutes. You want to remove a bit of moisture from the mixture.

4. Add the garam malsa, salt, sugar, and fennel seeds, and sauté for another 4 to 5 minutes.

5. Finally, add the green garlic, lemon juice, coconut, and cashews, and sauté for another minute. Remove from the heat. Let the mixture cool completely for about an hour.

To Assemble the Galette

1. Remove both discs of dough from the fridge. If it is hard, let it sit for 10 minutes. Prepare two baking sheets with parchment paper.

2. On your work surface, sprinkle some flour. Unwrap the plastic from one disc and cut the dough into four even pieces. Repeat with the second disc of dough.

3. Add more flour on one piece and shape it into a round disc. Use extra flour as required, rolling out the dough on a flat surface into an even circle about 7 inches (18 cm) wide.

4. Add about 1/3 cup (90 ml) of the cooled green pea mixture in the middle of the rolled dough and, using a small offset spatula, spread the mixture in a circle, leaving an inch border all around.

5. Gently wrap the 1-inch (2½ cm) border on top of the pea mixture, all around. It will form pleats. With your hands, gently pat the sides to form a circle.

6. Press the overlapped dough gently to seal it. Place the galette on the baking sheet. Drizzle 1 to 2 teaspoons of olive oil on the filling portion of the galette.

7. Repeat Steps 3 to 6 for six of the other pieces of dough.

8. You can repeat Steps 3 to 6 on the last disc, or use the disc to prepare leaf pie cutouts, and place them on the rim of the galettes to form a pretty design.

9. Place the baking sheets in the freezer for 10 minutes.

To Bake the Galettes

1. Preheat the oven to 400°F (200°C).

2. Remove the trays from the freezer. Use a pastry brush to brush the heavy cream generously on the border of the galettes so that they get a lovely brown crust.

3. Using aluminum foil, fold it to double it up and make seven to eight round discs, just enough to cover the filling, around 4 inches (10 cm) in diameter. Cover the filling portion of each galette with an aluminum disc so as not to dry the filling.

4. You can bake both trays simultaneously on the middle and lower racks of the oven. Bake the galettes for a total of 45 to 50 minutes, depending upon your oven, until the crust is golden brown in color. Switch the trays halfway through baking: Move the tray on the middle rack to the lower rack, and vice versa.

5. Remove the galettes from the oven and let cool, about 15 minutes.

6. Sprinkle the cilantro and coconut on top of the galettes. Serve with the Date Tamarind Chutney.

PRO TIPS

1. The masala pea filling can be made a day in advance. The galette dough can be made a day in advance as well.

2. If you'd prefer, you can bake just a few galettes at a time. The filling keeps up to a week and the galette dough freezes well for up to a month. Before using the galette dough, move it from the freezer to the fridge a day in advance.

3. The galettes can be assembled a day in advance and stored in the fridge (not the freezer), and baked the next day.

4. Substitute the green garlic with two grated garlic cloves, but add it in Step 1 of the Masala Matar Filling.

PRO TIPS

1. The batter itself can be stored in the freezer for up to a month. Defrost it in the fridge completely, bring to room temperature, and follow on from Step 3.

2. You can serve the Dahi Wadas as a do-it-yourself dish, to make the assembly interactive.

Dahi Wadas (Lentil Fritters in a Yogurt Sauce)

Makes 36 to 40 wadas

Mumbai has a ton of good street food and is a city of millions of street hawkers. I was lucky to grow up eating all of it, from vada pavs to pav bhajis, haats, and dosas, to name a few. I have to say my stomach is pretty immune to roadside foods. You can stand and eat breakfast, lunch, snacks, dinner, and even dessert, by the roadside vendors. If you ever get a chance to try this experience, do not miss it, but make sure that your tummy can handle it. When I go back to visit Mumbai, I have to stop at all my favorite places. These foods I grew up eating take me back to fond memories of my childhood with beloved family and friends.

Mum would often make melt-in-your-mouth Dahi Wadas. Some dinners would just be Dahi Wadas, and that was sufficient. They were a favorite among my friends, who would frequently visit my home just to eat Mum's delicious food! Feeding people was her charm.

My kids relish the Dahi Wadas and to see them enjoying my childhood favorites really makes my heart jump with joy!

INGREDIENTS

WADAS

1½ cups (300 g) urad daal or skinned split black gram lentils

2 cups (480 g) warm water + 6 tablespoons water (or more) for blending

2 green chilis

1 inch (2½ cm) ginger

2 teaspoons (12 g) table salt

Vegetable oil, for frying (vegetable oil level should be about half the height of the Dutch oven)

YOGURT SAUCE

2 cups (440 g) Greek yogurt

1½ cups (360 g) water

1 teaspoon (6 g) table salt

2 tablespoons (25 g) granulated sugar

TOPPINGS

2 tablespoons (12 g) cumin seeds

Date Tamarind Chutney (page 45)

2 tablespoons (16 g) red chili powder

2 tablespoons (34 g) table salt

2 cups thin sev (fried chickpea noodles)

½ cup finely chopped cilantro

METHOD

To Make the Wadas

1. In a medium bowl, add the urad daal and wash it under cold running water to remove any dirt. Wash it three to four times thoroughly. Drain out the water. Add the warm water, cover with a lid, and let them soak overnight (or at least for 4 hours).

2. The next morning, drain out all the water and add the lentils to a high-speed blender. Add the 6 tablespoons water, green chilis, ginger,

continued ➡

and salt and blend it for about 3 minutes until it becomes a smooth paste. You may need 1 to 2 tablespoons extra water, but only if the mixture is not smooth. When you feel the batter between your index finger and thumb, it should feel smooth to the touch. Cover it and keep it aside for half an hour.

3. Whip the mixture vigorously with either your hand, a balloon whisk, or a handheld mixer for 5 full minutes. This step is to aerate the batter properly so that the wadas fluff up in the final assembly of this dish.

4. In a large Dutch oven, heat vegetable oil on medium to high heat for 5 minutes. Add a drop of the batter into the hot oil. If it rises to the top immediately, the oil is hot enough. Otherwise, wait one more minute for the oil to heat to the ideal frying temperature of 350°F (175°C). Have a large bowl with cold water ready next to the Dutch oven.

5. Using a tablespoon-sized ice cream scoop, scoop the batter and drop it into the oil. If you don't have an ice cream scoop, you can use 2 tablespoons, with one for dropping the batter, the other for releasing the batter from the first tablespoon. I usually put the batter in the hot oil with my hands, but do not do this if you are not comfortable with it. Drop about six wadas at a time into the hot oil. Using a spider skimmer, splash the oil over the wadas for even browning. The little wadas will start browning. Cook on one side for 2 minutes and the other side for 1 minute or until they are golden brown on all sides.

6. Remove the wadas from the hot oil and place them in the large bowl of cold water. Keep them in the water for 30 minutes.

7. Repeat Steps 5 and 6 for the remaining batter, adding each new batch of wadas to the same bowl of water.

8. After 30 minutes, remove each wada one at a time and gently squeeze out the water between the palms of your hands. Place the wadas on a separate clean plate. You can keep them in an airtight container in the fridge for up to 3 days.

To Make the Yogurt Sauce

For the dahi, add all the ingredients in a medium bowl and whisk well to combine until the yogurt mixture is smooth. It should be the consistency of heavy cream. If it is thinner, add a tablespoon of yogurt at a time and whisk until thickened. If it is thicker, add a little bit of water a tablespoon at a time to thin it out.

To Roast the Cumin

1. In a small saucepan on medium heat, add the cumin seeds. Stir them occasionally every minute for up to 3 to 4 minutes. You will smell the fragrance of the roasted cumin seeds. Remove from the heat and let them cool completely.

2. Grind the cumin seeds to a fine powder in the coffee or spice grinder.

To Assemble

1. To serve on a large platter, spread all the wadas evenly on the platter in a crowded manner. Pour the yogurt slowly over the wadas. They should be covered completely with the yogurt mixture.

2. The Date Tamarind Chutney is thick. Add a bit of water, 2 tablespoons at a time, to thin it out. It should be the consistency of heavy cream. Drizzle ribbons of the Date Tamarind Chutney all over the platter.

3. Next sprinkle red chili powder, roasted cumin powder, and salt, one after the other to your liking. I usually sprinkle enough to cover each wada. Sprinkle the sev on the top, again to cover each wada.

4. Finally, garnish with freshly chopped cilantro.

Sprouted Moong Salad

Serves 6

In Mumbai, shoppers, students, office goers, families, and people in a rush frequent the thousands of street vendors selling all kinds of amazing, lip-smacking street foods at every nook and corner. You will see all kinds of crowds at the street vendors varying in age, economic class, culture, and religion. That is the beauty of the street food stalls—they welcome all and break down those barriers.

I have the fondest memories of Mumbai street foods with my mum, my family, my friends, and relatives. Even my mum would give in sometimes to her cravings and we would go to a stall to get all the snacks as dinner: sev puri, ragda pattice, pani puri, sprouted moong chaat, and more. We would order a bunch of stuff and share it between the four of us. And when accompanied by masala lemon soda and ending with malai kulfi, kesar pista ice cream, or paan, it would make for a very satisfying dinner!

One of my favorite street foods, which is healthy and filling, is the sprouted moong chaat, made with sprouted and boiled green moong and kala channa (black garbanzo beans) and served with fresh vegetables such as cucumber, tomatoes, red onions, boiled potatoes, and raw mango. The vendors make it within a minute, quickly putting each ingredient into a steel pot and mixing everything with all the masalas. Then they put the contents in magazine paper (so it does not get soggy) shaped into a cone and folded at the bottom. They give you a little spoon and you eat it immediately while it is still warm.

Sprouted moong has a lot of benefits. The high content of fiber in sprouts helps with digestion and good gut health. It is also great for hair and skin. Sprouts have innumerable benefits. Sprouted moong can be used to make salads, daals, and sandwiches.

INGREDIENTS

4 cups (320 g) sprouted moong or sprouted green moong daal

1 small (80 g) red onion, diced into small cubes

1 Persian cucumber (100 g), diced into small cubes

2 small (185 g) tomatoes, diced into small cubes

3 small boiled potatoes (210 g), diced into small cubes

½ raw mango (100 g), diced into small cubes

2 green chilis, finely chopped (optional)

2 teaspoons (4 g) chaat masala

1 teaspoon (2 g) red chili powder

1 teaspoon (2 g) amchur (dried mango powder)

1 to 1½ teaspoons (6 to 9 g) table salt or rock salt

2 tablespoons (30 g) lemon juice

¼ cup finely chopped cilantro

2 to 3 tablespoons (Date Tamarind Chutney (page 45)

GARNISH

¼ cup finely chopped cilantro

continued ➤

METHOD

To Sprout Green Moong Daal

1. In the evening, place 1 cup (200 g) green moong daal in a large bowl and wash it three to four times with warm water. After washing, add water about 1 inch (2½ cm) above the level of the green moong daal. Cover and set it aside overnight. By morning, the moong should have grown from all the water it absorbed.

2. Add 2 tablespoons of water and use a rubber spatula to wet the daal, cover, and set it aside. Check on the moong every 6 to 8 hours. You will see sprouts coming out slowly. Add 2 tablespoons of water again and stir every 6 to 8 hours that day.

3. Repeat Step 2 on the second day if you want longer sprouts. Your sprouts should have come out pretty well by the second day, especially if the weather is warm. In colder weather, the sprouts may be ready by day three. The sprouts should have tripled or quadrupled in quantity from the original 1 cup of dried green moong daal.

4. You can eat the sprouts as is, in this salad, or you can steam them, boil them, or make a soup out of them.

To Prepare the Salad

1. Bring 4 cups (360 g) water to a boil in a steamer. Add the sprouts to the steamer. Cover and steam for 5 minutes. Remove from the heat.

2. Let the steamed sprouts cool completely.

3. In a large bowl, add the finely chopped red onions, cucumbers, tomatoes, potatoes, mango, green chilis, and all the remaining ingredients. Using two salad spoons, mix the salad gently until everything is incorporated well.

4. Serve in bowls and garnish with additional cilantro.

PRO TIPS

1. The sprouted moong will keep in an airtight container, stored in the fridge, for up to a week.

2. You can add the Cilantro Mint Chutney (page 42) and sev (chickpea noodles) to this chaat.

3. Pomegranate seeds add a good sweetness and crunch as well..

Deconstructed Kachumber (Indian Salad)

Serves 4

Growing up in Mumbai, our lunch at home was a proper Gujarati lunch, consisting of shaak (vegetable), rotli, daal, kachumber, papad, and masala chaas to cool off from the Mumbai heat. It was a wholesome, nutritious meal that I am so much more appreciative of now that I'm older. As kids we complained about having variations of the same lunches, but I would give anything to have this every day now.

Kachumber is basically an Indian salad. It consists of finely chopped tomatoes, cucumbers, red onions, cilantro marinated in lime juice, salt, red chili powder, and sugar. It is probably my favorite thing to eat, especially on hot days. Mum knew she would have to make a big batch every day, because I would eat at least two bowls of it. The juice at the bottom of the bowl, which is sweet, sour, and spicy, is the best part!

I wanted to showcase the freshness and beauty of the California produce through this salad, so this is my Deconstructed Kachumber. I have used all the ingredients that go into a kachumber, along with in-season fresh peaches and radishes. It is a beautiful crowd-pleasing salad!

INGREDIENTS

CILANTRO OIL

½ cup (106 g) olive oil

1 cup cilantro, washed and patted dry

½ teaspoon (2.5 g) Maldon salt

SALAD

Juice of 2 limes

¾ teaspoon (2 g) red chili powder

1 teaspoon (5 g) Maldon salt

2 teaspoons (8 g) granulated sugar

3 differently colored heirloom tomatoes, cut into 8 pieces each, lengthwise

1 large peach, sliced into 8 pieces

1 Persian cucumber or ½ English cucumber, sliced thin

4 to 6 radishes, thinly sliced

1 shallot, skin removed and thinly sliced

METHOD

To Make the Cilantro Oil

In a high-speed blender, add all the ingredients and blend to form a fine emulsion. Strain it through a fine sieve and use a rubber spatula to gently press on the solids to get as much flavor from the cilantro as possible. Store in a squeeze bottle for later use.

To Make the Salad

1. In a small bowl, add the lime juice, red chili powder, salt, and sugar, and mix until the sugar has dissolved.

2. On each salad plate, evenly distribute the tomatoes, peach slices, Persian cucumbers, radishes, and shallots in whatever creative way you want. Drizzle a bit of the juice on all the vegetable-fruit pieces of each plate. Just before serving, add droplets of the cilantro oil for a pretty presentation. Serve immediately.

PRO TIPS

1. This salad is free form—use your imagination to make the presentation as creative as you want.

2. This salad is best prepared and served immediately.

Summer California Salad

Serves 6 to 8

The best way to cool off in the summer is with an easy, fruity, seasonal salad. There are many times I do not feel like cooking, especially in hot weather, and salads really save the day. Mangoes are in abundance in the summer, and I bring quite a few home with each trip to the grocery store. This California-inspired salad features those mangoes with avocados, cucumbers, and radishes. My favorite leafy green for salads is butter lettuce. I love the silky-smooth texture of the leaves and how they simply melt in your mouth.

With the proximity of California to Mexico, Californian cuisine is heavily influenced by Mexican cuisine, both in terms of the freshness of ingredients and how tasty the food is, with varied flavors and textures. This summer salad is inspired by numerous trips to Mexico. I love the pumpkin seeds and pistachios paired with the Cotija cheese in this salad, giving it the added crunch, saltiness, and creaminess needed. I use the Avocado, Cilantro, and Poblano Pepper Dressing (page 55), which is oil free and universal. It can be used as a dip, for drizzling on tacos, or as a dressing for this salad. Wow your guests at a summer party with this easy-peasy salad!

INGREDIENTS

1 head butter lettuce, washed and patted dry

2 just-ripe mangoes, cut into small to medium cubes

2 just-ripe avocados, cut into small to medium cubes

1 medium cucumber, cut into small to medium cubes

5 radishes, sliced thin

¼ cup (35 g) coarsely chopped raw pistachios

¼ cup (35 g) roasted pumpkin seeds

¼ cup (35 g) Cotija cheese

⅓ cup (80 ml) Avocado, Cilantro, and Poblano Pepper Dressing (page 55)

GARNISH

Sprinkling of Maldon salt

2 tablespoons finely chopped mint

METHOD

1. Place the butter lettuce leaves on a serving plate or in a shallow bowl.

2. In another large, deep bowl, add the mangoes, avocados, cucumbers, most of the radish slices, three-fourths of the pistachios, three-quarters of the pumpkin seeds, and three-quarters of the Cotija cheese. Add the dressing and gently mix, so as not to bruise the mangoes and avocados.

3. Place the salad in the bowl covered with butter lettuce. Add the remaining radishes, and sprinkle remaining pistachios, pumpkin seeds, and Cotija cheese on top of the salad. Garnish with a sprinkling of Maldon salt and finely chopped mint. Enjoy.

PRO TIPS

1. The dressing can be made 1 to 3 days ahead and stored in the refrigerator in an airtight container.

2. If you do not have Cotija cheese, you can substitute with feta or omit it completely.

Bhindi (Okra) Masala Tempura Fries

Serves 6

Growing up, I had a lot of friends from the Sindhi community. To give you a little bit of history, Sindh was a part of Pakistan before its 1947 independence. During that time there were Indians and Pakistanis living in Sindh. After independence, many of the Indians from Sindh migrated to India and were dispersed all over the country. Many of the Sindhis moved to Mumbai, and hence Mumbai has a huge Sindhi population. Sindhis are a very enterprising community in the sense that they have spread all over the world in the name of business, and with their hard work and tenacity, they have come up and done well in different pockets of the world. My father-in-law's family migrated from Sindh and settled in Pune when he was 3 years old. My husband was born in Pune, but his family migrated to the United States when he was 2 and they have been here ever since.

Bhindi Fry is a Sindhi dish. The first time I ate this dish was at the home of a dear friend, whose mom made the most amazing Sindhi food. My friend and I met in engineering college, and we used to frequent each other's homes. One of the most striking features of Mumbai is the diversity in cultures and how people from different races and religions come together over food. My friend's mother would prepare the Bhindi Fry by frying the cut okra in hot oil and then tossing it in spices. This bhindi is usually eaten with the famous Sindhi curry and rice.

Okra can be tricky to cook since it is quite slimy, but there are ways to make it taste good. One way is by frying the bhindi to remove the sliminess. My kids love Japanese fried vegetables—tempura. Tempura can be meat or vegetable, dipped in a batter and deep fried quickly to preserve the fresh taste of the meat or vegetable. The technique was brought over by the Portuguese in the 16th century. I came up with this dish by combining the two techniques of frying the bhindi in a tempura style with spices. The tempura batter requires chilled seltzer water for the batter to be light and crispy. You get the taste from all the beautiful spices in the batter, a slight crunch from the okra, and an additional sprinkling of spices on the top. This appetizer cannot be kept, and needs to be eaten fresh. The Fried Curry Leaf and Toasted Cumin Aioli (page 370) is a fantastic dip for the Bhindi Masala Tempura Fries. The combination makes it absolutely delicious! Raj, who hates okra (how can he?) loves this dish, which speaks for itself.

continued ➜

INGREDIENTS

1 cup (120 g) all-purpose flour
1 tablespoon (7.5 g) cornstarch
½ teaspoon (2 g) baking powder
½ teaspoon (1 g) red chili powder
½ teaspoon (1 g) ground cumin
½ teaspoon (1 g) ground coriander
1 teaspoon (2 g) chaat masala
1 teaspoon (2 g) ground turmeric
½ teaspoon (3 g) salt
1 pound (450 g) okra (bhindi)
1 cup (240 g) cold seltzer water
Oil for deep frying

GARNISH

½ teaspoon (1 g) Kashmiri red chili powder
¼ teaspoon (0.5 g) amchur (dried mango powder)
¼ teaspoon (0.5 g) chaat masala
2 tablespoons finely chopped cilantro
Fried Curry Leaf and Toasted Cumin Aioli (page 370)

METHOD

1. In a large bowl, add the all-purpose flour, cornstarch, baking powder, red chili powder, ground cumin, ground coriander, chaat masala, turmeric, and salt and whisk to combine.

2. There are two ways to clean okra. The first is to wash the okra and lay them out on a kitchen towel individually to completely air dry. The second is to use a wet kitchen towel, wipe each okra clean, and set it aside to dry. After cleaning and drying, cut off the top hats and bottom slim portions of the okra. Slit each okra into 4 equal parts lengthwise.

3. Add the cold seltzer water to the flour mixture and whisk until combined and no clumps in the batter remain. Set it aside. Place a baking sheet with a wire rack, on the side to keep the okra tempura fries crispy.

4. Place a large frying pan with oil halfway up over medium-high heat. It will take about 5 minutes for the oil to come to a frying temperature of 350°F (175°C). You can check the temperature with a kitchen thermometer or drop a tiny bit of batter into the oil. If it comes up immediately, you know that the oil is ready for frying. If it does not come up immediately, the oil needs 2 to 3 minutes to come to a frying temperature.

5. Once the oil is ready, add a handful of okra at a time into the batter and coat each piece with the batter. Remove each piece individually and drain off all the excess batter until there is a thin coating. One at a time, add each piece into the frying pan. Add about 12 to 14 pieces at a time. Fry for a minute until lightly brown on all sides. Using a kitchen spider, remove the okra, drain off the excess oil into the frying pan, and set the pieces aside on the wire rack setup.

6. Repeat Step 5 for the remaining okra.

7. In a small bowl, combine the Kashmiri red chili powder, amchur, and chaat masala, and mix with a spoon to combine.

8. Once all the okra pieces are fried, plate them, and sprinkle with the garnish spices. Garnish with the finely chopped cilantro. Serve immediately with the Fried Curry Leaf and Toasted Cumin Aioli and enjoy!

Summer Hariyali (Green) Paneer Skewers
WITH CILANTRO, PEANUT, AND TOASTED CORIANDER SEED PESTO

Makes about 6 skewers

Growing up in Mumbai, we had access to a ton of great restaurants and food. I had a few favorites. One of them was Copper Chimney. They had seriously the best Punjabi-style or North Indian–style food, and we used to go there for all our birthdays, especially when we were little. Mum did not make paneer that often at home, but we loved eating paneer when we went out to Indian restaurants. My absolute favorite dish was Hariyali Paneer or Green Paneer, made with a wonderful green yogurt-based paste, in which the paneer is marinated for a bit and then put on skewers with bell peppers and onions, grilled to perfection, and served with Cilantro Mint Chutney (page 42). My brother and I would fight over the last piece of paneer, and he would be left crying, because I would win. Fun memories!

With the beautiful summer California produce, and the wonderful fresh farmers' markets, I upped these Summer Hariyali (Green) Paneer Skewers with lemons from my backyard tree; firm, juicy, and sweet nectarines; and sweet bell peppers and onions. I serve them with the Cilantro, Peanut, and Toasted Coriander Seed Pesto (page 56), which goes perfectly with these skewers. The paste itself has kale, cilantro, and mint in it, giving a wonderfully fresh, seasonal taste to the paneer. You can taste the California summer in this dish. Eat it by removing all the contents of the skewer onto a plate, sprinkling with chaat masala, squeezing and drizzling the grilled, charred lemon onto the plate contents, and dolloping a bit of the pesto. Savor each bite while you sip on a beautiful sauvignon blanc from the Napa Valley!

INGREDIENTS

GREEN YOGURT SAUCE

1 cup (220 g) Greek yogurt

1 tablespoon (6 g) chickpea flour or besan

2 tablespoons (27 g) vegetable oil

1 tablespoon (15 g) lemon juice

½ teaspoon (1 g) ground cumin

½ teaspoon (1 g) ground coriander

1½ teaspoons (9 g) table salt

1 teaspoon (3 g) garam masala

1 teaspoon (2 g) chaat masala

½ teaspoon (1 g) amchur (dried mango powder)

½ cup washed and tightly packed cilantro

½ cup washed and tightly packed kale

¼ cup washed and tightly packed mint

2 green chilis

2 garlic cloves

1 inch (2½ cm) ginger, skin removed

4 tablespoons water

1 pound (453 g) paneer (Indian cottage cheese), cut into approximately 18 (1-inch) pieces

continued ➡

VEGETABLES AND FRUITS

½ medium onion, cut into roughly 1-inch
(2½ cm) chunks

1 red bell pepper, deseeded and cut into roughly
1-inch (2½ cm) chunks

1 lemon, cut into roughly 1-inch (2½ cm) chunks

1 small nectarine, pitted and cut into roughly
1-inch (2½ cm) chunks

GARNISH

2 tablespoons chopped cilantro

1 to 2 teaspoons chaat masala

Cilantro, Peanut, and Toasted Coriander Seed
Pesto (page 56)

METHOD

1. Soak six long bamboo skewers (about 10 inches or 25 cm long) in water for 20 to 30 minutes.

2. Meanwhile, in a large bowl, combine the Greek yogurt, chickpea flour, vegetable oil, lemon juice, ground cumin, ground coriander, salt, garam masala, chaat masala, and amchur and whisk to combine.

3. In a high-speed blender, combine the cilantro, kale, mint, green chilis, garlic, ginger, and water and blend until a smooth paste is formed.

4. Add this paste to the yogurt mixture and whisk again to make a smooth green yogurt sauce. To marinate, add the paneer pieces, cover, and place in the fridge for a minimum of 30 to 40 minutes.

5. Preheat the oven to 450°F (230°C). Build each skewer however you prefer. I add 2 to 3 red onion slices, red bell pepper, paneer, lemon wedge, paneer, nectarine wedge, paneer, red bell pepper, red onion slices. Place the skewer on a baking sheet.

6. Spray the skewers with cooking spray and place in the oven for 5 minutes.

7. Remove the baking sheet from the oven and gently, using kitchen mitts, turn the skewers to cook them on the other side. Spray again with cooking spray. Return to the oven for 5 minutes.

8. Change the oven setting to broil and broil for 2 minutes.

9. Remove from the oven. Place the skewers on a platter, making sure not to burn yourself. Sprinkle with cilantro and chaat masala. Remove the vegetables from the skewers and squeeze the grilled lemon all over them. Serve with the Cilantro, Peanut, and Toasted Coriander Seed Pesto.

PRO TIPS

1. For cutting the lemon wedges, red onion, and nectarines, I cut the produce in half and slice each half into quarters. You can use more nectarines or more lemons, based on your preference.

2. Grill the skewers on a stovetop grill on high heat if you do not want to turn on the oven. You can even grill them on a backyard grill, placing the skewers on a piece of alumnium foil, and then placing them on the grill.

3. The green yogurt sauce can be made a day ahead and stored in the fridge.

Aloo Tikki Arancini
WITH SAFFRON AIOLI

Makes about 26 large or 52 small balls

Anishka loves arancini. Her favorite Italian restaurant is Delfina, simply because they have arancini on their menu, and half of them are always hers. She claims them even before we reach the restaurant. The days I make risotto for dinner, I make extra so that I can prepare arancini for her the next day.

What is arancini? Arancini is an Italian snack or appetizer made from leftover risotto, coated with bread crumbs and deep-fried, to make these delicious balls. They are served with marinara sauce or aioli, and make perfect anytime snacks/appetizers.

My fusion arancinis have a mixture of boiled potatoes and spices that we use to make aloo tikkis or shallow fried potato patties. The mashed boiled potatoes help to bind the risotto together well, and the spices add a wonderful taste to the arancini. The spice is just enough, so as not to overpower the taste of the arancini. Together with Saffron Aioli (page 379), this snack is a fun fusion of East meets West. This has become Anishka's favorite snack. They store well in the fridge, and the best way to heat them up is by baking them in a toaster oven. Make them for your next party, or serve them on your cheese board to wow your guests.

INGREDIENTS

RISOTTO
1 tablespoon (13 g) olive oil
2 tablespoons (28 g) unsalted butter
½ small (65 g) white onion, finely chopped
2 garlic cloves, finely chopped
¼ zucchini (70 g), grated
1 cup (195 g) arborio rice
3 cups (660 g) vegetable stock (I prefer low-sodium)
½ cup (40 g) grated parmesan cheese
Lemon zest from 1 lemon
½ teaspoon (3 g) table salt
1 teaspoon (2.33 g) black pepper
3 tablespoons finely chopped fresh basil

ALOO TIKKI
3 small (230 g) potatoes, boiled and mashed completely
½ teaspoon (1 g) red chili powder
½ teaspoon (1 g) ground cumin
½ teaspoon (1 g) ground coriander
1 teaspoon (2 g) chaat masala
½ teaspoon (3 g) table salt
½ cup (60 g) all-purpose flour
2 eggs
1 cup (60 g) panko bread crumbs
30 to 50 small mozzarella cheese cubes (optional)
Vegetable oil, for frying

GARNISH
Freshly grated parmesan cheese
Microgreens
Saffron Aioli (page 379)

continued ➤

METHOD

To Make the Risotto

1. In a medium sauté pan or skillet pan on medium heat, add oil and butter.

2. Once the butter melts, add onions, and cook for 2 to 3 minutes, until translucent. Add the garlic and grated zucchini. Sauté for 1 minute.

3. Add the arborio rice, and toast for about 4 minutes, until translucent. You will smell the aroma of the rice.

4. Start adding ½ cup (110 g) stock to the pan and keep stirring until all the stock has been absorbed. There should not be any stock left in the pan, at which point you will add another ½ cup (110 g) stock. Keep repeating the process for a total of 20 to 25 minutes, until the rice is al dente. There will be a slight bite to the rice, but it should be soft. The risotto should look creamy at this stage.

5. Add the parmesan cheese, lemon zest, salt, black pepper, and basil. Mix well to combine.

6. Dump the risotto onto a baking sheet lined with parchment paper. Spread it with a rubber spatula into an even layer to cover the entire sheet pan. Place it to set in the fridge for 1½ to 2 hours, or up to a day.

To Make the Aloo Tikki Arancini

1. Remove the risotto from the fridge. In a large bowl, add the boiled mashed potatoes, all the spices, and salt. Add the risotto and mix well.

2. Keep a large baking sheet ready. Prepare an assembly line of bowls ready with flour, eggs (beaten well until combined), panko bread crumbs, and the mozzarella cubes (if using).

3. With a 1-tablespoon or 2-tablespoon ice cream scoop, take a scoop of the risotto mixture and make balls by rolling them between your palms to make them perfectly round.

4. If you want to stuff them with mozzarella cheese, then add a piece of cheese in the middle, wrap the risotto around the cheese to seal it, and roll the ball between the palms of your hands to secure the ball.

5. Place the balls on the baking sheet as you work. Continue until all of the mixture has been formed into balls.

6. Coat each ball in the flour, shake off excess, then the egg wash, shake off excess, and then the panko bread crumbs. Place each ball back on the baking sheet. To prevent sticky lumpy fingers, use a fork for the panko bread crumbs part, and a spoon for the egg part, or use two different hands, one for the egg wash and one for the panko bread crumbs.

7. Once all the arancini are ready, freeze them for 10 minutes in the freezer.

8. Place a paper towel or parchment paper on a large plate. Get a large pot or Dutch oven ready, filling it halfway up with the vegetable oil on medium to high heat. It will take a good 5 to 6 minutes for the oil to heat up to the frying temperature of 350°F (175°C). Once the oil is ready, fry a few balls at a time on medium heat to heat all the way through and melt the cheese, about 2 minutes. Rotate halfway through to brown the other side. Once they turn brown uniformly, remove them onto the plate.

9. Once all the arancini are fried, garnish with the freshly grated parmesan cheese and the microgreens. Serve with the Saffron Aioli.

Grilled Bombay Sandwich

Makes 4 large sandwiches; serves 6 to 8

The Bombay sandwich is the most common Mumbai street food fare you will find at every street corner. Around schools, colleges, bus stations, train stations, movie theaters—you name it! A sandwich made in no time, it serves as a quick snack, or even a meal, especially when you're on the go.

I have two favorite memories of this sandwich. My favorite sandwich is from a place called Rama's, in the Juhu Vile Parle area. Mum and I would visit this contemporary shop, next to the sandwich place, that had the most beautiful ethnic pieces from all over India. We would shop and then the next stop would be the sandwich wala. He made a triple-decker sandwich, which is really to die for! Mum and I would finish one between us. My second favorite place is Jay Sandwich, outside my engineering college, which actually has a spiced potato filling. I have the best memories outside Jay Sandwich, eating sandwiches with my dear friends, gossiping, and having a jolly good time! The meal was followed by a cooling glass of sweet and fresh sugarcane juice, which is a novelty here in the United States, and a must-have if you visit India.

To bring those memories to my family, I recreated the Grilled Bombay Sandwich. It is a veggie-loaded sandwich with extra butter, because, why not? Sometimes extra butter is needed in life! Each layer of sandwich is sprinkled with Sandwich Masala (page 61), which gives the sandwich that special flavor and punch. This sandwich is pretty big and filling, and makes for a great appetizer.

INGREDIENTS

2 medium (approximately 300 g) red or yellow beets

12 country white bread slices

6 to 8 tablespoons (¾ to 1 stick; 85 to 113 g) salted butter, room temperature, plus 4 tablespoons (½ stick; 56 g) for the panini grill

½ cup Cilantro Mint Chutney (page 42), plus more to serve

3 medium (approximately 400 g) white potatoes, boiled, peeled, and cut into ¼-inch (½ cm) slices

2 to 3 tablespoons Sandwich Masala (page 61)

⅔ cup (150 g) freshly grated Monterey Jack cheese

1 medium (approximately 135 g) English cucumber, cut into ⅛-inch (½ cm) slices

1 medium red onion (100 g), sliced thin horizontally

2 medium (approximately 350 g) heirloom tomatoes, cut into ¼-inch (½ cm) slices

Ketchup, to serve

continued ➡

METHOD

To Roast the Beets

1. Preheat the oven to 400°F (200°C). Wash the beets. Cut off the tops and ends of the beets. If they are large, cut them into halves. Place them in aluminum foil and cover to form a closed pouch.

2. Place the pouch in the oven for about 1 hour. The beets should have cooked by then. You can test by opening up the pouch and using a sharp knife to poke through the middle of a beet. Be careful as it will be very hot and steam will come out of it.

3. Open up the foil and let the beets cool completely for about an hour.

4. Remove the skin and cut into thin ¼-inch (½ cm) slices.

To Assemble the Sandwich

1. Heat your panini grill. If you do not have a panini grill, use your grill pan on the stove over medium-high heat.

2. On a big cutting board, lay out 12 slices of bread. Generously apply one-third of the salted butter on all the slices. Apply the Cilantro Mint Chutney on all the slices. Make sure you put an even layer on the slices.

3. Evenly layer four slices with the boiled potatoes. Sprinkle the Sandwich Masala on top of the potatoes. Layer the golden beets in an even layer. Sprinkle the Sandwich Masala on top of the beets. Add half of the Monterey Jack cheese to the tops.

4. Place four butter-chutney slices of bread on top of the cheese, upside down so the plain side is up. Slather one-third of the butter on the top, followed by the Cilantro Mint Chutney. Layer with cucumber slices and sprinkle the Sandwich Masala on top.

5. Layer with onion slices and sprinkle the Sandwich Masala on top. Layer with tomato slices and sprinkle Sandwich Masala on top. Add the remaining Monterey Jack cheese to the tops. Cover with four butter-chutney slices of bread, placing them upside down such that the non-buttered sides are facing up. Slather the remaining butter on top of the slices.

6. Put some butter on the panini grill, place the triple-decker sandwich on the grill, and gently close the grill. Make sure the top of the grill is even and straight such that the top of the sandwich grills properly. Grill the sandwich for about 3 to 4 minutes. It should be nicely browned and crisp on the top and bottom.

7. Using a spatula, gently place the sandwich onto the cutting board. Let rest for 2 minutes. Using a sharp serrated knife, cut the sandwich into triangles. The knife going through the sandwich should make a nice crunching sound.

8. Repeat Steps 3 to 7 for the remaining sandwiches.

9. Serve immediately to preserve the freshness, as the sandwich gets soggy over time.

10. Serve with ketchup and Cilantro Mint Chutney.

PRO TIPS

1. It is important to get sturdy bread as this is a triple-decker sandwich. I recommend country white bread.

2. Substitute Sandwich Masala with chaat masala if required.

3. If you do not have a panini grill, grill the sandwich on a grill pan. Place something heavy on top like a cast-iron pan to mimic the panini grill. Flip carefully to grill both sides of the sandwich.

Corn Mushroom Tomato Chili Cheese Danish

Makes about 14 to 16 Danish

One of our favorite dinners growing up was toast with corn, mushrooms, chili, and cheese. It came together very easily by simply mixing the ingredients. Mum would use Amul cheese, which makes the mixture creamy and delicious, and she would bake it in the oven. We had it with tomato soup and the pairing was to die for!

Laminating dough is a very therapeutic process. It's not hard at all but it does require some good muscle work to roll dough with a huge butter block in the middle, go through the folds, and finally roll it out thin enough to make beautiful pastries. And while it takes lots of patience, the end result is definitely worth it. Once you make it a couple of times, the process becomes easier, and you can experiment with different flavors, be they sweet or savory.

Reminiscing about my memories at home with this toast, I came up with a savory Danish that uses the same flavors as the toast, along with cherry tomatoes. I use pepper Jack and fontina cheese instead of the Amul cheese, and it works just as well together. It is truly a celebration of California summer produce, with the sweet corn, shiitake mushrooms, juicy cherry tomatoes—and green onions and chilis to add the flavor. You can make these Danish as appetizers for guests or serve as dinner, with a side salad and a glass of white wine.

INGREDIENTS

BUTTER BLOCK

2 cups + 1½ tablespoons (470 g) cold, unsalted European-style butter

DANISH DOUGH

6 cups minus 4 teaspoons (720 g) bread flour

⅓ cup (65 g) granulated sugar

4 teaspoons (12 g) instant yeast

1 tsp (2.2 g) finely ground black pepper

2 teaspoons (12 g) table salt

1 cup + 3 tablespoons (280 g) whole milk, room temperature

3 eggs

5 tablespoons (72 g) European-style butter, melted and cooled

DANISH FILLING

½ cup (70 g) corn kernels, fresh or frozen

½ cup shiitake mushrooms, diced small

½ cup (80 g) pepper Jack, shredded and packed

½ cup (60 g) fontina, shredded and packed

¼ cup finely chopped cilantro

2 to 3 tablespoons heavy cream

1 teaspoon (6 g) table salt

1 teaspoon (2.2 g) coarse black pepper

2 green chilis, finely chopped

2 garlic cloves, grated

1 green onion, finely chopped

36 to 40 cherry tomatoes, cut into halves

continued ➡

DANISH TOPPING

Flaky sea salt

Cracked black pepper

EGG WASH

1 egg

1 teaspoon water

1 teaspoon granulated sugar

GARNISH

Freshly grated Parmesan cheese

Cherry tomatoes

Flaky sea salt

Coarse black pepper

Finely chopped chives (3 to 4 stems)

or

Everything bagel seasoning

EQUIPMENT

Wide rolling pin

Bench scraper

Wide-haired brush, for excess flour

2-foot stainless steel ruler

Pastry brush

**5-wheel stainless steel pastry cutter
(a sharp knife will do)**

Half-sheet baking sheets

METHOD

DAY 1

To Make the Butter Block

1. Cut the chilled butter into rectangular blocks to form an even square on the center of a sheet of parchment paper. It is almost like playing Tetris with the butter on the parchment to form a square.

2. Cover with another sheet of parchment paper and start pounding the butter block with a rolling pin until the layer evens out. The goal is to smooth out the butter into an even layer of an 8-inch (20 cm) square butter block.

3. Keep measuring after a few poundings to see if it is reaching an 8-inch (20 cm) square but-

ter block. You can use a bench scraper to even out the edges and smooth out the top. You can even flip the parchment paper upside down, since the bottom will be smoother, and then use a rolling pin to smooth the butter. Keep pushing the sides to be straight and form a square.

4. The whole process takes anywhere from 5 to 10 minutes. The goal is for the butter to remain chilled during the entire time and not soften. If you feel the butter is getting too soft, put it in the fridge for 30 minutes and then try forming it into a square again.

5. Once the square is formed, tuck the parchment paper overhang around the butter block and set it in the fridge overnight.

To Make the Danish Dough

1. In the bowl of a stand mixer with a dough hook attachment, add all the dry ingredients—bread flour, sugar, yeast, black pepper, and salt and whisk to combine. Add the milk, eggs, and butter to the mixture. Start the stand mixer at low speed for a minute for the dough to mix together. Increase to medium speed for 3 minutes until the dough is smooth and the bowl is clean.

2. Mix for another 2 to 3 minutes for the dough to develop gluten and become sturdy.

3. Do the windowpane test: Take a small piece of dough and use your first three fingers and thumb on both hands to gently smooth and stretch the dough until thin. If you can stretch the dough without breaking it, the dough has been sufficiently kneaded and the gluten is well developed. If it breaks, knead the dough in the mixer for another 1 to 2 minutes and do the windowpane test again.

4. Place the dough on a clean surface. Shape into a rectangle, place it on a piece of parchment paper on a baking sheet, cover with plastic wrap, and refrigerate overnight.

DAY 2

To Laminate the Dough

1. Keep the extra flour, rolling pin, bench scraper, wide-haired brush, pastry cutter, and stainless steel ruler handy. See photographs of the lamination process on page 76.

2. Remove the dough from the fridge. Using extra flour sprinkled on a clean surface and extra flour on the rolling pin, roll out the dough to an 8-by-18-inch (20-by-46 cm) rectangle. You have to keep straightening the sides of the rolled-out dough with the bench scraper and rolling pin to ensure that the rectangular shape is maintained at all times while at the same time maintaining the thickness of the dough throughout. Use extra flour as needed to ensure that the dough does not stick to the surface.

3. Remove the butter block from the fridge and place in the middle of the dough. Remove the excess flour from the dough with the wide-haired brush. Wrap the left side over half the butter block, then wrap the right side over the other half of the block. Secure it from the top, bottom, and middle by pinching the dough together. This is called a classic enclosure. Square out the entire block by using the bench scraper to align all the sides in parallel.

4. We will do three turns to the dough to laminate it.

First Turn

5. Sprinkle flour on the work surface. With an open side of the dough-enclosed butter block toward you, roll lengthwise, up and down, to lengthen the dough. Make sure that the edges are straightened by using the bench scraper and rolling pin, keeping the thickness the same throughout the length of the dough.

6. Make sure that you spread flour beneath the dough by lifting it with one hand and sprinkling flour with the other. Always be sure to sprinkle flour on the top as well. You want to ensure your dough does not stick underneath or on your rolling pin.

7. Roll until you have an 8-by-18-inch (20-by-45 cm) rectangle. Make sure the corners are even and squared off. You can roll out to 8 by 19 inches (20 by 40 cm) and, using a pastry cutter, cut off half an inch (1¼ cm) from the width of the rectangle to even out the sides. Use the wide brush to gently remove any excess flour.

8. With the length of the rectangle parallel to you, wrap the dough by folding the left side of the dough two-thirds of the way in. Brush off the excess flour using the wide brush and then wrap the right side of the dough over the left side. Again, brush off the excess flour. Straighten out the dough with a bench scraper and the rolling pin to an exact 8-by-18-inch (20-by-46 cm) rectangle. Place it on the baking sheet, wrap it with plastic wrap, and put it in the fridge for an hour.

Second Turn

9. With an open edge of the dough toward you, roll lengthwise, up and down, to lengthen the dough. Make sure that the edges are straightened by using the bench scraper and rolling pin to maintain an even thickness throughout the length of the dough.

10. Repeat Steps 6, 7, and 8.

Third Turn

11. With an open edge of the dough toward you, roll lengthwise, up and down, to lengthen the dough. Make sure that the edges are straightened by using the bench scraper and rolling pin to maintain an even thickness throughout the length of the dough.

12. Repeat Steps 6, 7, and 8.

To Cut the Laminated Dough

1. With an open edge of the dough toward you, roll lengthwise, up and down, to lengthen the

continued ➤

dough. Make sure that the edges are straightened by using the bench scraper and rolling pin to maintain an even thickness throughout the length of the dough.

2. Make sure that you spread flour beneath the dough by lifting it with one hand and sprinkling flour with the other. Always be sure to sprinkle flour on the top as well. You want to ensure your dough does not stick underneath or on your rolling pin.

3. The desired size is 9 by 26 inches (23 by 66 cm) and about ¼ inch (5 mm) thick. You want an even rectangle. Cut off half an inch from the width and the length of the rectangle to even out the sides, using a sharp knife and the stainless steel ruler. Use the wide-haired brush to brush off the excess flour.

4. Using the stainless steel pastry cutter, and setting it to 3½ inches (9 cm), cut strips from the rolled-out dough, lengthwise first. When using the pastry cutter, cut at a 60-degree angle, putting even pressure across the entire cutter to make even and consistent squares. Using the same 3½-inch (9 cm) setting, cut widthwise to form the squares. You will get 14 exact squares, and additional scraps of dough to play with or to make cylinder pastries with. You can also use a knife and ruler to cut the squares if you do not have a cutter.

5. Place the squares 2 inches (5 cm) apart on a baking sheet with parchment paper, cover with plastic wrap, and put it in the fridge for 30 to 40 minutes.

To Make the Danish Filling

In a medium bowl, add all the ingredients except the cherry tomatoes and mix gently to combine. Set it aside.

To Shape, Proof, Fill, and Bake the Danish

1. **To shape the Danish:** Remove six squares at a time from the fridge. Roll them out slightly larger to about 4 by 4 inches (10 by 10 cm).

2. Place the squares on the baking sheet, make a slight indentation in each pastry using the bottom of a 3- to 3 ½-inch round glass (8 to 9 cm). This is where the filling will go.

3. **To proof the Danish:** To proof, you can choose two different methods. The first option is to put a large plastic bag or an unscented garbage bag over the baking sheet, sealing the tray. Make sure that the bag does not touch the Danish by putting inverted glasses on the four corners of the tray inside the bag to hold it up. Repeat for the other trays. Leave the trays in a warm place, around 75°F (25°C). The second option is to place the baking sheets in the oven with a pot of warm water (around 75°F [25°C]) to create the warm environment required for proofing. Proof for 2½ to 3 hours.

4. **To fill the Danish:** Add about 2 tablespoons of the filling to each cavity, press it down gently, and add 3 to 4 cherry tomato halves.

5. **To make the egg wash:** Combine the ingredients in a small bowl and whisk for 2 minutes until the mixture is smooth.

6. **To bake the Danish:** Preheat the oven to 415°F (215°C). Dip the pastry brush in the egg wash, remove excess, and gently brush on the border and sides of each Danish. Sprinkle flaky sea salt and freshly ground black pepper on the top of each. Place the baking sheet on the center and bottom racks of the oven. Bake for 5 minutes, then reduce the temperature to 375°F (190°C). Bake for another 20 to 25 minutes until golden brown, rotating the trays from top to bottom and front to back after about 10 to 15 minutes for an even bake.

7. **To decorate the Danish:** When the Danish come out of the oven, top each with grated Parmesan cheese, 2 halves of a cherry tomato, flaky sea salt, freshly ground black pepper, and a sprinkling of chives. You may also use everything bagel seasoning if you have it, in place of the other seasonings.

Example Timeline to Prepare Your Danish

See photographs of the lamination process on page 76.

DAY 1

Prepare the butter block and the Danish dough. Let them both rest overnight.

DAY 2

7 a.m. Enclose the butter block in the dough with the single turn method. Roll it out once to an 8-by-18-inch (20-by-45 cm) rectangle, then enclose the dough in the single turn method again. Wrap in plastic wrap and store in the fridge for approximately an hour.

8:30 a.m. Roll the dough out again to an 8-by-18-inch (20-by-45 cm) rectangle, fold the dough with the single turn method. Wrap in plastic wrap and store in the fridge for approximately an hour.

9:30 a.m. Roll the dough out again to an 8-by-18-inch (20-by-45 cm) rectangle, fold the dough with the single turn method. Wrap in plastic wrap and store in the fridge for approximately an hour.

10:30 a.m. Roll the dough out again to an 8-by-19-inch (20-by-48 cm) rectangle, enclose the dough in the single turn method. Wrap in plastic wrap and store in the fridge for approximately an hour.

11:30 a.m. Roll it out to the desired size of 9 by 26 inches (22 by 66 cm), and ¼ inch (5 mm) thick. Cut into 3½-inch (9 cm) squares and store in the fridge for half an hour.

12 p.m. Shape the squares into the desired shape and then set to proof for about 2½ hours. Preheat the oven as the proofing comes to an end and prepare the egg wash.

2:30 p.m. Add the desired filling, brush on the egg wash, and bake for half an hour in total or until the Danish are golden brown in color.

3 p.m. Remove the Danish from the oven, add any desired toppings, and let cool.

Dahi Papdi Chaat

Serves 10 to 12

Mumbai street food is so world famous that even Andrew Zimmern and the late Anthony Bourdain featured it on their travel shows. It is discussed on any travel show that showcases Mumbai eateries. The speed at which the street vendors make each dish is fascinating to watch, their hands moving rapidly to gather all the ingredients in a bowl to give you the best concoction ever! I grew up with the best street food that any city has to offer, and it makes me happy to be able to share this special street food with you.

When my mother-in-law, then 22, immigrated to San Diego, California, in the 1970s, she had no idea what to expect, or if there would be an Indian store around to make the food she grew up with. It was a culture shock, to come 9,000 miles away from home to a place where there is neither family, nor familiarity, nor Indian stores to turn to. She had to make do with the ingredients that she had at hand to try and whip up dishes that were familiar to her and my father-in-law and my husband, who was 2 when they moved to the United States. They craved all the dishes they grew up with, all the street food that is so easily available in Mumbai and Pune (where they are from).

She came up with the idea of frying flour tortillas as a quick fix to make the papdi for the Dahi Papdi Chaat. What is papdi? Round fried puri made with flour, ghee, carom seeds, and salt, that form the base of the Dahi Papdi Chaat, upon which the other ingredients are laid to create a mouthwatering dish! When we visited my in-laws in Los Angeles, my mother-in-law would make the Dahi Papdi Chaat for us. She made it with the fried tortillas and the taste was amazing! The fried tortilla chips were crunchy, lighter than the traditional puri or papdi, and made a fantastic bed for all those spicy chatpata umami ingredients. Thus I wanted to share a piece of what my husband grew up with, as an amazing hack to make your own Dahi Papdi Chaat, one that will wow your family and friends.

INGREDIENTS

5 large flour tortillas

Oil, to fry the tortillas

1 cup (320 g) Date Tamarind Chutney (page 45), plus water for thinning

½ cup (160 g) Cilantro Mint Chutney (page 42), plus water for thinning

2 cups + 1 tablespoon (500 g) Yukon gold potatoes, boiled, and cut into tiny pieces

¾ teaspoon (1.5 g) red chili powder

1 teaspoon (2 g) chaat masala

½ teaspoon (1 g) amchur (dried mango powder)

1 teaspoon (6 g) table salt

½ cup (60 g) finely chopped red onions

YOGURT MIXTURE

⅓ cup (80 g) water

½ cup (114 g) Greek yogurt

½ teaspoon (3 g) table salt

1 teaspoon (4 g) granulated sugar

continued →

GARNISH

½ to ¾ cup (40 to 60 g) thin sev or chickpea noodles

⅓ cup (58 g) pomegranate arils

Finely chopped cilantro

Additional chaat masala

METHOD

To Prepare and Fry Tortillas

1. Dry out the tortillas by placing them in a pre-heated oven at 350°F (175°C) for 5 to 7 minutes. Remove from the oven and let cool completely.

2. Set a frying pan with oil, about 2 inches in height, on high heat. The temperature of the oil should be around 350°F (175°C). It will take about 5 minutes for the oil to heat up.

3. Meanwhile, cut the cooled, dry tortillas into strips about 1 inch (2½ cm) in width, and cut each strip into 2-inch (5 cm) pieces. Prepare a baking sheet with a wire rack on top to drain off excess oil.

4. Once the oil is ready, fry a few tortilla pieces at a time, until golden brown in color. They fry up pretty quickly, so make sure that you are attentive. The tortilla pieces take about 5 to 7 seconds to fry on each side. Remove and set aside on the wire rack.

5. Repeat for the remaining tortilla pieces. Let cool completely.

To Prepare the Other Ingredients

1. For the Date Tamarind Chutney, add water a tablespoon at a time so it reaches the consistency of heavy cream. Mix to blend well.

2. For the Cilantro Mint Chutney, add water a tablespoon at a time so it reaches the consistency of heavy cream. Mix to blend well.

3. For the yogurt mixture, add the water, salt, and sugar to the yogurt. Mix to blend well.

4. In a bowl, add the potatoes, red chili powder, chaat masala, amchur, and salt, and mix to combine.

To Assemble

1. Arrange the fried tortilla pieces on the platter.

2. Distribute the spiced potatoes evenly on top of the tortilla pieces.

3. Distribute the chopped red onions evenly on top of the potatoes. Sprinkle a pinch of chaat masala evenly all over the platter.

4. Using a spoon, drizzle the prepared Date Tamarind Chutney all over the top, leaving about one-quarter of the chutney aside.

5. Using a separate spoon, drizzle the prepared Cilantro Mint Chutney all over the top, leaving about one-quarter of the chutney aside.

6. Using a separate spoon, drizzle the yogurt mixture all over the top.

7. Drizzle the remainder of the Date Tamarind Chutney and Cilantro Mint Chutney on top of the yogurt.

8. Sprinkle the thin sev all over the top.

9. Distribute the pomegranate arils on top evenly.

10. Finally garnish with the cilantro and a sprinkling of chaat masala all over the platter.

11. Serve immediately.

PRO TIP

You could use the Indian store-bought papdi or puri instead of the tortillas.

Brussels Sprouts, Dates, Walnuts, and Pomegranate Arils

WITH TOASTED CORIANDER-CUMIN VINAIGRETTE

Serves 5 to 6

When you immigrate to another country, you adapt to the different traditions and festivals celebrated in that country while trying to keep your own cultural traditions. Adapting to the United States was definitely a huge challenge, being away from my family with very few friends that I knew from Mumbai. I made new friends who were not Indian and I learned the American way of doing things. There was a lot to learn and unlearn, but as we come to a different place, we grow resilient and learn to adapt to the new ways with a smile. In the first year of my master's program in Los Angeles, I came to know of the most important holiday: Thanksgiving. My first Thanksgiving was with a couple friends from Mumbai and a whole set of new American and international friends. We all made dishes and it was like an international potluck. One of the dishes was a brussels sprouts dish that I did not like. But that was the first time I was introduced to brussels sprouts. I realized over the years what a big part this cruciferous vegetable played for the biggest tradition and holiday in the United States. I grew to really enjoy this humble vegetable, especially knowing its umpteen health benefits. It is high in antioxidants, helps in prevention and fighting of cancer, is high in fiber, and, just like its cousins cauliflower and broccoli, it helps decrease the risk of diabetes.

Since having kids and wanting to make sure they get the proper nutrition, I have been making brussels sprouts regularly when they are in season with different preparations. One of my favorite ways is to make a toasted cumin-coriander vinaigrette with smoked paprika and za'atar, tossing all the brussels sprouts in the vinaigrette and roasting them. Once roasted and nicely browned, I throw the sprouts together it with dates, walnuts, and pomegranate arils. The dish gets a lot of its flavor from the toasted cumin and coriander. The flavors are wonderful along with sweetness from the dates, crunch from the walnuts, and fall freshness from the pomegranate arils. The whole combination is so good and it has become a hit in our family and at any Thanksgiving get-together.

continued ➤

INGREDIENTS

1 teaspoon (2 g) cumin seeds

1 teaspoon (1 g) coriander seeds

¼ cup (32.5 g) olive oil

2 tablespoons (29 g) apple cider vinegar

2 tablespoons (40 g) maple syrup

2 teaspoons (4 g) za'atar

1 teaspoon (2 g) smoked paprika

1 teaspoon (1 g) red chili flakes

1½ teaspoons (9 g) flaky sea salt

1 teaspoon (2 g) freshly ground black pepper

1½ pounds (680 g) brussels sprouts, halved

¾ cup (100 g) coarsely chopped dates (about 12)

¾ cup (90 g) coarsely chopped toasted walnuts

½ cup (80 g) pomegranate arils

METHOD

1. Toast the cumin and coriander seeds: In a small saucepan on medium heat, toss the cumin and coriander seeds for around 2 to 3 minutes, until you start to smell their aroma and they are slightly browned. Turn off the heat. In a small coffee or spice grinder, coarsely grind the seeds.

2. Make the vinaigrette: In a glass jar, add the olive oil, apple cider vinegar, maple syrup, za'atar, smoked paprika, red chili flakes, flaky sea salt, black pepper, and ground toasted cumin and coriander seeds. Shake the jar vigorously for 15 to 20 seconds until the mixture has combined.

3. In a large bowl, toss the brussels sprouts with the vinaigrette. Set them aside to marinate for 30 minutes.

4. Meanwhile, preheat the oven to 400°F (200°C).

5. Place the marinated brussels sprouts on a baking sheet, flat side down, and place it on the middle rack of the oven for about 35 minutes in total. Halfway through, remove the tray and, using a flat spatula, move the sprouts around to redistribute.

6. Remove from the oven and let cool completely.

7. Return the brussels sprouts to the large bowl. Add the dates, walnuts, and pomegranate seeds and toss to combine.

PRO TIPS

1. The salad can be made a day ahead and served at room temperature.

2. The vinaigrette can be made a few days in advance and stored at room temperature.

Handvo (Savory Rice-Lentil Vegetable Cake)

Serves 10 to 12

Handvo is one of the most popular Gujarati *farsan*, or savory snacks, that I grew up with. It was one of those dishes that Mum made on rotation as a Sunday night dinner. Mum made a huge pan of the handvo, cut it into pieces, and served it with cilantro chutney and masala chai for dinner. The leftover handvo would be fantastic for breakfast the next day. Indians rarely eat a sweet breakfast. Savory breakfast is more the norm, and that is what I grew up with—fafda, dhokla, gathiya, and handvo, to name a few breakfast items.

Handvo is traditionally made with short-grain rice, like jasmine rice, along with two to three varieties of daals, or lentils. They are first rinsed in water, then spread on a cloth, and dried in the sun. Once dried, they are ground into a coarse powder, and then you proceed with mixing it with a bunch of ingredients to make the handvo batter. It is a therapeutic process, and the end results are what makes the effort worth it. To speed things up a bit, you can simply soak everything in water for 4 hours, drain out the water, and then make a coarse paste with the ingredients. Handvo is a very healthy dish, and really tasty too. It has a lot of vegetables in it, along with all the spices that are good for you. When I bake it, the smells from the oven always take me back home, to my mum's kitchen and me as an ecstatic girl, waiting to eat the warm handvo, and eventually fighting over that crust with my dear brother, which was the most coveted part of this iconic dish!

INGREDIENTS

RICE AND LENTILS
1¼ cups (125 g) short-grain rice, such as jasmine rice
1¼ cups (125 g) channa daal (split chickpeas)

FERMENTATION
½ cup (113 g) Greek yogurt
1 tablespoon (12.5 g) granulated sugar
4 tablespoons (50 g) semolina
2 green chilis (use 1 green chili if you prefer less spicy)
½ teaspoon (1 g) ground turmeric
2 inches (5 cm) ginger
1 tablespoon (15 g) table salt

VEGETABLES
2 medium (200 g) zucchinis, grated, squeezed of all the water
1 medium (80 g) carrot, peeled, grated
1 medium (100 g) red onion, grated, squeezed of all the water
2 garlic cloves, freshly grated
½ cup finely chopped cilantro
1 teaspoon (4 g) baking powder
½ teaspoon (2.4 g) baking soda
1 teaspoon fruit salt, such as Eno Fruit Salt
1 tablespoon (15 g) lemon juice

continued ➤

PRO TIPS

1. If you do not want to soak the rice and lentils for 4 hours, you could get handvo flour, which is readily available at Indian grocery stores. Soak 250 grams handvo flour with 1 cup of warm water, along with all the ingredients in the fermentation step. Continue from there onward to make the handvo.

2. Handvo can be stored in the fridge for up to a week. Heat it up in a toaster oven to crisp the top and enjoy as a snack.

TEMPERING

⅓ cup (72 g) vegetable oil

1½ teaspoons whole black peppercorns

¾ cinnamon stick, broken into pieces

8 whole cloves

1 teaspoon (3 g) mustard seeds

3 tablespoons (24 g) white sesame seeds

Pinch of asafoetida

GARNISH

Aadhu Masala Chai (page 315)

Cilantro Mint Chutney (page 42)

METHOD

To Soak

1. In a medium bowl, add the rice and channa daal. Wash them thoroughly by running under water and draining off any dirt in the rice and lentils. Soak in warm water, up to 2 inches (5 cm) above the level of the rice and lentils in the bowl, for 4 hours.

2. Drain off the water completely.

To Ferment

1. Add the soaked rice and lentils to a high-speed blender, and blend with the Greek yogurt, granulated sugar, semolina, green chilis, turmeric, ginger, and salt, until it forms a coarse paste. Do not grind to a completely smooth texture. When touched between the first finger and the thumb, you should feel very tiny grains between them. It should be a bit coarser than fine.

2. In a bowl, whisk the blended paste vigorously for a minute. Cover with plastic wrap, and set it in a warm place in the kitchen, for overnight fermentation, at least 8 hours.

3. For a warm place in the kitchen, keep it in the oven with the oven light on for an hour and then switch off the light.

To Prepare

1. The next morning, preheat the oven to 350°F. Grease or spray cooking spray in an 8-inch (20 cm) square baking pan. Add parchment paper to the bottom and spray again.

2. Add the grated zucchini, carrots, onions, garlic, and cilantro to the paste and whisk to combine.

3. To temper: In a small saucepan over medium heat, let the oil heat up for a minute. Add the peppercorns, cinnamon, cloves, mustard seeds, 1 tablespoon of the seseame seeds, and the asafoetida. Cover with a lid, as it will splatter. Turn off the heat after 30 seconds.

4. Add the baking powder, baking soda, and fruit salt to the batter. Add the lemon juice. It will start foaming. Add the tempering into the batter. Whisk vigorously in one direction and combine for 30 to 40 seconds. The mixture will expand in volume.

5. Add the batter into the pan. Sprinkle the remaining 2 tablespoons of sesame seeds evenly on top of the batter.

6. Bake the savory cake in the bottom rack of the oven for 1 hour 20 minutes. Put a toothpick tester in the middle of the cake to check for doneness. If it comes out clean, you know the cake is cooked inside. Once the crust looks crisp and brown and the toothpick comes out clean, broil for 3 to 4 minutes on high.

7. Remove from the oven and let it cool completely for an hour. Cut into 16 equal squares.

8. Serve with Aadhu Masala Chai and Cilantro Mint Chutney.

Khaman (Chickpea Flour Savory Cakes)

Makes about sixteen 1.75–inch (4½ cm) squares

Khaman, also known as khaman dhokla, is a *farsan*, or a snack/appetizer, served alongside the mains in a thali. It is also served separately as appetizers or snacks. Khaman originates from Gujarat and is very popular across India, because it's easy to prepare, light, protein-rich, and healthy. It is gluten-free if you do not add the asafoetida, and vegan as well. The cakes are spongy in texture, airy, salty, sweet, spicy, and sour, which is the essence of Gujarati food! Khaman is served at all Gujarati weddings. It is a set part of the menu, like a limb you cannot live without. It completes a Gujarati thali.

Khaman and dhokla are actually two different things. Dhokla is usually made from rice and lentils, and khaman is made from chickpea flour. People interchangeably call khaman "khaman dhokla" because both have that soft and spongy texture.

I grew up eating khaman. Our favorite way to eat it was with pickled raw shredded papaya and Cilantro Mint Chutney (page 42), and of course any Gujarati snack has to be served with very hot Aadhu Masala Chai (page 315). Because khaman is so easy to prepare, Mum would get it ready in no time, especially if we had guests over. She was a tornado in the kitchen and could whip up dishes very quickly, and this dish was no exception. When I got married, I found out about my husband's love of khaman dhokla. He loves the ones I make and cannot get enough of them!

INGREDIENTS

KHAMAN BATTER
1½ cups (135 g) chickpea flour (besan)
1½ teaspoons (6 g) granulated sugar
¾ teaspoon (4.5 g) table salt
½ teaspoon (1 g) ground turmeric
Pinch of asafoetida (optional)
1 inch (2½ cm) ginger
1 green chili
1 tablespoon (15 g) lemon juice
2 teaspoons + 1 tablespoon vegetable oil
¾ cup (180 g) warm water, plus 3 cups (720 g) water for steaming
2 teaspoons fruit salt, such as Eno Fruit Salt

TEMPERED SPICES
1 teaspoon mustard seeds
10 to 12 fresh curry leaves
3 green chilis, split in half
1 teaspoon (6 g) table salt
2 teaspoons (8 g) granulated sugar
1 tablespoon white sesame seeds
2 tablespoons (27 g) vegetable oil
1 tablespoon (15 g) lemon juice
⅓ cup (80 g) water

GARNISH
2 tablespoons finely chopped cilantro
2 tablespoons fresh or frozen (thawed) ground coconut
Cilantro Mint Chutney (page 42)
Aadhu Masala Chai (page 315)

continued ➡

EQUIPMENT

7-inch (18 cm) aluminum square cake pan or an
8-inch (20 cm) round cake pan
Large deep pot with a lid for steaming

METHOD

To Make the Khaman Batter

1. In a medium bowl, add the chickpea flour, granulated sugar, salt, ground turmeric, and pinch of asafoetida, if using, and whisk to combine.

2. In a mini food processor, add the ginger and green chili to make a paste.

3. Add the paste to the batter, along with the lemon juice, vegetable oil, and the warm water, and stir constantly until the batter is smooth and there are no lumps whatsoever. It should be a very silky, smooth batter. Let the batter rest for 10 minutes.

4. Meanwhile, prepare the pot for steaming. In a large pot on medium to high heat, add the water. Add a 4- or 5-inch (10 to 12½ cm) round steel ring, 1 to 2 inches (2½ to 5 cm) in height, inside the pot. Cover with the lid. Let the water come to a boil.

5. Coat the inside of the cake pan with the oil.

6. Add the fruit salt to the batter a minute before placing the pan into the steaming pot. Whisk vigorously in one direction only for 40 to 60 seconds. The batter will be frothy and foamy. Immediately pour it into the oiled pan. Smooth with an offset spatula and place the pan inside the steaming pot.

7. Cover the pot with the lid and steam for 15 minutes. Do not open the lid the entire time.

8. Turn off the stove after 15 minutes and let rest for 2 minutes. Open the lid, and poke with a knife to see if it comes out clean. If it does, the khaman dhokla is done.

9. Let cool completely for 15 more minutes. Use a knife and run it along the edges to release the khaman dhokla from the sides.

10. Place a plate on top of the pan and invert the pan to gently release the khaman dhokla onto the plate. Cut into 16 equal pieces.

To Temper the Spices

1. In a small bowl, gather the mustard seeds, curry leaves, split green chilis, salt, sugar, and sesame seeds.

2. In a small pot on medium heat, add the oil. Once it is hot after a minute, add the bowl ingredients and cover with a lid or else it will splatter. You will hear the splattering. Temper for 30 seconds. Remove from the heat.

3. Add the lemon juice and water and mix well to combine.

4. Using a large spoon, spoon the tempered spices over each dhokla piece, until all of them are covered with the mixture.

5. Garnish with the chopped cilantro and the coconut. Enjoy with Cilantro Mint Chutney and Aadhu Masala Chai.

PRO TIPS

1. Eno Fruit Salt can be found at an Indian grocery store, or it is available online as well.

2. The khaman dhoklas will keep in the fridge in an airtight container for up to 2 days.

Caramelized Onion, Fontina, and Samosa Tart

Makes two 10-inch (25 cm) square tarts; serves 10 to 12 people

Samosas! I do not know anyone who has not heard of samosas. It has become a universal appetizer available everywhere. Samosas are filled with a spiced potato-pea mixture, encased in a flaky dough, shaped into a triangle, and then deep-fried until golden brown. They are eaten with Date Tamarind Chutney (page 45) and Cilantro Mint Chutney (page 42) and make seriously the best snack ever. Do not watch your calories when you eat samosas. Enjoy the flavor, the crunch, and the texture and it is absolute bliss!

I came up with this creation as a non-deep-frying option for this very famous appetizer. About 15 years ago, I auditioned for a Food Network competition. We had to record a 3-minute recipe video, showcasing an easy appetizer that could be shown on TV. That is when I made a puff pastry samosa. I enclosed the filling in a puff pastry and shaped it into a rectangle rather than a triangle. You get the flakiness from the puff pastry, and avoid the deep-frying part that is quintessential to the samosa. And it tastes the same.

This tart has three layers: the caramelized onion part; the cheesy fontina, which is a really wonderful cheese that's quite underrated in my opinion, and it pairs perfectly with the spicy samosa filling. The tart is then baked, and garnished with pomegranate seeds and cilantro. It is typically served with the Date Tamarind Chutney and Cilantro Mint Chutney. This makes a fantastic party appetizer as you can cut the tart into individual pieces and leave them on the table for guests to help themselves. The best part is that the tart can be made a day or two in advance and frozen. When ready to bake, you simply keep it in the fridge for an hour and then bake. It saves so much time on the day of the party, giving you more time to spend with the guests.

INGREDIENTS

CARAMELIZED ONIONS

2 tablespoons (27 g) vegetable oil

1 medium (230 g) thinly sliced white sweet onion

½ teaspoon (3 g) table salt

SAMOSA FILLING

3 large (530 g) potatoes

1 teaspoon (2 g) coriander seeds

1 teaspoon (2 g) fennel seeds

1 green chili

1 inch (2½ cm) fresh ginger

3 tablespoons (40 g) vegetable oil

1 teaspoon (2 g) cumin seeds

½ cup frozen peas

¾ teaspoon (2 g) Kashmiri red chili powder

¾ teaspoon (2 g) garam masala

¾ teaspoon (2 g) amchur (dried mango powder)

¾ teaspoon (4.5 g) table salt

1 teaspoon (5 g) lemon juice

¾ teaspoon (3 g) granulated sugar

2 tablespoons finely chopped cilantro

⅔ cup (150 g) freshly grated fontina cheese

continued ➟

PUFF PASTRY

2 store-bought puff pastry sheets

Extra all-purpose flour for rolling out the puff pastry

HEAVY CREAM WASH

2 tablespoons (29 g) heavy cream

1 teaspoon (4 g) granulated sugar

GARNISH

½ cup (87 g) pomegranate seeds

Cilantro leaves

Date Tamarind Chutney (page 45)

Cilantro Mint Chutney (page 42)

METHOD

To Caramelize the Onions

In a medium skillet over medium to low heat, add the vegetable oil. After a minute, add the sliced onions and salt, and continuously sauté for 10 to 12 minutes until caramelized. Remove to a bowl to cool.

To Make the Samosa Filling

1. In a medium to large pot, add the potatoes. Poke the potatoes with a knife from all sides, so that they boil evenly and properly. Fill with water to cover the potatoes completely. On medium to high heat, cover the pot with a lid and boil the potatoes for about 20 minutes. Drain off the water and let them cool completely. Remove the skin of the potatoes and dice into ½- to 1-inch (¾ to 1 cm) pieces. Set aside.

2. Coarsely grind the coriander seeds and fennel seeds in a coffee or spice grinder. Set aside.

3. In a mini food processor, add the green chili and ginger, and grind into a paste. Remove with a mini rubber spatula and set it aside.

4. In a large nonstick skillet, on medium heat, add the vegetable oil. After a minute add the cumin seeds, green chili-ginger paste, and coarsely ground mixture of coriander and fennel seeds, and sauté for a minute. Add the boiled potatoes and peas and sauté for a minute. Add the Kashmiri red chili powder, garam masala, amchur, and salt and sauté the mixture for 2 minutes. Add the lemon juice, sugar, and cilantro and sauté for 2 to 3 minutes. Turn off the heat. Let the mixture cool completely.

To Assemble the Tart

1. If you have frozen puff pastry, make sure to place it in the fridge a day before using it. Otherwise, you can thaw the puff pastry out on the kitchen counter for an hour before rolling it out.

2. On a clean surface, sprinkle all-purpose flour. Open the store-bought, thawed puff pastry, and roll it out evenly to about 9½- to 10-inch (25 cm) squares.

3. Transfer the rolled-out puff pastry to a baking sheet lined with parchment paper.

4. Repeat Steps 2 and 3 for the second sheet of puff pastry on a separate baking sheet.

5. Layer half of the caramelized onions on one tart, leaving a 1-inch (2½ cm) border from the sides. Using a rubber spatula, flatten and distribute them evenly.

6. Repeat Step 5 for the second tart.

7. Distribute and spread the grated fontina cheese evenly between both the tarts, using a rubber spatula to flatten it over the caramelized onions.

8. Next, distribute and spread the samosa filling evenly between both the tarts, using a rubber spatula to flatten the layer. Make sure to leave a 1-inch (2½ cm) border from the edges of the tarts.

9. In a small bowl, add the heavy cream and sugar and whisk to combine. Use a small pastry brush to brush the edges of the tarts with the heavy cream mixture. This will give them a nice golden edge.

10. Place the baking sheets into the freezer for 10 minutes.

To Bake and Serve

1. Meanwhile, preheat the oven to 400°F (200°C). Once preheated, add the baking sheets with the tarts, one on the bottom rack and one on the top rack. Bake for 40 minutes in total, or until the crust is golden brown in color. Make sure to switch the placement of the baking sheets, halfway through baking, at around 20 minutes. This will ensure even baking for both the tarts.

2. Remove the baking sheets from the oven and let the tarts settle for 10 minutes.

3. Using a sharp knife or a pizza cutter, cut the tarts into neat squares.

4. Garnish with pomegranate seeds and cilantro.

5. Serve immediately with Date Tamarind Chutney and Cilantro Mint Chutney.

PRO TIPS

1. The tart can be assembled and the whole baking sheet can be wrapped in plastic wrap and stored in the freezer a day beforehand. On the day of serving the tart, place it in the fridge for an hour before baking it.

2. This tart is best served fresh, so the crust retains its flakiness.

Mains

"If you really want to make a friend, go to someone's house and eat with him. . . . The people who give you their food give you their heart."
—Cesar Chavez

My mother loved to feed people, and she gave it her all. She was known by everyone—family, friends, acquaintances—as the most humble and loving woman. You could taste the love in the food she made. As they always say, the taste comes from the hand that makes it. And she had magic in her hands. We always had a lot of guests visiting us, and they left with full bellies, full hearts, and big smiles.

It was never simply one main dish that she would make, for even just one guest at the table. There would be at least three dishes. Variety in food was her motto. This concept actually comes from the Gujarati way of cooking. In any Gujarati household, there are typically two to three vegetable stir-fries or shaak to choose from, and a daal or lentil to go with them. This provides a nourishing and hearty meal that is balanced in nutrition as well.

Mains for my family now are considered both lunch and dinner meals. They can work interchangeably. Meal prep starts on weekends, when I get the fresh, seasonal produce I need for the entire week from my trip to the farmers' market. That is really my favorite time of the week. The fresh produce with their vibrant colors make me very happy and in my zone. I plan out my weeknight meals on the weekend, with the intention of having enough leftovers to make a hearty lunch the next day, as well as for the kids' school lunches. Weeknights are hectic, so I do plan or make ahead, depending upon the recipe. For my Squash Blossom Tacos (page 214), for example, I always make the avocado dressing over the weekend for Taco Tuesday. Or when I am making the Tandoori Vegetable Wrap (page 205), the Butter Garlic Naan (page 357) are made in advance as well for an easy weeknight meal. What with the kids' schoolwork and other activities, it does get rushed. Nourishing, balanced meals are my go-to, and they also keep the hangry kids happy!

I look forward to Sundays because that is when I make something elaborate, which may require a bit more time, so that we can enjoy a leisurely lunch or dinner and carry forward the leftovers to Monday. My Ultimate Mumbai-California Veggie Burger (page 217) is something that I prepare on Sundays. Extra patties always help for a good weeknight meal or school lunch for the kids. Ragda Pattice (page 229) is another meal that takes some planning and prepping, and it makes the perfect Sunday meal.

The recipes in this chapter are all of my favorite things to make for my family and friends. Undhiyoo (page 184) is a very traditional Gujarati dish that I am extremely fond of, and brings back wonderful memories of spending hours in the kitchen prepping it with my mum. My version is a slightly faster one, but qualifies for a leisurely Sunday meal. In fact, it was the last meal that I shared with my group of friends before the pandemic hit. All the meals in this chapter are shareable, communal meals. Meals that you can have leftovers after, or meals that you can put in dabbas and give to your neighbors, family, or friends. These meals will become a part of your family, as much as they are a part of mine.

Gujarati Daal

Serves 6 to 8 people

Gujarati Daal is a quintessential dish, one that comes from the state of Gujarat and is a staple in every home. It was probably the second dish my dear mum taught me to make. It was a part of every lunch—no Gujarati meal is complete without this daal. Mum would start preparing for lunch pretty early in the morning, probably around 8 to 9 a.m. and would be done within the hour, while I, the lazy teenager, would be sleeping away. The delicious whiff of this daal would wake me up around 10 a.m. This daal is characteristic of any Gujarati meal, and it satisfies the whole palate with sweet, spicy, salty, sour, and bitter. The sweet comes from the jaggery, the spicy from the chilis, sour from the lemon juice and tomatoes, and the bitter from the fenugreek. Gujarati Daal is eaten on a thali (platter) with bhaat (plain rice), shaak (a sautéed vegetable), rotli (Indian flat bread), papad (crisp, roasted flatbread), and mango pickle.

We would have Gujarati Daal in our tiffins or dabbas too. If you are not familiar with the dabbawala system in Mumbai, it has been featured in various articles on renowned networks like the BBC, *The Independent*, and more. These articles talk about the 125-year history of dabbawallas. Each dabbawala goes to people's homes through a delivery system where they pick up the stainless steel tiffins or dabbas, put them on their bicycles, and deliver them to the home or office, effortlessly, flawlessly, and on time for people to eat their lunches. Each dabbawala carries about 30 tiffins at a time, and does a phenomenal job delivering the dabbas and collecting them to return them to the source, with no intermixing of dabbas. They do it all with a warm smile and that makes it so special. My brother and I would get our school lunches delivered in the same manner. We would eat our lunch together during recess time. Mum would pack us a proper Gujarati meal three out of the five days, at the least.

India has so many different regions and cuisines, but everyone will talk about THE Gujarati Daal because it is very popular throughout the country. I am thrilled to share my mum's recipe with you! I hope you like it as much as we all love it in our family.

INGREDIENTS

1 cup (190 g) pigeon pea lentils or toor daal

5 cups (1,183 g) water, plus 1 cup (236 g) water for thinning

2 small to medium (150 g) tomatoes, cut into small cubes

2 teaspoons (12 g) table salt

2 teaspoons (6 g) ground turmeric

1 teaspoon (2 g) cumin powder

1 teaspoon (2 g) coriander powder

1 teaspoon (3 g) Kashmiri red chili powder

1 teaspoon (3 g) garam masala

⅓ cup (25 to 30 g) jaggery or 1 tablespoon (12 g) brown sugar

2 teaspoons (13 g) freshly grated ginger

4 teaspoons (20 g) lemon juice

25 (20 g) raw peanuts, boiled separately in water for 5 minutes and drained

3 dried round red chilis or 2 dried long red chilis

continued ➝

1 teaspoon (2 g) cumin seeds

1½ teaspoons (6 g) mustard seeds

6 cloves

½ cinnamon stick (2 g), broken coarsely

⅛ teaspoon asafoetida (optional)

8 to 10 fresh curry leaves (optional)

1 teaspoon (4 g) fenugreek seeds

2 tablespoons (36 g) ghee

3 cups (715 g) water

GARNISH

¼ cup washed and finely chopped cilantro

METHOD

1. Soak the pigeon pea lentils in a medium bowl, with warm water covering the lentils by about 2 inches. Let them soak for half an hour. Wash the lentils by using your hands under water. Drain out all the water after three to four washes.

2. Using a pressure cooker on the stove at medium-high heat (see Pro Tips below if you don't have one), add the lentils, along with 3 cups (720 g) of the water, the tomatoes, salt, and 1 teaspoon turmeric. The salt helps to increase the boiling point of the water, which cooks the lentils faster and softens them. Remove from the heat once the whistle blows five or six times.

3. Open up the pressure cooker once it has cooled for 15 minutes. Add 2 cups (480 g) of the water and use a hand blender to blend the lentils until smooth.

To Make the Daal

1. In a large pot over medium heat, add the blended lentils, the remaining 1 teaspoon of turmeric, the ground cumin, ground coriander, Kashmiri red chili powder, garam masala, and jaggery, and combine with a whisk.

2. Add the grated ginger and lemon juice and whisk again to combine. Add the boiled peanuts.

To Temper the Spices

1. In a small bowl, combine the dried red chilis, cumin seeds, mustard seeds, cloves, cinnamon, the asafoetida and curry leaves, if using, and the fenugreek seeds.

2. In a small pot over medium heat, add the ghee. Once the ghee has melted, about 10 seconds, add the spices. The seeds and curry leaves will start to splatter after 30 to 40 seconds (watch out for the splatters!). Once the splattering starts, the tempering is complete.

Final Steps

1. Add the tempering mixture into the lentil pot and stir immediately to mix. Add another cup of water to the daal for good consistency. The consistency should be similar to or slightly thicker than whole milk. Bring the mixture to a boil and cook for about 15 minutes. Stir to combine.

2. Garnish with cilantro and eat as is or serve with rice, or as soup with some crackers.

PRO TIPS

1. If you do not have a pressure cooker, cook the lentils in a large pot with the lid on for about 40 minutes, or until the lentils squeeze very easily between your thumb and forefinger. It should become mush without any pressure.

2. Make it vegan by using oil instead of the ghee.

3. Make it gluten-free by omitting the asafoetida.

Bateta Nu Shaak (Potato Curry)

Serves 4 to 6 people

In every Gujarati home, this Bateta Nu Shaak or potato curry, is probably the first thing mums teach their kids. Why? Because it is one of the easiest, tastiest Gujarati dishes to make. Once you have all the ingredients mise en place (all put together on the counter), this dish is literally a one-pot dish anyone can make.

This was literally the first dish that my mum taught me to make when I was perhaps 8 or 9 years old during one winter vacation. I went on a cooking spree, and made a new dish every day for my family during the 10-day break from school. It was really fun experimenting, with some successes and some failures. My mum always encouraged me as she instilled her knowledge of cooking in me. The way she taught me how to make Indian dishes was, "You add a little bit of the turmeric powder and then a little bit of the coriander powder, a little bit of this and a little bit of that." There were no measurements, just approximations, and that's how she would get her food to taste so soulful and delicious! The whole process of adding spices, tasting at every level, adding more if required—bringing the dish to your desired spice level—and getting it to taste divine makes it really therapeutic and fun. It is a sensory game of tasting and smelling the food until the dish is perfect! My mum taught me those exact things, estimation and approximation, to get your desired taste with your senses.

If this is your first time making any Indian dish, I would highly recommend trying to make this easy one-pot meal that can be prepared in less than 30 minutes. It is perfect with Indian flatbreads like rotli, naan, paratha, or even daal and rice.

INGREDIENTS

3 tablespoons (40 g) vegetable oil

8 to 10 curry leaves (optional)

1½ teaspoons (3 g) mustard seeds

1 teaspoon (3 g) cumin seeds

⅛ teaspoon asafoetida (optional)

1 inch (2½ cm) ginger, finely grated

2 garlic cloves, freshly grated

1 green chili, sliced into half vertically and then sliced into half horizontally

1½ pounds (700 g) potatoes, washed, peeled, and chopped into 1-inch (2½ cm) cubes

1½ teaspoons (3 g) ground turmeric

1 teaspoon (2 g) Kashmiri red chili powder

1 teaspoon (2 g) ground coriander

1 teaspoon (2 g) ground cumin

1½ teaspoons (3 g) garam masala

1½ teaspoons (9 g) table salt

2 cups (480 g) water

2 teaspoons (8 g) brown sugar

1 medium (140 g) tomato, chopped into small pieces

GARNISH

3 tablespoons finely chopped cilantro

continued ➤

METHOD

1. In a medium saucepan, on medium heat, add the vegetable oil. After 30 seconds, once the oil is a little warm, add the curry leaves, cumin and mustard seeds, and the asafoetida, if using, and sauté until you hear the crackle, about a minute. The grated ginger and garlic, and the sliced green chili go in next. Sauté for 30 seconds. Add the potatoes, and sauté for 2 minutes. Add the turmeric, Kashmiri red chili powder, coriander, cumin, garam masala, and salt. Sauté for a minute. Add the water, brown sugar, and tomatoes. Mix to combine. Cover and let it boil away and cook for about 20 minutes.

2. After 20 minutes, remove the cover and cook for about 10 minutes until the potatoes are soft and water has reduced by about 60 percent. Mash about ⅓ cup of the potatoes with the back of a spoon to make a gravy-like texture. Garnish with the cilantro.

PRO TIPS

1. Eat this potato curry with naan, rotli, or any Indian flatbread, or it goes great as a side with Gujarati Daal (page 179) and plain cooked rice.

2. Omit the green chili and the Kashmiri red chili powder, if you do not like it spicy. It will still be flavorful.

3. Make it gluten-free by omitting the asafoetida.

Undhiyoo

Serves 8 to 10 people

What is Undhiyoo? It is a dish, made with winter vegetables like sweet potatoes, purple yams, potatoes, eggplant, and flat beans, as well as fenugreek fried dumplings and raw bananas. It is cooked in a green paste made with cilantro, green garlic, coconut, green chili, sugar, and salt. It is a feast of the senses, with sweet, salty, sour, tangy, spicy flavors all in one bite. Considered a winter dish on account of its seasonal produce, it is the most iconic dish of Gujarat. Gujarat typically gets cold in the winter and this is a meal that keeps you warm with starchy, carb-rich ingredients like sweet potato and yam.

I have the fondest memories of making this dish with my entire family. It was a family affair. The four of us—my parents, my brother, and me—would gather around the dining table and help to clean, peel, and prep vegetables. It would take a couple hours to do so, with loads of talking, poking fun, and laughter! This is a slow one-pot meal, where you prepare the green paste or green masala, stuff it into the vegetables and slow cook it for an hour or so, depending upon the quantity. The whole house will smell amazing! Mum would make at least 7 pounds of Undhiyoo and we would eat it over the course of the next three to four meals because it was that delicious. You could taste the love that went into it.

Undhiyoo is made at all Gujarati weddings. There are two ways to prepare it. The first way is with the green masala, which is how my mum prepared it, with no dry spices whatsoever. The second way is with dry spices. It is typically eaten with hot puri and shrikhand, a sweetened strained yogurt with saffron, cardamom, pistachios, and almonds. And the thing is, although commonly made by so many households, Undhiyoo tastes different from one home to the next. That is the beauty of home-cooked Indian food.

This is a dish meant to be shared with your community—it's made with a lot of sweat and love. Before we went into the Covid lockdown last year, I was recipe-testing Undhiyoo, and I invited my friends over for a meal. There were around 25 of us. I made hot puri, and shrikhand to go along with it. They were from different parts of India, except for Gujarat. I was pretty sure I would have leftovers, since they may not like Undhiyoo. By the end of the meal, however, I was absolutely shocked to see an empty pot. This dish is irresistible, full of flavor and love, and you will be able to taste it. That is how I remember having our last meal of last year with all my friends.

continued ➡

INGREDIENTS

MUTHIA (FENUGREEK DUMPLINGS)

¾ cup (115 g) whole wheat flour

1 tablespoon (7 g) chickpea flour (besan)

⅛ teaspoon asafoetida

½ teaspoon (1 g) ground turmeric

¾ teaspoon (1 g) red chili powder

½ teaspoon (3 g) table salt

2 teaspoons (6 g) vegetable oil

¼ cup (25 g) packed fresh fenugreek

¼ cup (60 g) warm water

Oil, for frying

GREEN MASALA

1½ cups (190 g) frozen or freshly
  shredded coconut

4 cups (140 g) packed fresh cilantro,
  washed and patted dry

5 tablespoons (75 g) lemon juice

1 tablespoon + 1 teaspoon (23 g) table salt

2 tablespoons (25 g) granulated sugar

4 green chilis

¾ to 1 cup (100 g; about 3 to 4 stalks) green garlic

4 to 5 garlic cloves

VEGETABLES

500 grams purple yam (if not available,
  substitute with different variety of yam)

500 grams sweet potatoes

500 grams small potatoes

250 grams raw bananas

1 small (500 g) eggplant

¾ cup (168 g) vegetable oil

½ teaspoon asafoetida

2 teaspoons (6 g) cumin seeds

1 teaspoon (5 g) baking soda

GARNISH

1 to 2 stalks green garlic, finely chopped

½ cup (65 to 67 g) frozen or freshly
  shredded coconut

METHOD

To Make the Muthia (Fenugreek Dumplings)

1. In a large bowl, mix all the muthia ingredients together and bind the dough until it is smooth to the touch. Add an extra tablespoon of flour if the dough is still sticky. Form the muthias about 1½ inches (4 cm) long—they should be less round and more elongated. You can use extra oil on your hands to mold the muthias.

2. In a small saucepan over medium heat, let the oil for frying heat up for 3 to 4 minutes to about 350°F (175°C). Once heated, slowly add four muthias at a time to cook them all the way through until golden brown, about 2 minutes. Set them aside on a plate with a paper towel to drain off the excess oil.

To Make the Green Masala

In a food processor, add the coconut, cilantro, lemon juice, salt, sugar, green chilis, green garlic, and garlic cloves and blend until it forms a paste. The paste should not be completely pureed, but at the same time it should not be chunky. It should look like a coarse pesto. Set the green masala aside in a bowl.

To Make the Vegetables

1. Peel the yam, sweet potatoes, and potatoes, and cut them into 2-inch (5 cm) pieces. Cut the raw bananas into 2-inch (5 cm) pieces. Slit all of the pieces and eggplant into a criss-cross pattern lengthwise, not all the way to the end—just enough to stuff them with the green masala. Take each piece and stuff each with about 2 tablespoons of the green masala.

2. You will have some green masala remaining that will be added later to the dish.

3. In a large nonstick saucepan or Dutch oven, big enough to hold all the vegetables, add the vegetable oil on medium heat. Add the asafoetida and cumin seeds. Let it splatter for 30 seconds.

4. Add the potatoes and eggplant, along with the baking soda, into the pot, stir it gently, cover it and let it cook on medium to low heat for about 15 minutes. Stir it every 7 to 8 minutes. Add the raw banana, sweet potato, and yam after 15 minutes. Cover and let it cook. Keep stirring every 7 to 8 minutes. Let it cook covered for a total of about 50 minutes to an hour, until all the vegetables are cooked all the way through.

5. Add the muthias to the pot of vegetables and stir. Keep the pot covered.

6. To serve, garnish with the green garlic and fresh coconut. Serve with rotli or puri, and shrikhand (which is essentially strained yogurt).

PRO TIPS

1. This can be made a day ahead and it keeps well in the fridge for up to a week.

2. Undhiyoo usually contains papdi as well, called flat beans or field beans in English, but they are not easily available in most stores, so I have not included them in the recipe. They are, however, available in the frozen section of Indian food stores. If you do find frozen papdi, you can add 200 to 250 grams at the beginning of Step 5.

3. If yams are not available, you can increase the quantity of sweet potatoes and potatoes.

4. Green garlic is typically available in the winter, so keep that in mind and make this dish in the winter when you see green garlic at your local markets.

5. Green garlic can be grown in the backyard as well. Take a couple of garlic bulbs, put them in a glass of water, and place on a windowsill. You will see tiny sprouts in 3 to 4 days. After a week, transfer to a pot with soil and water regularly. You will see beautiful stalks growing within 2 weeks. Within 6 to 8 weeks, they will be ready to eat.

Pav Bhaji Sliders

WITH SHAVED HEIRLOOM CARROT SALAD

Serves 8 people

Pav bhaji is one of the most iconic Mumbai street food dishes. The bhaji is made on humongous tawas or flat pans and you can see the vendors making the whole dish in front of you, starting with the copious amounts of butter, laden with loads of boiled and finely chopped vegetables, and finally garnished with lots of finely chopped cilantro, red onions, and more buttah! It is a mesmerizing sight to watch the vendors make the entire dish from start to finish. Then they put butter on the soft pillow-like pav or the buns, and grill them on a separate pan until they are golden brown in color. The piping-hot pav bhaji is a college student's comfort food. If you watch any Mumbai street food video, you will definitely see pav bhaji on the list. In fact, Andrew Zimmern did a Mumbai street food episode that featured pav bhaji.

This was the first dish my mum taught my brother when he was off to the United States to study for his master's program. Cooking is an essential life skill that everyone should learn. He put together a whole recipe book with the help of my mum that would help him with his cravings whenever he fancied them. Pav bhaji comes together very easily, once you have all the vegetables boiled and the remainder finely chopped. The only spices are red Kashmiri chili for a very pretty reddish hue, and pav bhaji masala. This dish is filled with vegetables and that makes it healthy in some ways. You could use vegan butter as well. The shaved heirloom carrot salad is a perfect pairing with the bhaji. I love serving it as a slider, and it all started because of how I saw my son, Rishan, eating it when he was 5. He would put the bhaji on the pav with a spoon, then put the side salad on the top, and that is how he loved to eat it. Hope you enjoy it as much as we love this dish.

continued ➤

INGREDIENTS

SHAVED HEIRLOOM CARROT SALAD

10 to 12 (350 g) heirloom carrots, washed and peeled, stems removed

1 tablespoon (15 g) lemon juice

2 tablespoons (26 g) olive oil

1 generous teaspoon (8 g) honey

1 teaspoon (6 g) salt

1 teaspoon (2 g) black pepper

1 tablespoon finely chopped shallot

1 tablespoon finely chopped cilantro

BHAJI

10 small (600 g) potatoes

2 small (100 g) carrots

¼ head (200 g) cauliflower

 cup (100 g) frozen peas

4 cups (960 g) water

½ cup (1 stick; 113 g) unsalted butter

1 medium (150 g) red onion, finely chopped

3 garlic cloves

2 teaspoons (2 g) red Kashmiri chili

2 teaspoons (12 g) salt

1 medium (150 g) green bell pepper, finely chopped

2 to 3 medium (300 g) tomatoes, finely chopped or pureed

4 tablespoons (60 g) tomato paste

2 to 2 ½ tablespoons (12 to 15 g) pav bhaji masala

1 tablespoon (15 g) lemon juice

¼ cup (9 g) finely chopped cilantro

BUNS

½ cup (1 stick; 113 g) salted butter

16 buns

GARNISH

¾ cup (95 g) finely chopped shallot

¾ cup (28 g) finely chopped cilantro

METHOD

To Make the Shaved Heirloom Carrot Salad

1. Use a vegetable peeler or a mandoline to shave the carrots into thin ribbons from top to bottom. Peel carefully to ensure each shaved ribbon stays intact. Keep aside in a bowl.

2. For the dressing, whisk together all the remaining ingredients, except the cilantro, in a small bowl, until combined and mixture is homogeneous.

3. Pour the dressing over the shaved carrots and gently toss the carrots in the dressing, with your bare hands to give it a light touch of dressing throughout. Add the cilantro and repeat the tossing again. Set aside.

To Make the Bhaji

1. To prep the veggies, wash and peel the potatoes and carrots. Cut each carrot into ⅓ inch (1 cm) rounds. Cut the branches off the cauliflower to get the florets.

2. In a pressure cooker (see Pro Tips if you don't have one), add the potatoes, carrots, cauliflower, peas, and water. Pressure cook the vegetables on medium-high heat until the whistle blows five times.

3. Cool the veggies until they are ready to be handled. Drain the water, reserving 2 cups (480 g) to set aside.

4. Mash the vegetables with a potato masher to an almost mushy consistency with some chunks remaining.

5. In a large pot, on medium heat, add 6 tablespoons of the butter. Once melted, add the red onions and sauté for 4 to 5 minutes or until the red onions are golden brown in color.

6. While the onions are being sautéed, add the garlic, red chili powder, and salt in a mortar

and pestle and crush it to make a paste, or you can use a mini food processor to do it as well.

7. Add the paste to the onions, and sauté for a minute.

8. Add the green bell pepper and sauté for 2 minutes to soften the bell pepper.

9. Add the tomatoes and the tomato paste and sauté for 3 to 4 minutes. Use the potato masher to mash the mixture to make it paste-like. You will see the butter separating slightly at this stage.

10. Add the pav bhaji masala and mix until blended.

11. Add the mashed vegetable mixture and 1 cup (240 g) of the reserved water, along with the lemon juice and mix well until blended. If the mixture is too thick, you can add another ½ to 1 cup (120 to 240 g) of the reserved water. The color will change to a reddish-brown color.

12. Turn the heat to low, as the mixture will start to splatter. Cover half of the pot with the lid.

13. Cook the mixture for about 8 to 10 more minutes, stirring from time to time to not let it splatter. Remove from heat. The bhaji is ready.

14. Garnish with the remaining 2 tablespoons of the butter and cilantro.

To Assemble

1. Use the salted butter to butter the insides of each bun. Set them aside.

2. On a large grill pan, on medium heat, add as many buns as you can fit on your grill pan to grill for about 2 minutes, to get the perfect grill marks.

3. Set the grilled buns aside.

4. Add the bhaji on top of each bottom bun. Top with the shaved carrot salad, and garnish with a bit of the shallots and the cilantro.

5. Repeat for the remaining buns and serve.

PRO TIPS

1. If you do not have a pressure cooker, cook the vegetables in a large pot with water covering 1 inch (2½ cm) above the vegetables. Cut the potatoes in quarters to cook faster. Check after 20 minutes if the potatoes are cooked—they will take the longest to cook. If a knife goes all the way through you know that the potatoes are ready. If they are not cooked after 20 minutes, cook for an additional 10 minutes every time and check for the potatoes being cooked.

2. Pav bhaji masala is readily available in Indian stores, or online as well.

3. The bhaji can be eaten with grilled and buttered sourdough slices too.

4. The dish keeps well for about 2 days in the fridge. It makes for fantastic leftovers.

Teen Daal or Three-Lentil Daal

Serves 6 to 8 people

It is really hard to get proteins from a vegetarian diet. The best way to get the proteins is through lentils. Growing up as a vegetarian in our family, Mum made lentils for practically every meal, along with a cooked vegetable and roti. This daal is called Teen Daal or Three-Lentil Daal, or as it's called in Gujarati—maag, channa, adadh ni daal—and is made up of three types of lentils: split black gram daal, split green gram daal, split bengal gram daal. This daal was typically served in our home with a sweet puri, sweetened with jaggery (raw sugar) called dhebra or simply with Triangle Paratha (page 354). The daal stays well in the fridge for up to 3 days. My kids and Raj are very fond of this daal and I make it quite often. It is great by itself as a lentil stew as well, and I love having it with yogurt too. This is a family recipe and I am really happy to share it with you.

INGREDIENTS

½ cup (100 g) split urad
   daal (split black lentil with skin)

½ cup (100 g) split moong daal (split green gram)

¼ cup (50 g) channa daal (split bengal gram)

5 cups (1.2 kg) water

2 ½ teaspoons (15 g) table salt

2 tablespoons (28 g) vegetable oil

⅛ teaspoon asafoetida

2 teaspoons (6 g) cumin seeds

1 medium (150 g) white onion, finely chopped

2 teaspoons freshly grated ginger

3 garlic cloves

2 small (150 g) tomatoes, finely chopped

2 tablespoons (30 g) tomato paste

DRY MASALAS

1½ teaspoons (3 g) ground turmeric

1 teaspoon (2 g) red chili powder

1 teaspoon (1 g) ground coriander

1 teaspoon (1 g) ground cumin

1½ teaspoons (4 g) garam masala

GARNISH

1 tablespoon lemon juice

¼ cup finely chopped cilantro

METHOD

1. In a medium bowl, add the daals and mix well. Rinse them well with warm water to remove any dirt in the daals by running water through the daals, draining the water, and repeating the process four to five times.

2. Once all the water is drained, add 3 cups (720 g) of the water and let them soak for 3 to 4 hours, so the lentils can soften. Drain the water.

3. Transfer the daal, 2 cups (480 g) of water, and salt into a pressure cooker (see Pro Tip if you don't have a pressure cooker). Pressure cook for about five to six whistles of the cooker. Let the pressure cooker cool and, once the lid releases from the cooker, open it and set it aside.

4. In a medium saucepan on medium heat, add the vegetable oil, asafoetida, and cumin seeds. Once the seeds start to splatter, let cook for an additional 15 seconds. Add the onions, and sauté it until brown, for about 5 to 6 minutes, stirring occasionally.

continued ➝

5. Add the ginger and garlic and sauté for 30 seconds. Add the tomatoes and tomato paste and sauté for 1 minute.

6. Add all the dry spices—ground turmeric, red chili powder, ground coriander, ground cumin, and garam masala—to make it a homogenous paste, about 2 minutes.

7. Add the cooked lentils with the water and mix everything together well. If the mixture is too thick, add another ½ cup (120 g) water and let it boil for about 7 to 10 minutes, stirring at regular intervals so that the daal does not splatter.

8. Once cooked, add the lemon juice and stir.

9. Garnish with cilantro. It is ready to eat with rotli, rice, or paratha.

PRO TIPS

1. If you do not have a pressure cooker, add the daal and 3 cups (720 g) of water to a large saucepan, and cook on medium-high heat with the lid half on, for about 30 to 40 minutes, or until the lentils soften when pressed between your index finger and thumb, very easily

2. Reduce the red chili powder or omit it if you do not like the daal to be too spicy.

3. You can make it gluten-free by omitting the asafoetida.

Daal Dhokli
(Noodles in a Lentil Stew)

Serves 4 to 6

Most families have a Sunday meal that they make regularly, which is comfort food. Something that they look forward to and make for a good, relaxing Sunday. Ours was Daal Dhokli. This dish was prepared almost every Sunday by Mum. It is my dad and brother's absolute favorite comfort food. There is absolute silence for the entire lunch period when this dish is served. It is masala noodles made with whole wheat dough and spices, soaked in Gujarati Daal (page 179), or lentil stew, again spiced with warming, wonderful spices like cinnamon, clove, garam masala, dried red chilis, and more. The bowl is topped with ghee or clarified butter, lemon juice, fried raw peanuts, and cilantro and eaten piping hot. It is a very wholesome meal, where you get in your carbs, protein, vitamins, and minerals, all in one meal. It is one of the most popular dishes in Gujarat, and each home has its own way of preparing it. I remember those times when Daal Dhokli was consumed, we would all be in food coma! The meal was followed by a long-awaited afternoon nap. My dad and brother have still continued the tradition and have this meal every Sunday, back home in Mumbai.

INGREDIENTS

DHOKLI (WHOLE WHEAT NOODLES)

1 cup + 1 tablespoon (130 g) whole wheat flour

2 tablespoons (16 g) chickpea flour

½ teaspoon (1 g) red chili powder

½ teaspoon (1 g) ground turmeric

½ teaspoon (3 g) table salt

2 teaspoons (9 g) vegetable oil

½ cup (120 g) warm water

Extra flour for rolling the dough

Gujarati Daal (page 179)

GARNISH

¼ cup cilantro

25 (20 g) raw peanuts,
shallow fried in vegetable oil

Warm, pourable ghee

Lime or lemon wedges

METHOD

1. In a medium bowl, combine the whole wheat flour, chickpea flour, red chili powder, ground turmeric, and salt. Whisk to combine. Add the vegetable oil and mix.

2. Add the warm water, first put half and bind the dough with one hand, massaging the dough as you progress. Add the water a little bit at a time, as it comes together. You might not need to use all the water.

3. The dough should come together in a matter of a few minutes. Knead until the dough is smooth. Let it sit for 15 minutes.

To Make the Dhokla

1. Divide the dough into six 40-gram pieces, and roll them between the palm of your hands to make round balls.

continued ➤

2. Using a marble board and the rolling pin, sprinkle extra flour on the board and the round ball, flatten it on the board with your palm and start rolling the dough into a 6-inch round disc. Sprinkle extra flour if the dough sticks to the board.

3. Cut the round disc into three equal sections vertically and then three cross sections horizontally to make nine pieces. You can even make 16 pieces if you prefer smaller pieces. Remove and keep it aside on a plate.

4. Repeat with the remaining five pieces of dough.

To Make the Daal Dhokli

1. The daal consistency should neither be too thin nor too thick. If it is too thick, add 1 cup (240 g) of water at a time until the consistency is slightly thicker than whole milk. If the daal is too thin, let it boil on medium heat to reduce the water in the daal.

2. The daal must be on a rolling boil. Take a few pieces of the cut dough or dhokli at a time, and put it in the daal. Put in a few pieces at a time, or else the dhokli will stick together. You want it to be separate.

3. Add all the dhoklis in the daal and let it cook for about 7 to 10 minutes on medium heat.

4. In a soup bowl, pour the daal with the dhokli. Garnish with cilantro, fried peanuts, a drizzle of ghee, and a squeeze of lime or lemon juice, and enjoy it piping hot.

Vegetable Koftas in Tomato Cashew Curry

Serves 6 to 8

Vegetable Koftas in Tomato Cashew Curry is a very famous, restaurant-style dish typically served with naan or tandoori rotli. It is a celebrated dish at weddings as well. It hails from Northern India and is usually made with heavy cream and loaded with cashews. I love to make this curry, especially when I am entertaining. My friends invariably ask me for this recipe whenever I make it.

I have made this dish vegan by using cashew puree without heavy cream. The cashew puree makes it luxurious yet keeps it light on the tummy. This curry can be eaten with rice and some raita on the side.

This dish was made quite often by Mum, but she usually served it with simple phulka or ghee-smeared rotli. It would be a luxurious meal, and we would eagerly wait for the meal to be served. We didn't go often to restaurants to dine, so when we did it would be a special treat. This might explain why, when Mum would make restaurant-style dishes, we would get ecstatic. Everyone loved her recipe. I am sharing this recipe with you, and I hope you like it as much as we do in our home! The curry is best eaten with garlic naan, kulcha, or paratha.

INGREDIENTS

VEGETABLE KOFTAS (MAKES 14 TO 16 BALLS)

2 medium or 1½ cups (200 g) potatoes, cut in half with skin on

1 carrot or ½ cup (90 g), peeled and cut into small pieces

½ cup (70 g) green peas

½ cup (60 g) green beans, cut into pieces

1 cup (84 g) cauliflower florets

5 tablespoons (40 g) chickpea flour

4 tablespoons (24g) bread crumbs

1 teaspoon (2 g) garam masala

½ teaspoon (3 g) table salt

½ teaspoon (1 g) amchur (dried mango powder)

½ teaspoon (1 g) red chili powder

2 tablespoons finely chopped cilantro

Vegetable oil, for frying

continued ➤

TOMATO CASHEW CURRY

1 cup (150 g) whole cashews

½ cup (120 g) warm water for cashews, plus 1¼ cups (300 g) water for curry

½ large (130 g) onion, cut into big pieces

2 inches (5 cm) ginger

2 garlic cloves

1 green chili

3 tablespoons (42 g) vegetable oil

1½ teaspoons (3 g) cumin seeds

Pinch of asafoetida

1 bay leaf

1 inch (2½ cm) cinnamon stick, broken into pieces

3 cardamom pods

2 medium (325 g) tomatoes

3 tablespoons (42 g) tomato paste

1 teaspoon (2 g) ground turmeric

1 teaspoon (2 g) Kashmiri red chili powder

½ teaspoon (1 g) amchur (dried mango powder)

2 teaspoons (4 g) garam masala

1 teaspoon (2 g) ground cumin

1 teaspoon (2 g) ground coriander

1 tablespoon (12.5 g) brown sugar

2 teaspoons (12 g) table salt

1 tablespoon (1 g) kasuri methi (dried fenugreek leaves; optional)

GARNISH

¼ cup finely chopped cilantro

METHOD

To Make the Vegetable Koftas

1. Fill a medium pot three-quarters with water, place over medium to high heat, bring the water to a boil, and add the potatoes. After 15 minutes, add the carrots, green peas, green beans, and cauliflower. Let the vegetables cook with the lid on for a total of 20 to 25 minutes until softened.

2. Drain the water and let the vegetables cool down completely for about an hour. Remove the skin of the potatoes. Using a vegetable masher, mash the vegetables but not completely; let it be slightly coarse.

3. Add chickpea flour and bread crumbs, and all the dry spices and cilantro. Mix it together, but do not overmix.

4. Divide the mixture to make 14 to 16 small balls. Make them round by rolling them between the palms of your hands into perfect balls. You can use a little bit of oil on your palms to make them round.

5. Set them aside on a plate. Meanwhile, let's make the curry.

To Make the Tomato Cashew Curry:

1. In a small bowl, set aside the whole cashews in the warm water.

2. In a high-speed blender, puree the onion, ginger, garlic, green chili, and ¼ cup (60 g) of the water into a paste.

3. In a large pot on medium heat, add the vegetable oil, cumin seeds, a pinch of asafoetida, bay leaf, cinnamon, and cardamom. Sauté with a wooden spatula for 30 seconds.

4. Add the onion puree and sauté for 5 minutes, until all the water has almost evaporated. Meanwhile, puree the tomatoes in the high-speed blender.

5. Add the pureed tomatoes and tomato paste and sauté for 3 to 4 minutes.

6. Add the ground turmeric, red chili powder, amchur, garam masala, ground cumin, ground coriander, salt, and brown sugar. Sauté for 3 to 4 minutes. Meanwhile, puree the cashews along with the warm water in a high-speed blender into a smooth puree.

7. Add the pureed cashews into the pot and mix until well combined. Add the remaining 1 cup (240 g) of the water depending upon how thick the mixture is. The mixture should be a good consistency—not too thick, not too thin.

8. Cook the mixture on low heat for about 10 minutes, stirring it occasionally so that it does not stick to the bottom and does not splatter anywhere.

9. Add the dried fenugreek leaves as the last step if using, and stir to combine. Remove from the heat.

To Fry the Koftas

1. In a medium pot, add vegetable oil about halfway up the pot on medium to high heat.

2. Let the oil heat up for about 5 to 7 minutes. Drop a piece of the kofta dough into the oil. If it floats up, you know that the oil is ready to fry.

3. Set a plate aside with parchment paper.

4. Add about 3 balls at a time into the pot of oil, and, using a spider spatula, fry them for about a minute on each side until golden brown all around. Remove them and set aside.

5. Repeat for all the balls. Resist frying more than 3 at a time, so as not to bring the temperature of the oil down, which makes the koftas very oily.

To Assemble

In a serving dish, add the tomato cashew curry. Drop in the kofta balls in a pretty manner. Garnish with cilantro.

PRO TIPS

1. Dried fenugreek leaves are optional but they give the meal fantastic taste and balance out the flavors.

2. The tomato cashew curry can be made a day ahead and stored in a container in the fridge. When ready to serve, warm it up on the stove, and add some water to loosen the consistency a bit.

3. Koftas need to be made on the day of.

4. Best eaten with Triangle Paratha (page 354), Butter Garlic Naan (page 357), or Wild Mushroom and Green Garlic Kulcha (page 351).

Palak Paneer
Mushroom, and Corn Sabzi

Serves 6

Mum loved corn and mushroom together. She would make a variety of dishes with this combination. She made a mean baked dish with spinach, corn, and mushrooms on Sunday nights, when she would make something special or influenced by Western dishes that we could enjoy together around the table. We would eagerly wait for Sunday dinners because it would be something different from the usual rotli, shaak, daal, and bhaat. Mum had graduated from home science, so she had a vast knowledge of all sorts of cuisines from around the world. She knew how to make jams, jellies, ketchup, shrubs, cakes, biscuits, souffles, you name it, from scratch!

Going back to her love for mushroom and corn, we were lucky to have corn vendors or *butta* (corn in Hindi) vendors on the beach, from where we could get fresh corn every single day. As a family, we hated mushrooms, so she would try to sneak them in any way that she could, whether in a curry or a pasta bake.

Mum would make a mushroom and corn curry, but in a tomato gravy, where the base was tomatoes, spices, heavy cream, and some cashews. She made a lot of palak paneer as well, which is spinach and paneer curry, so I combined her two famous dishes into one, to make this wonderful Palak Paneer, Mushroom, and Corn Sabzi. I know Mum would be so delighted if she had a chance to try this curry with all her loves in one dish. The sabzi is flavorful, luxurious with just a little heavy cream, and makes a perfect dish for entertaining! We love to eat it with rotli or paratha, but I know kulcha would pair well with this curry too.

INGREDIENTS

5 tablespoons (68 g) vegetable oil

2 heaping cups (130 g) chopped mushrooms (crimini/shiitake)

1 cup (130 g) fresh or frozen corn kernels

1 cup (250 g) paneer, cut into 1-inch (2½ cm) cubes

2 cups (480 g) water

1¼ cups (300 g) spinach (washed thoroughly)

1 medium (130 g) red onion

1 inch (2½ cm) ginger

3 garlic cloves

1 green chili

3 tablespoons (40 g) ghee

1½ teaspoons (3 g) cumin seeds

Pinch of asafoetida

1 bay leaf

1-inch (2½ cm) cinnamon stick, broken into pieces

3 cardamom pods

2 small to medium (230 g) tomatoes

2 tablespoons (28 g) tomato paste

1 teaspoon (2 g) ground turmeric

1 teaspoon (2 g) Kashmiri red chili powder

1 teaspoon (2 g) ground coriander

1 teaspoon (2 g) ground cumin

2 teaspoons (12 g) table salt

1½ teaspoons (3 g) garam masala

1 tablespoon (1 g) kasuri methi (dried fenugreek leaves; optional)

1 tablespoon (12.5 g) brown sugar

¼ cup (60 g) heavy cream

continued ➜

METHOD

To Fry the Paneer, Mushroom, and Corn

1. In a medium nonstick saucepan over medium heat, add 2 tablespoons vegetable oil and the chopped mushrooms. Sauté for 5 minutes, until the mushrooms are slightly browned and shriveled. Set aside in a bowl.

2. In the same saucepan over medium heat, add 1 tablespoon vegetable oil and the corn kernels. Sauté for 5 minutes until the corn is charred slightly. Add to the mushroom bowl.

3. In the same saucepan over medium heat, add 2 tablespoons vegetable oil and add the cubed paneer. Sauté for 5 minutes and turn each cube with tongs to brown each side slightly. Do not char the paneer. Set aside in a bowl.

To Make the Spinach Puree

1. In a medium to large pot on high heat, bring the 2 cups (480 g) of water to a boil. Have a medium bowl of ice water ready next to the stovetop.

2. Add the spinach and push it with a spatula as it starts wilting and let it boil for 1 minute. Remove from the heat and let it sit covered for 2 minutes. Using the tongs, immediately move the spinach to the bowl of iced water to blanch it and help retain its color. Keep it in the ice water for 2 minutes. Reserve spinach cooking water.

3. Remove the spinach from the cold water, draining out as much water as possible, and place the spinach in a high-speed blender to puree it.

To Make the Spinach Curry

1. In a high-speed blender, puree the onion, ginger, garlic, green chili, and ¼ cup (60 g) of the reserved spinach water into a paste.

2. In a large pot over medium heat, add the ghee, cumin seeds, asafoetida, bay leaf, cinnamon, and cardamom. Sauté with a wooden spatula for 30 to 40 seconds.

3. Add the onion puree and sauté for 5 minutes, until all the water has almost evaporated. Meanwhile, puree the tomatoes in the high-speed blender.

4. Add the pureed tomatoes and tomato paste and sauté for 3 to 4 minutes.

5. Add the dry spices and brown sugar. Sauté for 5 minutes. Add the spinach puree to this mixture and sauté for 3 to 4 minutes. Add the heavy cream and mix to combine.

6. Add three-quarters of the corn, mushroom, and paneer into the curry and stir to mix. Let the curry cook for another 5 minutes and it is done.

7. Place the curry in a serving pot, garnish with the remainder of the corn, mushroom, and paneer.

8. Serve hot with the Triangle Paratha (page 354), Wild Mushroom and Green Garlic Kulcha (page 351), or Plain Rotli (page 345) and a side of Radish Mint Cumin Raita (page 366).

PRO TIPS

1. Make the curry vegan by substituting the paneer for tofu, ghee for vegetable oil, and heavy cream for coconut or almond cream.

2. Paneer can be bought from an Indian store or specialty grocery stores.

3. To make the paneer soft, submerge the paneer in warm water for 15 minutes. Dry with paper towels and cut in cubes.

4. You can make it gluten-free by omitting the asafoetida.

Tandoori Vegetable Wrap
WITH MANGO CABBAGE SLAW

Serves 8

Tandoors or clay ovens date back to 5,000 years ago in the Indus Valley civilizations, where remnants of the clay ovens were found. Tandoors were brought over to India by the Mughals from Persia. Tandoors were encouraged by Guru Nanak Dev, who was the founder of the Sikh religion (practiced by my husband's family). He invited the use of communal clay ovens, where the community would gather around the clay ovens and cook their food. This was to eradicate the caste barriers and bring togetherness among people and advocate the community feeling.

Tandoors are clay ovens with heat generated from the charcoals burnt in the oven base. There is a whole science behind the use of the marinade—made of yogurt, lemon juice, dry and wet spices—in which the meat is dunked so that the flavors penetrate into the meat, making it juicy and moist. After putting them onto a skewer, it is put into the tandoor, where the heat grills the meat and chars it, which gives it its smoky flavor. Tandoori rotli and naan are typically placed on the inside of the tandoor, giving it its quintessential charred edges and base and the naan's bubbles. The flavor generated by the tandoors is simply amazing. If you go to the small towns in the north and northwest part of India and eat at the dhabbas (small eateries), you will get the most authentic and simple food. Not even the finest fine dining restaurants can mimic the taste of these dhabbas.

We cannot replicate the same experience at home, but to get similar flavors, I often make tandoori vegetables that I marinate in the yogurt-spice marinade and grill in the oven at a high temperature, mimicking the tandoors. The vegetables are charred to give that wonderful smoky flavor and when added to the Butter Garlic Naan (page 357), along with a beautiful and simple Mango Cabbage Slaw, and the Cilantro Mint Chutney (page 42). This makes for a fulfilling meal that is ever-so-slightly reminiscent of the dhabba experiences that I have had on my several trips to the northern parts of India with my family, which I will never forget.

INGREDIENTS

TANDOORI VEGETABLES

1½ cups (335 g) Greek yogurt

2 tablespoons (16 g) chickpea flour (besan)

1 tablespoon (15 g) lemon juice

1 tablespoon (14 g) vegetable oil

1½ teaspoons (9 g) table salt

1 teaspoon (2 g) ground turmeric

1 teaspoon (2 g) Kashmiri red chili powder

1 teaspoon (2 g) garam masala

1 teaspoon (2 g) chaat masala

2 to 3 garlic cloves, freshly grated

1 inch (2½ cm) ginger, freshly grated

750 grams vegetables, such as small potatoes, cauliflower, red onions, zucchini, bell pepper, cut into 1- to 1½-inch (2 to 4 cm) cubes (potatoes must be parboiled, refer to Pro Tips)

8 to 10 bamboo skewers

Olive oil or cooking spray

continued ➤

MANGO CABBAGE SLAW

2 mangoes, cut into cubes (about ⅓ inch, 8 mm) or thin slivers (2 inches, 5 cm long)

1 cup (200 g) thinly shredded savoy cabbage or green cabbage

2 tablespoons (20 g) apple cider vinegar

1 teaspoon (6 g) table salt

1 teaspoon black pepper

2 to 3 tablespoons finely chopped mint

2 to 3 tablespoons finely chopped cilantro

Butter Garlic Naan (page 357)

Radish Mint Cumin Raita (page 366)

Cilantro Mint Chutney (page 42)

METHOD

To Make the Tandoori Vegetables

1. In a large bowl, add the Greek yogurt, chickpea flour, lemon juice, vegetable oil, salt, turmeric, Kashmiri red chili powder, garam masala, chaat masala, garlic, and ginger. Whisk until well combined.

2. Add all the cut vegetables in the marinade and toss gently so that all the pieces are well coated. Set it aside, covered, for 30 to 45 minutes. Meanwhile, soak the bamboo skewers in water, and keep them immersed for 15 minutes.

3. Preheat the oven to 400°F (200°C).

4. Set a baking sheet aside. Place a medley of vegetables onto the soaked skewers, distributing them evenly between the skewers. Place them on a baking sheet so that they hang crosswise across the width of the sheet. Spray the skewers with the olive oil or cooking spray.

5. Place the baking sheet in the oven on the bottom or middle rack and cook for 10 to 15 minutes, until nicely charred. Remove from the oven, turn the skewers, and spray them with olive oil or cooking spray. Return them to the oven and cook for another 10 to 15 minutes, until charred.

6. You can also broil the skewers on high for 2 minutes to char them well. Be sure to watch for the entire 2 minutes, because you do not want to burn the skewers.

7. Remove from the oven.

To Make the Mango Cabbage Slaw

1. In a medium bowl add the mangoes and cabbage.

2. In a small bowl, combine the apple cider vinegar, salt, and pepper, and whisk to combine.

3. Add to the mango-cabbage mixture, along with the mint and cilantro. Toss gently to combine.

To Assemble

On a plate, place a warm Butter Garlic Naan and top with one of the skewers. Serve with the Mango Cabbage Slaw, Radish Mint Cumin Raita, and Cilantro Mint Chutney.

PRO TIPS

1. Par-boil the potatoes: In a pot of boiling water, add the whole potatoes and boil for 15 minutes, to soften them slightly. If used raw for the Tandoori Vegetables they will not cook through completely in the oven.

2. The Tandoori Vegetables can be cooked earlier in the day and warmed in the oven before serving.

3. The Mango Cabbage Slaw is best made just before serving to preserve its freshness and crunch.

4. You can soak the bamboo skewers in a baking pan so that they are completely immersed in water.

5. Line the baking sheet with tinfoil to help with cleanup.

Fajeto (Mango Kadhi or Mango Yogurt Soup)

Serves 6

Fajeto is a very traditional Gujarati dish. Fajeto is a derivative of the actual dish Gujarati Kadhi, which is a spiced yogurt soup. Yogurt is blended with chickpea flour, ground ginger, and green chili and the mixture is tempered with warm whole spices and ghee and stirred until the texture is smooth to perfection. Fajeto is mango kadhi, where mango is added to the kadhi ingredients to give a slight sweetness to the otherwise spicy, sour, and tangy soup. Kadhi is very cooling for the body because of the yogurt in it.

Fajeto is common in the months of April and May, which is mango season in India. Mango has its own season. Mango is the national fruit of India because of its popularity. I do not know one person who does not love this gorgeous fruit! There are over 1,500 varieties of mangoes in India if you can believe it! Mangoes have a natural sweetness and are high in vitamin C and dietary fiber. As a budding foodie at a year old, my mum would put a plate of cut mango pieces in front of me and, within seconds, it would all be gone! In the summer months, we would have aam ras (or mango puree) in different forms multiple times a day. Aam ras with our lunch, mango milkshake for a snack, and mango ice cream again with dinner. It used to be a 2-month-long mango fest with a huge amount of mango intake at home.

Coming back to this kadhi, it is perhaps one of my all-time favorite dishes to have. Mango Kadhi and the Vegetable Pulao (page 369) was the last comfort meal that I had before giving birth to my first born Anishka. This is what I want my last meal on Earth to be.

INGREDIENTS

MANGO KADHI

1 large (250 g) mango, peeled, de-seeded, and cut into pieces

1¼ cups (285 g) Greek yogurt

2 tablespoons (12 g) chickpea flour

1 green chili

1½ to 2 teaspoons (2½ to 3½ g) ground ginger

2 teaspoons (12 g) table salt

¾ teaspoon (2 g) turmeric

3 cups (720 g) water

1½ tablespoons (23 g) jaggery

TEMPERING

2 tablespoons ghee

1 teaspoon (4 g) mustard seeds

1 teaspoon (2 g) cumin seeds

1 teaspoon (4 g) fenugreek seeds

Pinch of asafoetida

5 to 6 cloves

10 curry leaves

1-inch (2½ cm) cinnamon stick, broken into pieces

2 to 3 dried red chilis

GARNISH

¼ cup finely chopped cilantro

continued ➡

METHOD

1. In a high-speed blender, add the mango, Greek yogurt, chickpea flour, green chili, ground ginger, salt, turmeric, and 2 cups (480 g) of the water, and blend until smooth.

2. In a medium to large pot on medium heat, add the ghee and let it heat up to a minute. Add the spices for tempering and until it splatters for 30 to 40 seconds.

3. Next, add the mango-yogurt mixture into the tempering. Do this step carefully because the spices can splatter everywhere. Add the remaining water and jaggery to the kadhi.

4. This step is important. Continuously stir the kadhi with a spatula in a number 8 shape for the next 15 minutes. It will come to a boil after 7 to 8 minutes into stirring the kadhi. The kadhi will come to a boil to the top of the pot, and then eventually subside and keep boiling. Keep stirring for the whole 15 minutes to ensure a smooth, even texture for the kadhi.

5. The kadhi is done after 15 minutes. Garnish with cilantro, and have it while it is piping hot with some delicious Vegetable Pulao (page 369).

PRO TIPS

1. If you prefer a thinner texture of the kadhi, you can add an additional ½ to 1 cup (120 to 240 g) water while stirring.

2. Kadhi will keep overnight in the fridge in a closed container. It thickens as it cools, so add a bit of water when reheating it.

3. It can be kept in the fridge for up to 2 days, but it is best eaten the day of.

4. Kadhi can also be served as a soup.

Makai Paka (Corn on the Cob in a Coconut Curry)

Serves 6 to 8

To give you a little history behind this dish, it comes from East Africa. Agriculturally East Africa has an abundance of corn, peanuts, and coconut. The original dish has only a couple of spices, namely turmeric and red chili, and some lemon juice, but it lacks onion, ginger, and Indian spices such as garam masala, cumin-coriander powder. Of course, the huge population of Gujaratis in East Africa Indianized this curry by adding a bunch of spices and making it even more flavorful.

My grandmother got married in the late 1940s. She came to Uganda with my grandfather on a boat since he had his business in Kampala. She was 16 when she got married. She had learned cooking from her mother but she learned many more recipes while living in Africa as she grew older and had her kids. She assimilated herself into the African culture, and learned their dishes from her African helper, along with learning Swahili as well. This was one of the curries she made often and passed it on to her daughters. My mum used to make this dish as well, since Mumbai also has an abundance of corn. She did not make it as often as my masi (my mum's younger sister) Ranju, who makes it beautifully and so tasty that you are left craving for more. When we visit London, she makes it for us. She graciously shared her recipe with me, and I am grateful that my family loves this recipe too! We enjoy this curry with Triangle Paratha (page 354), Butter Garlic Naan (page 357), or plain rice.

INGREDIENTS

4 ears of corn, husk removed

4 tablespoons (57 g) vegetable oil

1½ teaspoons (3 g) cumin seeds

Pinch of asafoetida

1 medium (150 g) red onion, finely chopped

1 cup (130 g) roasted peanuts

2½ medium (260 g) tomatoes

1 green chili

1 inch (2½ cm) ginger

1 teaspoon (3 g) ground turmeric

1½ teaspoons (4.5 g) Kashmiri red chili powder

1 teaspoon (2 g) ground cumin

1 teaspoon (2 g) ground coriander

1 teaspoon (3 g) garam masala

½ to 2 teaspoons (9 g to 12 g) table salt

3 tablespoons (45 g) tomato paste

½ cup (60 g) freshly grated coconut
    or frozen coconut

½ cup (120 g) reserved corn cooking water

1½ cups (342 g) whole coconut milk

GARNISH

¼ cup fresh cilantro

continued ➝

METHOD

1. In a large deep saucepan, fill three-quarters full with water, place over high heat, and bring to a boil. Meanwhile, cut the corn in 2-inch- (5 cm) thick pieces. It should be around four to five pieces per ear of corn. Once the water comes to a boil, add the corn and let it cook for 10 minutes. The corn should be submerged in the boiling water. Once the corn is boiled, remove the corn and reserve the water.

2. In a separate large saucepan on medium heat, add the oil. After about 30 seconds, add the cumin seeds and asafoetida and let the seeds splatter, about 20 seconds or so. Once the seeds start splattering, add the onions. Sauté for 5 to 7 minutes until the onions are golden brown in color.

3. Meanwhile, grind the roasted peanuts in a high-speed blender to a fine powder and set it aside.

4. Grind the tomatoes, green chili, and ginger in the high-speed blender and set it aside.

5. After the onions have browned, add the tomato mixture and sauté for a minute. Dry masalas or spices go in next and then the tomato paste.

Sauté continuously for 2 minutes, until the oil starts separating. The mixture will come together.

6. Add the ground peanuts and coconut and sauté for 2 minutes. Add the coconut milk and ½ cup (120 g) of the reserved corn cooking water and stir the entire mixture together until well combined. Let it cook for 2 minutes.

7. Add the boiled corn and cover the corn well with the curry. Let it cook for about 7 to 9 minutes. It will come to a boil. Garnish with cilantro in the end and your curry is done.

PRO TIPS

1. Use a sharp knife to cut through the corn. If you are not comfortable cutting it prior to boiling, cutting it after boiling the whole corn is much easier.

2. Omit the green chili if you do not want the curry to be spicy. Or deseed the green chili to eliminate the spiciness.

Squash Blossom Tacos
WITH KACHUMBER SALSA

Serves 6 (2 tacos per person)

My family and I are obsessed with these tacos. We make them at least a few times every summer. I change up the toppings but the stuffed and fried squash blossoms inside stay the same. I had discovered zucchini squash blossoms a few years ago at the farmers' market. I asked the vendor what the flower was and how it should be used. He told me it could be used in many different ways, including in tacos, frittatas, pizzas (I love squash blossoms on pizzas!), stuffed with ricotta and fried, used in quiches, savory pies—the possibilities are endless. It is amazing how much you can learn from the farmers regarding ingredients and how to cook them. Ask and they will tell you.

I started planting zucchinis a couple of years ago so that I could grow my own zucchinis and harvest squash blossoms from my plants. The results were amazing. Every time I would see a flower on the plant, it would get me excited. We were able to get a meal out of the zucchinis and the squash blossoms on our plant.

I used a kachumber salsa for these tacos. Kachumber is the Indian salsa if you may call it that. Or Indian salad. Growing up, kachumber was our salad for every meal. It consists of essentially finely diced tomatoes, cucumbers, red onions, and cilantro, mixed with red chili powder, salt, sugar, and lemon juice. I essentially added peaches to this mixture to make a delicious kachumber salsa. When I told my kids that this is a salad I grew up eating, they were a bit confused. For them, salad means some green leaves with diced or sliced vegetables and a vinaigrette. It is pretty amazing how a concept from one country is perceived in another country, when you have never heard of it. It takes time to assimilate, and understand, but when you do and you taste it, you relish and appreciate it. My kids love kachumber now, and that is our designated "salsa" for tacos!

INGREDIENTS

MARINATED RED CABBAGE AND ONION

¼ small red cabbage (80 g), packed
   tightly into 1 cup

½ small (40 g) red onion, thinly sliced

½ teaspoon (3 g) Maldon salt

½ teaspoon (1 g) black pepper

¼ cup (57½ g) red wine vinegar

¼ cup (57½ g) apple cider vinegar

KACHUMBER SALSA

1 medium tomato, diced into small pieces

1 Persian cucumber, diced into small pieces

¼ red onion, finely chopped

½ large peach, diced into small pieces

½ teaspoon Maldon salt

¼ teaspoon red chili powder

1 teaspoon granulated sugar

Juice of 1 lime

2 tablespoons finely chopped cilantro

continued ➤

PRO TIPS

1. Medium corn tortillas are best for these tacos, so they can be filled up to enjoy a hearty taco.

2. Make the stuffed and fried squash blossoms just before you eat as they taste best when they are freshly made.

TEMPURA FRIED SQUASH BLOSSOMS

1 tablespoon (14 g) butter

½ cup (63 g) zucchini, diced into small pieces

½ cup (87 g) fresh corn kernels

½ teaspoon chipotle powder

½ teaspoon smoked paprika

½ teaspoon garlic powder

1 heaping cup (120 g) Oaxaca cheese

12 stems squash blossoms, stamens removed, washed gently and patted dry

1 cup (120 g) all-purpose flour

½ teaspoon table salt

1 cup (240 g) cold seltzer water

Oil for deep frying

12 medium corn tortillas

½ cup (64 g) Cotija cheese

Avocado, Cilantro, and Poblano Pepper Dressing (page 55)

Cilantro, for garnish

Thinly sliced radish for garnish (about 3 to 4)

METHOD

To Make the Marinated Red Cabbage and Onion

The mixture needs to marinate for maximum flavor, which is why we prepare it first. In a medium bowl, add the red cabbage, red onion slices, salt, pepper, red wine vinegar, and apple cider vinegar, and mix well. Set it aside to marinate for half an hour.

To Make the Kachumber Salsa

Add all the ingredients in a medium bowl, and mix well to combine. The juices from the tomatoes and peaches will release with the salt in the mixture. Mix again after 15 minutes. Set it aside.

To Make the Tempura Fried Squash Blossoms

1. Prepare the stuffed squash blossom mixture: In a medium saucepan on medium heat, add the butter. Once melted, add the zucchini and corn and sauté for a minute. Add the spices and sauté for 5 to 7 minutes. Remove from the heat.

After 2 to 3 minutes, add the grated Oaxaca cheese and sauté to mix. The cheese will melt and form a nice melty filling.

2. Fill about a heaped teaspoonful of filling into each squash blossom and set aside on a plate. Fill all of the squash blossoms with the mixture. Do this step very gently as the squash blossoms are delicate.

3. Prepare the tempura batter: In a medium shallow bowl, add the flour and salt and whisk to combine. Add the cold seltzer water and whisk until the batter is smooth. Do not over whisk or else the fizz in the batter will subside.

4. In a deep saucepan on medium-high heat, add oil for frying the squash blossoms. Once it reaches a temperature of 350ºF (175ºC), the squash blossoms are ready to fry. Have a plate with paper towels on the side to drain off the excess oil.

5. Take a stuffed squash blossom and dip it in the tempura batter and coat it well. Let the excess drip off, and then fry it in the oil for a minute in total, rotating the blossom to lightly brown it on all the sides. Remove it with a kitchen spider.

6. Repeat the process with the remaining squash blossoms. They fry up pretty quickly so you have to watch it for the entire process.

To Assemble the Tacos

1. Char the corn tortillas on the stovetop, using tongs to char the edges of the tortilla. Arrange the tortillas on a platter. If you do not have a gas stove, you can cook the tortillas on a skillet or grill to heat them up.

2. Add a squash blossom to each corn tortilla. Add a bit of the kachumber salsa, marinated red cabbage and onions, a bit of the crumbled Cotija cheese, drizzle of the Avocado, Cilantro, and Poblano Pepper Dressing, cilantro, and radish on each tortilla. The tacos are ready to eat.

Ultimate Mumbai-California Veggie Burger

Makes about 8 patties

About six years ago, when my kids were quite little, my mother-in-law was visiting us from Los Angeles for the July 4th long weekend. All of us are vegetarians except Raj, so I decided to make veggie burgers for the celebration. I made veggie masala burgers, with a medley of vegetables, quinoa, and grated cheese in the burger patty, along with Indian spices—and they turned out delicious. Everyone enjoyed the patties, along with the heirloom tomato and peach burrata salad with reduced balsamic glaze to go along with the meal. Since then I have modified my burger patty recipe a few times, but have kept the spices the same.

The Indian spices in the patty remind me of the mouthwatering McDonald's patty in Mumbai that I absolutely love! When I came to California, I had a very hard time finding a good patty. I am not a fan of the chewy, bland texture of the soy patties. Then came Roam Artisan Burger, which has the best veggie burger in my opinion. Combining my love for the Mumbai Macdonald's patty and the Californian patty, I came up with this recipe. I love the combination of potatoes, beets, and quinoa, along with the Indian spices in the patty. This burger is truly delicious and turns out just the way I like it. As my daughter said, "I could eat this patty by itself, it is so delicious!" The tempura masala fried onions give it the right amount of crunch and texture. I mean who does not love fried onions?! The grilled pineapple reminds me of the millions of pineapples I ate as a kid growing up in Mumbai. The buttery lettuce tastes of California with its sweet tender leaves. This burger is truly an amalgamation of the flavors from Mumbai and California into one.

INGREDIENTS

PATTY MIXTURE

3 medium (270 g) potatoes, boiled, cooled, and peeled

½ cup (75 g) uncooked quinoa or 1 cup (160 g) cooked and cooled quinoa

¾ cup (70 g) plain bread crumbs

2 tablespoons (29 g) vegetable oil

2 teaspoons fennel seeds

1 cup (120 g) finely chopped white onion

3 garlic cloves

1 inch (2½ cm) ginger, freshly grated

1 teaspoon red chili powder

1 teaspoon turmeric powder

1½ teaspoons garam masala

1 teaspoon freshly ground roasted cumin

2 teaspoons table salt

3 medium (300 g) beets, washed, peeled, and grated

1 tablespoon cilantro

Cooking spray or olive oil spray, for grilling the patties

continued ➤

TEMPURA MASALA RED ONIONS

Oil for frying

½ teaspoon (1.4 g) red chili powder

½ teaspoon (1 g) chaat masala

½ cup (60 g) all-purpose flour

½ cup (118 g) cold seltzer water

1 medium red onion, thinly sliced horizontally, rings separated out

BUN AND TOPPINGS

6 to 8 pepper Jack cheese slices

6 to 8 pineapple slices

8 brioche burger buns

Chipotle Mayonnaise or plain mayonnaise

Butter lettuce leaves, washed and pat dry

2 large tomatoes, sliced thinly

Pickled cucumber

METHOD

To Make the Patty Mixture

1. In a large bowl, add the boiled potatoes and mash them almost completely. Add the cooked quinoa and bread crumbs.

2. In a sauté pan, on medium heat, add the vegetable oil and heat for 30 seconds. Add the fennel seeds and onions and sauté for 5 minutes until onions are translucent and slightly brown in color.

3. Add the garlic, ginger, and dry spices and salt and sauté for a minute.

4. Add the grated beets and sauté to mix well. Cook for 5 minutes, until the mixture has cooked down a bit. Sauté throughout the process to ensure the entire mixture is coated well with the spices. Remove from the heat and let the mixture come to a slight cool, about 10 minutes.

5. Add the spiced beet mixture to the potatoes, bread crumbs, and quinoa. Add the cilantro. With your bare hands mix the entire mixture really well to get the spices into every bite.

6. Weigh the mixture and divide equally into eight patties.

7. Roll each portion between the palm of your hands to form a ball. Flatten into a round disc, about ⅓-inch (8 mm) diameter smaller than the bun. Repeat for the remaining portions. Set aside on a plate and let it rest for 15 minutes.

To Make the Tempura Masala Red Onions

1. In a medium deep-frying pan, add oil about one-third up the pan, and let it heat on medium to high heat until it comes to a temperature of about 350°F (175°C).

2. Meanwhile, prepare the batter. In a medium bowl, add the all-purpose flour, red chili powder, and chaat masala, and whisk to combine. Add the cold seltzer water and whisk to combine. Do not overmix, as you do not want to flatten the fizz.

3. Add the thinly sliced red onions into the batter and mix to coat each slice properly.

4. To check if the oil is ready, add a drop of the batter. If the batter rises up immediately, you know the oil is ready to fry. Keep a plate near you with a paper towel to drain off the excess oil.

5. Using your hand, take a bit of the onions, drain off the excess batter, and put it into the oil. This process has to be quick as you do not want to burn yourself. It will start bubbling, and will take a minute for the onions to brown. Using a kitchen spider, turn the onions to brown on all the sides. Remove the fried onions, drain off the excess, and put it on the plate on the side.

6. Repeat for the remaining onions.

continued ➝

To Prepare the Burgers

1. Heat up your grill pan to medium-high heat. Spray cooking spray or olive oil spray on the pan. Once heated after 3 to 4 minutes, add 3 to 4 patties at a time. Cook for 3 minutes on one side to char properly. Spray the top of the patties with the cooking/olive oil spray as well. Turn the patties onto the other side. Add a slice of cheese on the top of each patty. Cover the grill with a lid on the patties to melt the cheese. Cook for another 3 minutes. Remove off the grill and let the patties rest on a plate for 1 to 2 minutes.

2. Once the patties are grilled, grill the pineapples by spraying with cooking/olive oil spray on the pan. Cook for a minute on each side. Remove and set aside.

3. Grill the buns next. Add a layer of mayonnaise or dressing of your choice on the bottom bun. Patty goes next. Top with the butter lettuce leaves, grilled pineapple, a sliced tomato, and pickled cucumber. Finally, top with the tempura masala red onions and the top bun. Enjoy with some fries or the Masala Potato Chips (page 375).

PRO TIPS

1. Switch up the toppings per your fancy. These are the toppings that I love on my burger.

2. I also love the Avocado, Cilantro, and Poblano Pepper Dressing (page 55) on this burger.

Summer California Pizza

WITH BUTTERED CORN, ZUCCHINI RIBBONS, SQUASH BLOSSOMS, OLIVES, RED ONIONS, AND HARIYALI PANEER

Makes 4

I have tried several pizza dough recipes from the *New York Times* to Food Network, but then I stumbled upon this article on the *Serious Eats* website by J. Kenji López-Alt, which was eye opening for me. He talks about pizza dough and the ingredients as a percentage of the flour used in the dough. The flour is 100 percent, and all other ingredients are a percentage of the flour. I have tweaked the percentages and what worked for me was 60 percent water, 2 percent salt, 1.5 percent yeast, 6 percent olive oil and 3 percent sugar or honey. The sweet factor in the dough caramelizes the dough when baked. If you know the baker's percentage for pizza dough, you can increase or decrease the quantity of the dough for the amount of people that you are making pizzas for.

The recommended flour for pizza is the "00" flour or "doppio zero" flour from Italy, which is a fine-milled flour that makes the best pizzas. I buy the "00" flour online, and it gives the dough great flavor and so much chewiness. So, if you are able to get the "00" flour, you must go for it. You can also use bread flour instead of the "00" flour, which has a higher protein content and helps develop the gluten. This gives the dough its strength, elasticity, and chewiness.

This Summer California Pizza reminds me exactly of that! Summer and California with a glass of Sauvignon blanc. All the beautiful summer produce like zucchini ribbons, squash blossoms, fresh buttered corn, Castelvetrano olives, red onions and the beautiful spiced paneer dunked in freshly mixed green yogurt sauce on the pizza, brought together by the melty, delicious fontina cheese is seriously a fantasy in one bite. A sip of wine to follow, and it is heaven! This is one of our family favorites, and I am happy to share it with you all.

continued ➤

INGREDIENTS

PIZZA DOUGH

4 cups (500 g) bread flour or "00" flour

1 tablespoon (15 g) granulated sugar or honey

¾ tablespoon (12 g) table salt

2½ teaspoons (7.5 g) active dry yeast

1⅓ cups (320 g) water

2¼ tablespoons (30 g) olive oil

Additional flour for kneading

2 tablespoons (27 g) olive oil

PIZZA TOPPINGS

2 cups (8 ounces) paneer, cut into cubes
(about ¼ to ¾ inch, 1 to 2 cm)

½ quantity of the Green Yogurt Sauce from Summer
Hariyali (Green) Paneer Skewers (page 145)

1 tablespoon (14 g) butter

Corn kernels from 1 corn on the cob or
½ cup frozen

½ teaspoon (3 g) table salt

¼ cup (40 g) cornmeal

¼ cup (32.5 g) olive oil

Cilantro, Peanut, and Toasted Coriander Seed
Pesto (page 56)

2 cups (8 ounces) grated fontina cheese

1 zucchini, sliced thin into ribbons using
a mandoline

½ small red onion, sliced thin

20 Castelvetrano olives, pitted and cut in
half horizontally

8 squash blossoms

EQUIPMENT

Baking steel or pizza stone or baking tray

Parchment paper

Pastry brush

Pizza wooden spatula

METHOD

1. In a large bowl, add the flour, sugar, salt, and yeast, and whisk to combine. Add the water and olive oil, and mix the dough until no dry bits are left. The dough will be very sticky.

2. On a clean surface, sprinkle flour. With flour on your hands, scrape the dough onto the floured surface. Sprinkle more flour on top of the dough and knead the dough for about 7 minutes with the palms of both hands, adding flour as needed, until you get a smooth dough. You are building the gluten in the dough so that it can stretch and gain strength.

3. Add a tablespoon of olive oil in the same large bowl and spread it all over the bowl. Form the dough into a nice round ball, and place it in the bowl. Pour a tablespoon of olive oil on top of the dough and massage it. Cover the bowl with a kitchen towel or plastic wrap, and set it aside to rise for 2 to 8 hours, until it doubles in size. I usually keep it in the oven. Punch down the dough. Form it into a ball by pulling the dough and tucking it underneath to the bottom. Store in a covered bowl, in the fridge for 2 to 3 days.

4. After 2 to 3 days, remove the dough from the fridge at least 2 hours before forming the pizzas. Divide into four equal pieces, and round them into balls, again by pulling the dough and tucking it underneath to form a ball. Place them on a baking sheet with parchment paper, cover with plastic wrap and let rise in the oven or any warm place. The dough will rise slightly after 1½ to 2 hours.

5. If you have a baking steel, place it in a 500°F (260°C) oven, 1 hour before making the pizzas. The baking steel helps to form a nice crust on the pizza as it generates heat from the bottom up into the pizza. If you do not have a baking steel you can use a pizza stone or simply an

continued →

inverted baking tray. Make sure to place it in the 500°F (260°C) oven an hour before baking.

6. In a medium bowl, add the paneer cubes to the Green Yogurt Sauce, mixing gently to combine. Set aside for 20 minutes.

7. In a small skillet on medium heat, add the butter. Once melted, add the corn and salt and sauté for 2 minutes. Place the corn in a small bowl and set aside.

8. To form the pizza, place a ball of dough onto parchment paper that has some cornmeal sprinkled on top. Using the tips of your fingers on both hands, start pressing the dough in an outward direction. You are massaging the dough to form a round circle and you want it as thin as possible like a Neapolitan pizza. Form the dough into a 9-inch (23 cm) circle. The outer rim will be a little higher and will form the beautiful crust of the pizza, once baked.

9. Using a pastry brush, brush the entire surface of the pizza dough with the olive oil.

10. Spread about 3 tablespoons of the pesto onto the pizza. Scatter the toppings onto the pizza, first the fontina cheese, then the vegetables, and finally spread the hariyali paneer onto the pizza. I generally add about 6 to 8 cubes of paneer per pizza.

11. Using the pizza wooden spatula, transfer the parchment paper with the pizza onto the baking steel in the oven. Bake for 10 minutes, and then set it to broil for 1½ to 2 minutes. This is to char the edges and some of the toppings slightly. It tastes good that way.

12. Remove immediately. Wait for 2 minutes and then cut into quarters and serve immediately with a glass of Sauvignon Blanc and enjoy.

13. Repeat the process for the other pizzas.

PRO TIPS

1. For Sunday pizza night, I start making the dough on Thursday evening, so that my dough is ready by Sunday evening. The pizza dough can be made up to 5 days ahead. You can make the pizza dough even on Saturday in the morning, and let it rest for a little over 24 hours for a Sunday evening dinner.

2. Use a marinara sauce and change up the toppings.

Bharela Ringan Nu Shaak (Peanut and Chickpea Flour Masala–Stuffed Eggplants)

Serves 4

Eggplant is underrated and also a vegetable that is not easily likeable. It is an acquired taste in my opinion. Eggplant needs to be seasoned well and prepared well to be able to enhance its flavor. It took me a while to really enjoy it and I only liked my mum's way of preparing it. She made it at least three different ways: as Ringan auro (mashed eggplant with Indian spices), with lots of garlic cloves sautéed along with it, and stuffed eggplants—this is my absolute favorite way to eat it.

Eggplant was Mum's favorite vegetable. Perhaps the only vegetable that she ate frequently and took double portions of. She was quite cunning—she would make sure we ate good portions of vegetables in our meals, but it was okay if she ate a small portion of vegetables. We were not allowed to get up from the dining table, unless and until our plates were clean and wiped out of whatever she had served us. She was strict when it came to food and food waste. Coming back to the eggplant, she loved eating it with millet flour rotli or *rotla* in Gujarati. It was her favorite meal, along with some spicy green chilis on the side, and Masala Chaas (page 335) to wash down the meal.

Did you know eggplant has a lot of nutritional benefits? It works as an antioxidant, and is known to benefit cholesterol levels. It's high in fiber and low in calories. This vegetable takes only about 20 minutes of cooking. The stuffing can be made a day ahead and stored in the fridge. It is really that simple and a fantastic way to add flavor to the eggplant.

INGREDIENTS

1.3 pounds (600 g) small eggplants

PEANUT AND CHICKPEA MASALA STUFFING

¼ cup (25 g) chickpea flour

½ cup (70 g) toasted unsalted peanuts

½ cup washed and tightly packed cilantro

2 green chilis (more if you like it spicy)

1 inch (2½ cm) ginger

1 tablespoon dried fenugreek (optional)

½ teaspoon red chili powder
   (more, if you like it spicy)

1 teaspoon ground cumin

1 teaspoon ground coriander

1 teaspoon ground turmeric

1½ teaspoons table salt

2 tablespoons (15 g) grated jaggery or
   1 tablespoon (12.5 g) brown sugar

¼ cup (32 g) frozen or fresh coconut

¼ cup (60 g) vegetable oil

1½ tablespoons (22 g) lemon juice

TEMPERING (VAGHAR)

3 tablespoons (40 g) vegetable oil

Pinch of asafoetida

1 teaspoon cumin seeds

1 teaspoon mustard seeds

1 cup (240 g) water

GARNISH

¼ cup coarsely chopped cilantro,
   washed and tightly packed

2 tablespoons frozen or fresh coconut

continued ➞

METHOD

Wash the eggplants, dry them, cut a slit crosswise at the bottom of each up to the top, while still keeping it intact. This is where the stuffing will go.

To Make the Peanut and Chickpea Masala Stuffing

1. In a small skillet on medium heat, add the chickpea flour. Constantly stir it for 3 minutes, and you will see it brown slowly. Once it is a light brown color after 3 minutes, remove from the heat. Let it cool.

2. In a high-speed blender, add all the ingredients and mix until it forms a paste. It should have some texture, and not be completely smooth. You do not want it to be coarse or fine. It needs to be in between for the best texture.

3. Once the mixture is ready, remove it into a bowl using a small rubber spatula to get all the bits from the processor.

4. With your hands, add a heaped teaspoon of stuffing into both the slits of the eggplant. Repeat for all the eggplants. You will have extra stuffing left, which we will add to the entire dish.

To Temper and Cook

1. In a medium pot on medium heat, add the oil. Let it heat up for 1 minute. Add the asafoetida, cumin seeds, and mustard seeds, and let it come to a splatter for 30 seconds.

2. Add stuffed eggplants and all the remaining stuffing into the pot. Sauté to cover the eggplants with oil. Cover with a lid completely and cook for 5 minutes. Sauté occasionally to turn the eggplants over to cook all the sides.

3. Add ¼ cup (60 g) of the water in the pot, cover the lid, and cook. Stir the eggplants occasionally to cook all the sides. Cook for 5 minutes. The water helps to steam and cook the eggplants through and through.

4. Repeat, and add ¼ cup (60 g) more water, cover the lid, and cook.

5. Repeat Step 3 with the remaining water. The total cooking time of the eggplants after tempering is 20 minutes.

6. The eggplant will look mushy after the 20 minutes of steaming and cooking. Remove from the heat.

7. Garnish with the cilantro and coconut. Serve with warm Plain Rotli (page 345) or Spinach Puri (342).

PRO TIPS

1. The same method can be used for okra, potatoes, and sweet potatoes as well. The total cook time will vary.

2. This dish can be stored in the fridge for up to 2 days. To reheat, warm in the microwave, or you can warm it in a pot on the stove.

Ragda Pattice (Potato Patties in a White Pea Lentil Curry)

Makes about 12 patties; serves 6

Ragda Pattice! It brings back only one image in my mind. One of my favorite vendors was on the streets of Juhu Scheme, opposite my school. Here I reminiscence many a wonderful times with my family, friends, and relatives where we ate all the possible chaat (Mumbai Street Food) there was to sample. Those are some of the best memories—where my friends and I would each get chaat dishes and we would share, standing on the streets, in a communal way, laughing and sweating in the 100 percent humidity of Mumbai, tears in our eyes from the spice levels in the dishes. Despite the tears, we had the biggest smiles on our faces because we were together and enjoying each other's company over chaat. It is a sensory and soulful experience to eat on the streets of Mumbai that is like no other, one that is a MUST to experience and enjoy.

Ragda Pattice are spiced potato patties that are shallow fried, then drenched with white pea daal (called ragda), drizzled with the three essential chaat chutneys—Date Tamarind Chutney (page 45), Cilantro Mint Chutney (page 42), and Lahsun Ni Chutney—then sprinkled with sev or thin chickpea noodles (available in Indian grocery stores), and finally garnished with red onions and cilantro. This is Dad's absolute favorite dish. Given a choice, his preference would always be Ragda Pattice for Sunday dinners. My brother enjoys it as much as Dad does, and it is almost a competition over who can eat the most patties. Of course, my six-foot-tall brother wins!

Make this dish for your family or friends, or serve it as a main or an appetizer. It will definitely be a hit!

INGREDIENTS

LAHSUN NI CHUTNEY (GARLIC CHUTNEY; OPTIONAL)

16 garlic cloves

2 teaspoons Kashmiri red chili

1 teaspoon table salt

4 to 6 tablespoons (60 g) water

RAGDA

1½ cups (270 g) white peas or safed vatana

2 teaspoons table salt

3 tablespoons (40 g) vegetable oil

1 teaspoon cumin seeds

1 medium (150 g) red onion, finely chopped

1 inch (2½ cm) ginger

1 green chili

3 garlic cloves

1 teaspoon ground cumin

1 teaspoon ground coriander

1 teaspoon ground turmeric

1 teaspoon Kashmiri red chili powder

1 teaspoon garam masala

¼ cup Date Tamarind Chutney (page 45), plus more for topping

½ cup (120 g) water, plus more for soaking and boiling

¼ cup cilantro

continued ➤

PATTICE

- 2 inches (5 cm) ginger
- 2 green chilis
- 2 garlic cloves
- 2 pounds (800 g) white potatoes (raw weight), boiled and peeled
- 2 teaspoons (4 g) cumin seeds
- 1½ teaspoons (3 g) Kashmiri red chili powder
- 1½ teaspoons (3 g) garam masala
- 1½ teaspoons (9 g) table salt
- Oil, for shallow frying
- 1½ cups Date Tamarind Chutney (page 45)
- 1 cup Cilantro Mint Chutney (page 42)
- Lahsun Ni Chutney (optional)
- 2 cups thin sev or chickpea noodles
- 1 small onion, finely diced
- ½ cup cilantro, finely chopped

METHOD

To Make the Lahsun Ni Chutney

In a small food processor, add all the ingredients and grind until well combined. It should be paste-like. Alternately, you can do it in a mortar pestle as well, using no water first, making a fine paste, and then diluting it with the water to make the chutney.

To Make the Ragda

1. In a medium bowl, add the white peas, and soak them in hot water, with 2 inches (5 cm) of water covering the peas. Let them soak for 8 hours.

2. After soaking, rinse the white peas under water at least three or four times.

3. In a pressure cooker, add the white peas, salt, and enough water to cover the peas by 2 inches (5 cm). On medium to high heat, let the pressure cooker do its magic and wait for five to six whistles. Remove from the heat. Wait for the lid to come off from the pressure. If you do not have a pressure cooker, in a large pot, add the white peas, salt, and enough water to cover the peas by at least 4 inches (10 cm). On high heat, with a lid on the pot, boil the mixture for about 45 minutes. Check on the water levels. If the water level goes below the white peas within the 45 minutes, add more water to cover, close the lid, and bring back to a boil for a total of 45 minutes. The white skins should come off the peas, and the peas should be mashed easily between the tip of your finger and your thumb. That is what you are looking for when boiling the white peas. If the peas are still hard, you will have to boil them for another 15 minutes, and try the test again until the peas are easily mashable.

4. In a large pot on medium to high heat, add the oil. Let it heat up for 1 minute. Add the cumin seeds and onion. Sauté for 5 minutes until the onions begin to sweat and become translucent.

5. Add the ginger, green chili, and garlic to a small food processor and process to form a paste.

6. Add the ginger-garlic paste paste into the mixture and sauté for a minute. Add the dry masalas and sauté until it forms a paste, about a minute.

7. Add the boiled white peas, Date Tamarind Chutney and ½ cup (120 g) of water to the mixture and mix until it all combines well together. Cook for 10 minutes on medium heat. Stir occasionally to not burn the bottom of the ragda. Garnish with chopped cilantro.

To Make the Pattice

1. Add the ginger, green chili, and garlic to a small food processor and process to form a paste.

2. In a medium bowl, add the boiled potatoes, ginger-garlic-green chili paste, cumin seeds, Kashmiri red chili powder, garam masala, and salt, mash it up well with a potato masher, or if you want to get your hands in, use your hands to mash it up well. There should not be any chunks. It should be a smooth mashed mixture like mashed potatoes.

3. Weigh about 70 to 75 g, and make round flat patties about 3 inches (7½ cm) in diameter. They are about less than an inch in height. You shape it with your hands into a nice round, forming and flattening as you go around the patty with both your hands. Set it aside on a plate. Repeat the process and make a total of 12 patties or pattice.

4. In a large nonstick skillet on medium to high heat, add about 3 to 4 tablespoons of oil. Heat it for a minute. Add six patties at a time, and shallow fry them for about 3 minutes on each side, until they are brown in color. Flip them over with a flat spatula, and brown for another 3 minutes. Remove and set it aside on a plate. Repeat with the remaining six patties.

5. In a pasta bowl or a shallow bowl, add two pattice. Ladle the hot ragda on top of the pattice. I generally put ragda so that the pattice is covered completely. Drizzle Date Tamarind Chutney, Cilantro Mint Chutney, 2 to 3 spoonfuls of the optional garlic chutney. Sprinkle generously with sev and garnish with finely chopped red onions and cilantro. Serve immediately.

PRO TIPS

1. The pattice can be made a day ahead and stored in an airtight container lined with aluminum foil, in the fridge.

2. The ragda can be made a day ahead as well.

3. Leftovers can be stored in the fridge for up to a day.

Kala Chana Daal (Black Chickpea Daal)

Serves 6 to 8

Kala chana or black chickpeas are similar to garbanzo beans but they are dark brown. Unlike garbanzo beans, which cause bloating and can make you feel gassy, kala chana does not cause the same gassy bloated feeling after consumption. It is very high in protein and helps to regulate blood sugar levels and control diabetes. There are many benefits to this legume. It is consumed as boiled kala chana in the morning as breakfast to keep one fueled for a long time.

Gujaratis make Kala Chana Daal quite often. It is not made with the typical onion, garlic, and ginger combination as is the case with North Indian daals. My mum would make this quite often, especially during the Navratri (nine nights) festival, where she would fast for 9 days, with only milk, fruit, and nuts. On the 9th day, she would break her fast with a lovely meal consisting of Kala Chana Daal, hot puri, and sheero (sweet semolina dessert, made with ghee, nuts, milk, cardamom, saffron, and raisins). It is served as an offering to Ambe Mata (goddess). The tradition is to call a few (10 to 15) unmarried girls under the age of 12 for a meal and Mum and I would serve this meal to the girls from the slums. The joy on their faces eating a warm, home cooked meal and the giggling and chatters really filled up the house and brought joy to her and us. She would send them off with a token of some bangles and money. She never missed a year with this tradition. Her generosity knew no bounds, she was always ready to give to the needy and the poor, help with the maid's kids' education, and so on. She had a big heart and a big smile. And her Kala Chana Daal, although simple, tasted wonderful, because it was made with love.

INGREDIENTS

1½ cups (300 g) kala chana (brown chickpeas)

3½ cups water (900 g), plus more for soaking

2 teaspoons table salt

1 inch (2½ cm) ginger

1 green chili

2 tablespoons (27 g) vegetable oil

Pinch of asafoetida

1 teaspoon cumin seeds

1 teaspoon mustard seeds

1 teaspoon ground turmeric

1 teaspoon ground cumin

1 teaspoon ground coriander

½ teaspoon red chili powder

1 tablespoon (7 g) chickpea flour

3 tablespoons Date Tamarind Chutney (page 45)

GARNISH

¼ cup finely chopped cilantro

continued ➤

METHOD

1. Soak the kala chana or brown chickpeas in a medium bowl with about 2 inches (5 cm) of warm water covering the chickpeas. Let it sit overnight or for 8 hours. Rinse the chickpeas using your hands under running water. Drain out all the water after three or four washes.

2. Using a pressure cooker on the stove at medium high heat, add the chickpeas, 3 cups (720 g) of the water, and the salt. The salt helps to increase the boiling point of the water, hence cooking the chickpeas faster and making them soft. Let the whistle blow seven to eight times, then turn off the heat. Let the pressure cooker cool for 20 minutes, and then open it up.

3. If you do not have a pressure cooker, in a large pot, add the kala chana or brown chickpeas, salt, and enough water to cover the chickpeas by at least 4 inches (10 cm). Over high heat, with a lid on the pot, bring to a boil and let cook for about 45 minutes. Check on the water levels. If the water level goes below the chickpeas within the 45 minutes, add more water to cover, close the lid, and bring back to a boil for a total of 45 minutes. The chickpeas should be mashed easily between the tip of your finger and your thumb. You can even bite on it and the texture should be mushy. That is what you are looking for when boiling them. If the chickpeas are still hard, you will have to boil them for another 15 minutes, and try the test again until they are easily mashable. Use a mini food processor to grind the ginger and green chili into a paste. Using a mini spatula, keep it aside.

4. In a medium pot on medium-low heat, add the oil. Let it heat up for a minute. Add the asafoetida, cumin seeds, and mustard seeds and let it splatter for 30 seconds. Add the ginger-green chili paste and sauté for 15 seconds.

5. Add all the dry spices and the chickpea flour, and sauté for 1 minute.

6. Add the pressure-cooked chickpeas, Date Tamarind Chutney, and ½ cup (120 g) of water and stir to combine.

7. It will come to a boil, and all the flavors will merge together. Cook for a total of 10 to 15 minutes on medium heat. Mash about ¼ cup of the cooked chickpeas, to give the daal a nice texture. Remove from the heat. It will thicken as it cools slightly. Add an additional ½ cup (60 g) of water if you want a bit more gravy in this daal.

8. Garnish with the chopped cilantro.

9. Serve with plain rice, Vagharela Bhaat (Turmeric Rice, page 380), with Plain Rotli (page 345) or Masala Puri (page 360).

PRO TIPS

1. If you do not have Date Tamarind Chutney on hand, you can add 1 tablespoon jaggery and 2 tablespoons tamarind water.

2. To make tamarind water, add 2 tablespoons dried tamarind to ¼ cup (60 g) hot water, cover it, and let it sit for 15 minutes. The tamarind will become soft. Squeeze the tamarind in the water to release all its juices. Use about 2 tablespoons tamarind water in the daal.

3. The daal can be put in an airtight container and stored in the fridge for up to 3 days.

Vegetable Frankie
WITH CARAMELIZED LEEKS AND RED ONION

Makes 4

Frankie is another street food that is mouthwatering delicious. I have many memories of having Frankie as a school-going kid with friends and family. What is the origin of this iconic Mumbai street food? It comes from Amarjit Singh Tibb, who, in 1969, was traveling to Beirut, Lebanon. He came across the stuffed pita, and he wanted to recreate something similar back home in India. After much experimentation by his wife, they finally came up with the classic Frankie, and it got very popular across the country. The brand is called Tibb's Frankie and is very famous in Mumbai.

I grew up eating Quality Frankie, which was a tiny store, walking distance from my school. Same concept, different brand. My friends and I would frequent this Frankie stall from time to time after school hours. It was about a 7- to 10-minute walk from school. Frankie is a buttery maida (all-purpose flour) rotli, filled with an absolutely delicious vegetable patty, onions, some lime juice, and Frankie masala sprinkled on top and covered in parchment paper, so your hands do not get greasy from the Frankie—an indulgent yet humble street food, so satisfying that it was hard to just be able to eat one. We would have our Coca Colas along with the Frankie to quench our thirst from all that sodium rush! I would take a couple home for my parents and brother to enjoy as well.

My recipe for the Vegetable Frankie is a modified version, with potatoes, peas, and carrots. I caramelized fresh beautiful leeks and red onions that I love to get from this one vendor at the farmers' market. They add a bit of natural sweetness to the Frankie, and the sprinkle of the Frankie Masala (which is a MUST!) just hits the spot and you end up wanting more. I love making this for my family, so that my kids can get a taste of what I grew up with, but with the influence of the beautiful produce of California.

INGREDIENTS

FRANKIE MASALA

4 teaspoons (10 g) Kashmiri red chili powder

2 teaspoons (6 g) ground turmeric

2 teaspoons (4 g) ground coriander

2 teaspoons (4 g) ground cumin

2 teaspoons (12 g) table salt

1 teaspoon (2 g) finely ground black pepper

2 teaspoons (6 g) garam masala

1 teaspoon (4 g) amchur (dried mango powder)

1 teaspoon (6 g) sanchar (rock salt)

FRANKIE PATTY

1 pound (60 g) potatoes

1 carrot (75 g), peeled and cut into big pieces

⅓ cup (45 g) green peas, frozen or fresh

2½ tablespoons (33 g) vegetable oil

3 garlic cloves

2 inches (5 cm) ginger

3 tablespoons Frankie Masala

¼ teaspoon (1.5 g) table salt (if required)

2 tablespoons tomato ketchup

¼ cup finely chopped cilantro

continued ➡

PRO TIPS

1. The patties can be prepared, cooked, and kept in the fridge, covered in aluminum foil, for up to 2 days.

2. The Frankie is best eaten hot and fresh.

3. Add 1 to 2 green chilis finely chopped in the Frankie patty mixture if you like it spicy.

½ teaspoon (1.5 g) lemon juice

Vegetable oil or olive oil, for shallow frying the patties

CARAMELIZED LEEKS AND RED ONIONS

2 tablespoons (27 g) vegetable oil

1 leek (120 g), cut into half lengthwise and then cut into thin slices

½ small (80 g) red onion, sliced thin

¼ teaspoon salt

FOR ASSEMBLY

4 teaspoons salted or unsalted butter

4 flour tortillas (about 7½-inch [19 cm] diameter)

½ small (80 g) red onion, finely diced

¼ cup finely chopped cilantro

Masala Potato Chips (page 375)

Cilantro Mint Chutney (page 42)

METHOD

To Make the Frankie Masala

Put all the ingredients in a glass jar and mix until well combined. Store in a cool place for up to a year.

To Make the Frankie Patty

1. In a pressure cooker on medium-high heat with four whistles or on a stove in a large pot filled three-quarters with water over medium-high heat for about 20 to 30 minutes, boil the potatoes, carrots, and green peas until the potatoes feel tender when poked with a knife. The pot should be covered with a lid the entire time. Drain thoroughly and let the vegetables cool completely.

2. Peel the potatoes, and mash all the vegetables completely until it is a mush.

3. In a shallow, medium frying pan on medium heat, add the vegetable oil and heat for 30 seconds to 1 minute. Using a fine grater, grate the garlic and ginger and add to the pan. Sauté for 30 seconds or so. Add the Frankie Masala, salt, and ketchup, and sauté for 1 minute.

4. Add the mashed vegetable mixture into the pan and sauté for 5 to 6 minutes. Add the

cilantro and lemon juice and mix to combine. Remove from the heat. Cool the mixture.

5. With a little bit of oil on both hands, form 4 equally sized long patties out of the mixture. The mixture weighs around 520 g, each patty will weigh around 130 g. Make a 5½-by-2-inch (14-by-5 cm) rectangle shape out of the patty.

6. In the same frying pan, on medium to high heat, add about 2 teaspoons of oil on the pan, add two patties at a time. Brush the top of the patties with oil, with a silicone brush, or pastry brush. Cook the patties for 3 minutes on each side. They will be nicely browned. Set them aside. Repeat for the remaining patties.

To Make the Caramelized Leeks and Red Onion

While the vegetables boil, prepare the leeks and onions. In a medium saucepan on medium heat, add the oil. Add the leeks and red onion slices and sauté until it's covered with the oil. Add the salt and sauté. Let the mixture cook for a total of about 8 minutes, until the mixture is browned slightly, and sauté it occasionally. Remove from the heat. For a crunchier texture (no caramelization), cook for 3 minutes.

To Assemble

1. In the same pan the patties were cooked in, on medium heat, add 1 teaspoon of butter. Add one flour tortilla and cook for 30 seconds on each side.

2. Add a Frankie patty on the tortilla while in the pan. Add some of the Caramelized Leek and Red Onion mixture, garnish with more red onion, and some cilantro on the top. Finally sprinkle some Frankie Masala on the top and close the wrap by overlapping the flaps of tortilla on the sides.

3. Turn the Frankie over, to seal the flaps, and cook for 20 seconds or so. Remove to a plate.

4. Serve with Masala Potato Chips and Cilantro Mint Chutney.

Desserts

"Life is uncertain. Eat dessert first."
—Ernestine Ulmer

I wish we all could live with that motto, right? Would it be wrong to say that dessert is my favorite meal of the day?! My mother was a dessert lover. There was always something baking in our home. She had a degree in home science, which meant she knew how to bake many different things—not very common in 1980s India. We were the lucky recipients of her delicious treats. She made everything from Indian desserts or mithais to puddings to cakes for our birthdays to soufflés, all in different flavors. I am sharing her famous Eggless Chocolate Fudge Cake (page 303). The cake was part of several birthday parties that we had in our home, and part of other people's birthdays, too. She got requests from family and friends to bake cakes for their special occasions, and she always obliged, with a bashful smile on her ever-glowing face. Her famous Gajjar No Halvo (Carrot Halva, page 257) is seriously the best. When warmed slightly, it simply melts in your mouth. She taught us the tricks to getting the halvo silky smooth, and I am sharing it with you.

My grandmother, or ba, was famous for her biscuits—we lovingly called them "pump wara biscuits," meaning biscuits made with the pump, or spritz biscuits, as they are famously known. Hers contained a special ingredient: love. My ba and masis (aunts) still make them in the United Kingdom every year, and I carried on the tradition in the United States. This recipe is very special to all of us, and I hope you will enjoy making it as much as we have enjoyed baking, eating, and sharing it over the years.

I love incorporating Indian spices like chai masala, thandai masala, and masala milk powder into my desserts, and you will see the fusion desserts like my popular Thandai Shortbread Cookies (page 248) in this chapter, along with the very delicious Chai Masala Crème Brûlée (page 263), which is creamy, silky, and beautifully light.

There is something unique about mithais that are a fusion of Indian and Western desserts. You can find this combination in my Plum Kalakand Cake (page 276), which is addictive, and you will not stop at round one. The Mango Shrikhand Panna Cotta Tart (page 270) is a very easy dessert to make, one that is tart, sweet, and a crowd-pleaser.

Italian and French desserts get an Indian twist with my Peacock Macarons with Apricot Saffron Jam Buttercream and Chopped Pistachios (page 291), which are very elegant in appearance and flavor. Or my absolute favorite of the lot—the Masala Chai Tiramisu with Rose Mascarpone, Whipped Cream, and Pistachio Sprinkle (page 299). This dessert is an ode to my mother, whose love for tiramisu knew no bounds. I think she would have approved of my version.

Baking brings people together, and it brings a smile to your face. Desserts bring joy to people gathered around the table. It is pure therapy that has no limit. Dessert makes everything better!

Kumquat and Black Sesame Bundt Cake
WITH LEMON ICING AND CANDIED KUMQUATS

Serves 10 to 12

Kumquats are jewel-like sweet-tart fruits from the citrus family. The skin of the kumquat is edible, and you can simply pop them in your mouth and eat them like grapes. I love kumquats so much that I decided to plant one in our backyard. The bush is still small and, like all citrus, it requires a lot of water to grow. I cannot wait until the day I have an abundance of kumquats and I can make kumquat marmalade. I first spotted this fruit at the farmers' market while picking up my Sunday haul a few years ago and ever since I've been a fan of this underrated fruit! It is loaded with vitamin C.

This cake is a celebration of kumquats that grow in abundance in California—! When pureed, kumquats are quite potent and give a wonderful aroma to the cake. They pair beautifully with black sesame, so I added a black sesame swirl in the middle of the cake to give it some depth of flavor with the nuttiness of the black sesame, along with the citrus freshness of the cake. My favorite part is the candied kumquats on the top that adorn the cake beautifully! The cake is pure sunshine in the winter months and would be a great dessert to share at a brunch table.

INGREDIENTS

CANDIED KUMQUATS

4 ounces (113 g) kumquats

½ cup (120 g) water

½ cup (100 g) granulated sugar

1 tablespoon (7 g) grated ginger

1 cinnamon stick

KUMQUAT PUREE

4 ounces (113 g) kumquats, washed, dried, and cut in half

¼ cup (50 g) granulated sugar

BLACK SESAME PASTE

⅓ cup (44 g) black sesame

⅓ cup (68 g) granulated sugar

KUMQUAT AND BLACK SESAME BUNDT CAKE

3 cups (360 g) all-purpose flour

½ cup (62 g) almond flour

2 teaspoons (6 g) baking powder

1 teaspoon (6 g) table salt

2 teaspoons (4 g) ground ginger

1 teaspoon (2.6 g) ground cinnamon

1 cup (2 sticks; 226 g) unsalted butter, room temperature

1½ cups (300 g) granulated sugar

4 large eggs, room temperature

½ cup (138 g) kumquat puree

1 tablespoon vanilla extract

1 cup (240 g) whole milk, room temperature

Cooking spray

continued ➤

LEMON ICING

1½ cups (180 g) confectioners' sugar

2 tablespoons (30 g) lemon juice

EQUIPMENT

10-cup Bundt cake pan

Pastry brush

METHOD

To Make the Candied Kumquats

1. Cut the ends off of the kumquats, and then cut each into four slices. Remove any seeds. Collect all the juice in a bowl.

2. In a small saucepan on medium heat, place the water and sugar, and dissolve for about 2 minutes. Add the ginger, cinnamon stick, and kumquat, and boil for 7 minutes until the kumquat is translucent. Remove from the heat.

3. Gently remove the slices onto a wire rack on a baking sheet and set them to dry. Strain the remaining liquid into a small jar. Discard the ginger and cinnamon. The kumquat simple syrup is used to glaze the cake, once it is baked, to moisten it. Cover and refrigerate the syrup and it will keep for about 3 weeks.

To Make the Kumquat Puree

Puree the kumquats and sugar in a high-speed blender until absolutely smooth with no tiny bits in it. It will take 3 to 4 rounds of pureeing in the blender; be sure to push the mixture down with a spatula. Remove and store in a covered jar. Refrigerate for a week.

To Make the Black Sesame Paste

Place the black sesame and sugar in a food processor or a high speed blender and make a paste. Turn it on for about 2 to 3 minutes until it forms a paste/powder consistency.

To Make the Kumquat and Black Sesame Bundt Cake

1. Preheat oven to 350°F (175°C).

2. In a medium bowl, whisk the all-purpose flour, almond flour, baking powder, salt, ground ginger, and ground cinnamon until blended.

3. In the bowl of a stand mixer fitted with a paddle attachment, add the butter and sugar. Start whisking at medium speed, increasing slowly to high speed. Beat for 2 to 3 minutes. Mixture should be fluffy and pale yellow in color.

4. Add eggs one at a time. Scrape the sides as you go along with one egg a time to get the butter off the bottom of the bowl. Add the kumquat puree and mix again to blend. Add the vanilla extract and mix again.

5. Add the flour mixture and milk, alternating both of them in three iterations, ending with the flour. Do not overmix.

6. Remove ¾ cup of the batter into a small bowl. Whisk the black sesame paste into this smaller portion of batter until it is smooth.

7. Apply cooking spray on a 10-cup Bundt cake pan. Spray it in all the nooks and crannies. Add half of the kumquat batter and smoothen it out. Add dollops of the black sesame batter throughout the Bundt. Top it off with the remaining kumquat cake batter. Using a wooden skewer, making swirls with a figure 8 in the batter, going around the entire cake pan twice to mix the two batters ever so slightly. You do not want a black batter so do not overmix it.

8. Place it in the oven for 60 minutes. Use a toothpick to ensure that it is baked all the way through. At that point remove the Bundt pan gently from the oven and let the cake rest for about 20 minutes.

9. Gently remove it from the Bundt pan, by turning it onto a wire rack on a baking pan. While the cake is hot, once out of the pan, poke holes with a bamboo skewer all around the cake gently. Using a pastry brush, brush the entire cake with the kumquat simple syrup (leftover from the candied kumquats) so that it seeps into the Bundt to make it moist.

10. Once completely cool, gently drizzle the lemon icing (recipe below) all around the Bundt cake, depending upon the shape of the Bundt.

11. Decorate all around with the candied kumquats. The cake is ready to be sliced and eaten with some tea.

To Make the Lemon Icing

In a medium bowl, add the sifted confectioners' sugar. Add the lemon juice. Whisk until the consistency is smooth. It should not be runny, but rather, a thick pourable consistency. It should be thick enough to form a nice layer on the cake. If it is runny, add more confectioners' sugar ¼ cup (30 g) at a time, until it reaches a desired consistency.

PRO TIPS

1. Puree the kumquats well to form a smooth consistency so there are no lumps in the batter or icing.

2. You can make the candied kumquats up to a week ahead of time.

Blood Orange and Hibiscus Tart
WITH CANDIED BLOOD ORANGES

Serves 12

I first discovered blood oranges a few years ago, at the local farmers' market. I loved the beautiful shades on the outside—the ombre colors really struck me and I wanted to taste them. As I got them home and cut them open, there were different colors inside too. Some were a deep magenta in color, some were more reddish, some were a pretty orange-reddish in hue. It was like a sunset in the form of a fruit and I had to create desserts with them.

I love playing with flavors, especially spices and dried flowers. Combining spices and dried flowers with seasonal fruits can really enhance the flavor of that particular fruit. Blood orange by itself can be a bit too saccharine, but when combined with hibiscus, it brings a sweet and tart aroma to the dessert.

I made this tart a few years ago, and I have made it several times since. It is always a hit with my kids. It is a perfect balance of sweet and tart, along with the smoothness of the whipped cream on the top. The candied blood oranges are the cherry on top, the perfect accompaniment to this decadent tart. The blood orange and hibiscus curd can be added to ice cream or used in a Linzer cookie (it's also really good by the spoonful). It's definitely a showstopper on the table!

INGREDIENTS

CANDIED BLOOD ORANGES
1½ cups (300 g) granulated sugar

1½ cups (360 g) water

2 blood oranges, thinly sliced (about ⅓-inch-thick), seeds removed

BLOOD ORANGE AND HIBISCUS CURD
1 cup (200 g) granulated sugar

¾ cup (125 g) blood orange juice

¼ cup (60 g) lemon juice

⅓ cup (13 g) dried hibiscus (see Pro Tip)

2 teaspoons blood orange zest

½ teaspoon salt

3 eggs

2 egg yolks

6 tablespoons (¾ stick; 85 g) cold, unsalted butter, cut into cubes

GINGERSNAP CRUST
20 small (90 g) gingersnap cookies, crushed (about 1½ cups)

1¼ cups (150 g) all-purpose flour

3 tablespoons (36 g) granulated sugar

1½ teaspoons (2.5 g) powdered ginger

½ teaspoon (3 g) table salt

½ cup (1 stick; 113 g) cold unsalted butter, cut into cubes

1 egg, divided (reserve the egg white)

WHIPPED CREAM
1 cup (240 g) heavy cream, cold

½ cup (60 g) powdered sugar

1 teaspoon vanilla extract

continued ➤

EQUIPMENT

9-inch (23 cm) fluted tart pan

Pie weights

METHOD

To Make Candied Blood Oranges

1. In a large saucepan on medium heat, add the sugar and water. Bring to a boil until sugar dissolves, about 3 to 4 minutes. Add the blood orange slices, separating them into the pan. Lower heat and simmer for 40 minutes, gently turning them with tongs, about halfway through.

2. Meanwhile, line a large baking tray with parchment paper, and set a cooling rack on top. Once the blood oranges are done, gently remove them with tongs, allowing any excess syrup to drip off and arrange them in a single layer to dry on the rack. Let rest for a day at least until all the slices are dried.

3. Let the remaining liquid in the pot simmer at medium-high heat for 5 to 7 more minutes to reduce it a little. Remove from the heat and cool. Store the syrup in a jar for another use, such as cocktails or mocktails, drizzle over ice cream or desserts.

4. After the blood oranges are completely dry, store them in an airtight container.

To Make Blood Orange and Hibiscus Curd

1. In a medium saucepan on medium heat, combine all ingredients except the butter and whisk continuously, constantly cleaning the sides and corners, to gather up the bits, until the mixture thickens, about 8 minutes. You know it is done when you coat a wooden spoon in the curd and run your finger on the back of the spoon. It should leave a clean line and the sides should not run.

2. Immediately strain the mixture through a sieve over a medium bowl. Once strained, stir in the butter pieces and keep stirring until the curd is well blended and smooth. Cover it with plastic wrap applied directly to the surface and let cool for 30 minutes. Place it in the fridge to firm for at least an hour.

To Make the Crust

1. Place the oven rack in the middle position and preheat to 375°F (190 °C).

2. Pulse gingersnap cookies, flour, sugar, ginger, and salt in a food processor until combined.

3. Add butter and pulse until mixture resembles coarse meal with some small (roughly pea-size) butter lumps. Add the egg yolk and pulse just until incorporated and dough begins to form large clumps.

4. Put dough in a tart pan and, with well-floured fingers, press into an even layer on the bottom and up the sides so it extends to the rim. Chill in the fridge for 30 minutes.

5. Lightly prick crust all over with a fork, then line with parchment paper and fill with pie weights. Bake the crust until golden around the edge, about 15 minutes. Carefully remove the paper and weights and bake until the shell is golden all over, about 5 more minutes. Cool shell completely in pan on a rack.

To Make the Tart

1. Preheat the oven at 350ºF (175ºC).

2. Using a pastry brush, brush the tart crust with the reserved egg white.

3. Pour in the blood orange curd and smoothen the top. Bake in the middle rack of the oven for about 30 to 40 minutes. You will see small bubbles on the surface towards the end of the 30 minutes. When you gently shake the pan, it should wobble a bit. Remove from the oven and cool on a rack for an hour. Cool in the fridge for another 3 hours to set before it is ready to assemble.

4. Make the whipped cream. In a large bowl, pour the cream. With a hand whisk, whisk the cream for a minute, until it has thickened slightly. Add the powdered sugar and vanilla extract and whip until it forms peaks. When you turn the whisk upside down, the whipped cream should form a peak, not too soft but slightly stiff. If it is too soft, whip the cream for 20 more seconds and check again.

5. On the chilled tart, you can pipe the whipped cream on the border of the tart or in the center of the tart. Arrange the candied blood orange slices around it or on top of it in concentric circles.

PRO TIPS

1. The curd can be made a couple of days ahead and stored in an airtight container in the fridge.

2. The blood orange simple syrup can be used in cocktails or mocktails or drizzled over ice cream. Or brush it on a blood orange cake to keep it moist before applying the frosting.

3. The dried hibiscus can be ordered from Amazon or your online retailer of choice.

Thandai Shortbread Cookies Dipped in White Chocolate
WITH PISTACHIOS AND ROSE PETALS

Makes 60

I love shortbread cookies. Something about them being so buttery and sweet. They are simple, with very few ingredients, and they take on different flavors quite easily, transforming the taste of a butter cookie.

What is Thandai? Thandai is an alcoholic milk-based drink, made by steeping a mix of nuts, spices, and dried rose petals in warm milk. It is then served cold, with the addition of bhang (which is an alcohol made from cannabis—very popular in the northern parts of India). You can also simply make a Thandai Masala (page 38), which comprises a ground up mixture of almonds, pistachios, cashews, poppy seeds, cardamom, nutmeg, cinnamon, cloves, black peppercorn, star anise, fennel seeds, dried rose petals, and saffron. The powder can be used in various ways, and one of my favorite ways is to incorporate them into baked goods. The baked goods take on the tastes and flavors of this iconic powder beautifully, leading to a delicately flavored baked treat.

These Thandai Shortbread Cookies are simply divine! I have been making them for a few years now, especially during the holiday time, and they are super popular among my family and friends. They have a beautiful depth of flavor from the Thandai Masala in the short-bread cookies, which makes it deliciously nutty, floral, fragrant, and earthy at the same time. The white chocolate and decoration of pistachios and rose petals makes them extra special for gifting. My favorite way to have them is dunking them in some masala chai.

INGREDIENTS

1¼ cups (2½ sticks; 284 g) unsalted butter, softened

1 cup (200 g) granulated sugar

1 tablespoon (13 g) vanilla extract

3 cups + 2 tablespoons (375 g) all-purpose flour

½ cup + 2 tablespoons (70 g) Thandai Masala (page 38)

½ teaspoon (3 g) table salt

2 cups (340 g) high-quality white chocolate morsels

2 teaspoons (10 g) coconut oil

¾ cup (85 g) finely chopped pistachios

4 tablespoons (1 g) powdered dried rose petal

continued ➡

METHOD

1. In the bowl of a stand mixer fitted with the paddle attachment, beat butter and sugar at medium speed until creamy, 3 to 4 minutes, stopping to scrape sides of bowl. Beat in vanilla.

2. In a medium bowl, whisk together flour, Thandai Masala, and salt. With the mixer on low speed, gradually add flour mixture to butter mixture, beating just until combined. Turn out dough, and divide in half. Shape into discs, and wrap in plastic wrap. Refrigerate for 2 hours.

3. Preheat the oven to 350°F (175°C). Line two baking sheets with parchment paper.

4. On a lightly floured surface, roll half of the dough to ¼ inch (5 mm) thick. Using a 2-inch (5 cm) fluted round cutter, cut dough, and place on prepared pans. Place the pans in the freezer for 10 minutes.

5. Bake on lower and middle racks of the oven until golden brown, about 16 minutes, rotating pans halfway through baking. Let cool on pans for 5 minutes. Remove from pans, and let cool completely on wire racks. Repeat with remaining dough.

6. In a small, microwave-safe bowl, combine white chocolate morsels and coconut oil. Microwave on high in 30-second intervals, stirring between each round, until the white chocolate is melted and smooth (about 2 minutes total). Have the pistachios and rose petals ready in two small bowls.

7. Line a baking sheet with parchment paper.

8. Dip one-third of each cookie in chocolate mixture, letting excess drip off. Sprinkle pistachio and dried rose petals onto the chocolate. Place on the prepared pan. Freeze until chocolate is set, about 5 minutes. If chocolate begins to thicken while dipping cookies, microwave for 10 to 15 seconds to rewarm. Store cookies in an airtight container for up to 2 weeks.

 PRO TIP Dough will keep refrigerated for up to 1 week or frozen for up to 1 month

Chikki (Cashew, Rose, and Cardamom Brittle)

Makes about 24 (2-inch or 5 cm) squares

Chikki is Indian brittle, made with jaggery or sugar, and mixed with nuts, sesame seeds, or even chickpeas or roasted chana. Growing up in Mumbai, we would make frequent trips to Lonavala, which was a hill station, around 2 hours away. It was our getaway staycation spot. Chikki comes from 19th-century Lonavala, where it was initially made with jaggery and peanuts. Chikki is often seen being sold by chikki street vendors who are always at the railway stations screaming, "Chikki! Chikki Walla!" Those words ring in my ears as I type this and it brings a smile to my face to remember the umpteen trips we took by rail and bought chikki from the chikki vendors. They now come in so many varieties, like peanuts, cashew nuts, almonds, roasted chana, sesame, and more. The jaggery one is more caramelly in taste and softer in texture than the normal brittle. Our trips to Lonavala would be incomplete without boxes of chikki for our home, and for our friends and families.

Mum made chikki during Diwali—the Festival of Lights—celebrated in the October-November timeframe (it varies depending on the Hindu calendar). She would make a variety of snacks and sweets to serve guests. During this festival season, it was tradition when we were growing up to visit each other's home to meet family and friends all dressed up in our traditional outfits adorned with jewelry. When people came to visit our home, Mum would put together small plates with different sweets and snacks, almost like your own mini meze platter. Chikki would be one of the sweets, along with churma na ladoo, penda or Gujarati sweets like mohanthal (made out of besan or chickpea flour, with sugar, nuts, and spices).

I love edible flowers in my desserts. It takes them to the next level and gives it a pretty look as well. So, I made my cashew nut brittle with cardamom and rose, as an ode to the wonderful memories of our frequent trips as a family of four to Lonavala, and the tons of chikki that we have consumed in our lifetime, and to all the times I helped Mum make chikki during the festive season. This brittle is very easy to make, but it does require a quick hand to ensure that all steps are followed fast enough to achieve the best results. This brittle, when added to an Indian flavored ice cream, turns out so delicious.

continued ➡

INGREDIENTS

1½ cups (210 g) cashew halves

1½ cups (300 g) granulated sugar

1 teaspoon (2 g) ground cardamom

½ teaspoon (3 g) Maldon flaky sea salt

2 teaspoons edible rose petals or 2 to 3 edible dried rose buds crushed by hand

METHOD

1. Line a baking sheet with parchment paper. Keep it ready along with a rolling pin and extra parchment paper near the saucepan. Keep all the ingredients ready to go—the process happens very quickly.

2. Toast the cashew nuts in a medium saucepan, over medium heat, mixing them occasionally to toast them ever so slightly, for 5 to 7 minutes to a light brown color. You want them lightly toasted.

3. In a medium heavy saucepan, cook sugar over moderate heat. Do not touch it for the first 2 minutes—you will start seeing the sugar melting on the outer rim. Start stirring with a rubber spatula occasionally, so as not to scorch the sugar at the bottom of the pan.

4. Let the sugar melt at medium heat for another 3 minutes. Do not take your eyes off the sugar, as you do not want to burn it. Reduce the heat to low and, stirring constantly, let the sugar melt for another minute until golden brown in color. Turn off the heat. Add the cashews, cardamom, and salt and stir quickly until coated well.

5. You have to be quick with the steps from now on. Immediately pour the mixture onto the parchment paper on the baking sheet and spread it as evenly as you can with the rubber spatula. It may be hard and that's why we require Step 6. Sprinkle half of the rose petals on top of the brittle.

6. Cover with the additional parchment paper and start rolling with the rolling pin to smoothen it out as much as possible. The brittle should be ½ inch (1¼ cm) in thickness. You can make it thinner if you want.

7. Gently remove the top parchment paper and sprinkle the remaining rose petals and gently press it into the brittle with the rubber spatula. Sprinkle with additional flakey sea salt if desired.

8. Let cool until you can touch it, not more than 10 to 15 minutes.

9. Cut into neat 2-inch (5 cm) squares.

10. Store in an airtight container, separated by parchment paper so as not to stick to each other. It keeps for 3 to 4 weeks.

PRO TIPS

1. The brittle is done very quickly so make sure you have all the ingredients and equipment ready to go before you start making it.

2. They make for fantastic gifts to give your loved ones. Layer each piece with parchment paper before placing it in plastic wrap or a container..

Masala Milk Popsicles

Makes 12 popsicles in a steel popsicle mold or 10 silicone popsicle molds

These Masala Milk Popsicles are an ode to all the cold masala milk we had as kids growing up in hot Mumbai summers, and I converted them to popsicles. The popsicles are really easy to make and would be an elegant dessert to serve when entertaining on summer nights. My kids really enjoy these pops be it summer or winter. Make them elegant by dipping in dulce chocolate feves, and drizzling it over them, along with a sprinkling of finely chopped nuts and dried rose petals, or even place edible gold leaf on top.

INGREDIENTS

1 cup (240 g) heavy cream

2 cups (480 g) whole milk

3 tablespoons (25 g) Masala Milk Masala (page 52)

2 tablespoons (40 g) light corn syrup

 cup (150 g) granulated sugar

¼ teaspoon saffron strands

2 teaspoons (9 g) vanilla extract

1 tablespoon (8 g) raw almond slivers

1 tablespoon (8 g) raw pistachio slivers

DULCE CHOCOLATE FEVES DIP (OPTIONAL)

1 pound (453 g) Valrhona Dulcey Chocolate Feve, or use white chocolate

4 teaspoons (18 g) coconut oil

GARNISH

Leftover 2 tablespoons melted Dulcey chocolate (optional)

4 pistachios, finely chopped

2 almonds, finely chopped

2 edible dried rose petals, crushed by hand

METHOD

1. In a heavy medium saucepan, on medium heat, add the heavy cream, whole milk, Masala Milk Masala, light corn syrup, granulated sugar, and saffron strands. Whisk the mixture to combine. Let the mixture come to a boil—it will take about 3 to 4 minutes. Let it boil for 30 seconds. Whisk occasionally to prevent milk from scorching at the bottom of the pan.

2. Reduce the heat to medium-low, and let it simmer for around 4 to 5 minutes. Remove from the heat. Add the vanilla extract and stir to combine. Cool the mixture completely for about 15 minutes.

3. Strain through a sieve and transfer the mixture to a pourable bowl, cover with plastic wrap and chill in the fridge for about an hour.

4. Remove the mixture from the fridge, and pour it into the steel molds leaving about ⅓-inch (1 cm) gap from the top. Sprinkle a few of the almond/pistachio slivers into each mold. Place the lid on, and put the popsicle sticks into the slots on the lid. If using the silicone molds, insert the popsicle sticks into molds first and then pour the mixture into the molds. Sprinkle a few of the almond/pistachio slivers into each mold.

5. Put it in the freezer for an hour.

continued ➙

6. After an hour, straighten the sticks. They tend to move around in the liquid and not stay straight.

7. Let the popsicles solidify for another 3 hours in the freezer.

8. Keep a baking sheet with parchment paper ready on the side. Run the steel popsicle mold base under warm water. For the silicone molds, the popsicles should come right out.

9. Remove the popsicles from the mold and place them on the parchment paper and into the freezer again for 30 minutes.

To Make the Dulce Chocolate Feves (Optional)

1. Melt the feves in a double boiler over medium-low heat along with the coconut oil.

2. Once three-quarters of the chocolate has melted, remove it off the heat, and keep stirring with a rubber spatula to melt the remaining feves. The temperature of the mixture will be above 100°F (38°C). Cool it down to about 90°F (32°C).

3. Pour it into a tall slim glass, wide enough to fit the popsicle.

4. Place a baking sheet with parchment paper on it ready.

5. Remove the popsicles from the freezer. Take a popsicle and dip it into the melted chocolate, coat it completely, remove it, and let the excess drip off completely. Place it carefully on the baking sheet. This process has to be quick.

6. Repeat the process for the remaining popsicles as quickly as possible or use two baking sheets. As soon as half of the popsicles are done, put them back in the freezer and start the next half.

7. As the chocolate level decreases, tilt the glass to coat the edge of the popsicle.

8. Put the popsicles back in the freezer for 30 minutes.

To Decorate the Popsicles

1. Meanwhile, if you used it above, add about 2 tablespoons of the melted dulcey chocolate in a ziplock bag fitted in a tall glass, so it is easy to pour the chocolate into the bag. As soon as you are ready to drizzle the popsicles, cut a tiny tip of the ziplock bag.

2. Drizzle the chocolate over the top of the popsicle on the top in a zig-zag fashion. Add a bit of chopped pistachios and almonds on top for decoration, along with a sprinkle of the crushed dried rose petals as well.

3. Place them back in the freezer for an hour. They are ready to eat.

4. They will keep in an airtight container in the freezer for a couple of weeks if they last that long.

PRO TIPS

1. The popsicles can be made a week in advance, which is optimal if you are planning to serve these popsicles as a dessert for entertaining guests.

2. Decorate it however you want. Skip the dipping in the dulcey chocolate feves, and go with a simple decoration of placing gold leaf on the popsicles to make them look elegant.

3. While the dipping part is completely optional, it gives a great contrasting taste to the popsicles.

4. Silicone popsicle molds are easier to pop out of the mold.

Gajjar No Halvo (Carrot Halva)

Serves 10–12

Gajjar No Halvo is a sweet Indian dessert from the Mughal period about 500 years ago. Halvo means "sweet" and it comes from the Arabic word, "Halwa." Gajjar No Halvo is usually a winter sweet because of the abundance of carrots in this season. Carrots have a lot of nutritional value and vitamin A, and, along with ghee, milk, spices and nuts, it makes it a healthy, sweet dessert that would help to keep the body warm in the cold winters of North and West India, and give strength and energy.

Gajjar No Halvo is very popular in our home. Mum made it very often and of course grating all the carrots was our job, which saved her a lot of time. It is a good activity to get the kids involved in. The Halvo comes together quite easily. It requires fewer ingredients, and it is more like a one-pot dish where you put everything in and let it slow cook for 45 minutes until all the milk has evaporated. It is smooth in texture and a darker orange in color. It is a popular dessert at Indian weddings and is served as a sweet dish in a Gujarati Thali, too.

I usually make this dessert once a year during Diwali. I make a large batch and freeze some for my father-in-law (the halvo freezes really well.), because he loves it. So, when we meet during the Christmas holidays, he gets a fine treat to enjoy. My son is a huge fan of this dessert and I love seeing his face light up with joy when he smells the aroma in the kitchen. The best kind of delight to look at!

INGREDIENTS

- 1.3 pounds (600 g) carrots, peeled, tops cut, and washed
- ½ cup (97 g) ghee
- 2 cups (480 g) whole milk
- ½ cup (120 g) heavy cream
- ¾ cup (150 g) granulated sugar
- 10 to 12 cardamom pods, ground to a powder in a coffee or spice grinder
- 1½ teaspoons (3.5 g) freshly grated nutmeg
- ½ teaspoon heaped saffron strands, crushed
- ⅓ cup (50 g) golden raisins
- 12 raw almonds, sliced thin
- 15 to 20 raw pistachios, sliced thin
- 10 raw cashews, sliced thin

GARNISH

- 10 raw almonds, sliced thin
- 15 raw pistachios, sliced thin
- ½ teaspoon ground cardamom

METHOD

1. Grate the carrots by hand, with a fine grater. You could use a food processor or use the thick side of a grater but I do prefer the texture of the halvo when the carrots are finely grated. This is the secret to making velvety, smooth, melt-in-your-mouth halvo! Grating carrots takes about 15 to 20 minutes but it is worth all the effort.

continued ➤

2. In a large, nonstick pot on medium heat, add the ghee. Add the grated carrots and sauté for 10 minutes. The water from the carrots will start to reduce. Add the milk, heavy cream, sugar, cardamom, nutmeg, and saffron, and stir gently. The milk should evaporate and reduce after 25 minutes. Add the raisins and the sliced almonds, pistachios, and cashews and mix gently.

3. The mixture will be bubbling, so keep stirring occasionally so as not to burn it from the bottom. Sauté for another 10 to 15 minutes. The mixture will reduce a lot to less than half from the original amount of carrots, all the milk will be evaporated, and the color of the halvo will be a dark orange. When it looks like a mushy clump, you know the halvo is done.

4. Remove onto a serving bowl and garnish with the almonds, pistachios and sprinkling of the cardamom. Serve warm.

5. You could also spread it on a jelly roll pan, and even it out with an offset spatula. Sprinkle the sliced pistachios, almonds, and sprinkling of cardamom. Cool it in the fridge for a couple of hours. Cut it into squares to serve. It can be served cold as well.

PRO TIPS

1. The Gajjar No Halvo can be made a few days or up to a week in advance. It needs to be warmed up either in the microwave or on the stove on low heat, and garnished with the pistachios, almonds, and ground cardamom before serving, as it is best eaten warm with a scoop of vanilla ice cream.

2. The Gajjar No Halvo can be frozen for up to 2 months. Thaw in the fridge for a day and then warm it in the microwave or on the stove on low heat before serving.

3. It can be served by making little mounds of the halvo with a mini Bundt cake pan, and garnished with chopped pistachios, almonds, and edible gold leaf.

Gajjar No Halvo (Carrot Halva) Ice Cream

Makes about 2 pints (1 L) or 1 loaf pan of ice cream

A few years ago, Natural Ice Cream in Mumbai had a carrot halva ice cream flavor. My trips to Mumbai to visit family and friends are never complete without a few trips to Natural Ice Cream. Growing up in Mumbai, Natural and Vadilal were really the only ice cream places. Sunday was the day when my mum and dad would treat us kids to ice cream after dinner, and Varun and I would always look forward to it. We would taste each other's ice creams and had real fun conversations too in the car ride to the ice cream parlor. They had standard flavors like chocolate and vanilla, fun fruity flavors, and nut-flavored ones like pistachio and badam pista. I always preferred the fruity flavors, but I also liked to try the exotic ones, such as jackfruit, one of my absolute favorites.

So, when I saw carrot halva ice cream on the menu, I had to get it. The ice cream left a lingering taste in my mouth that I just had to recreate. I set out to make my signature Gajjar No Halvo (page 257), which is well loved by all. My secret is to grate the carrots fine, which gives the halvo its velvety, melt-in-your-mouth texture. Grating the carrots fine is a bit of work, but it is so worth the effort! The wonderful aromatic flavors of gajjar no halvo from the sweetened carrots, fragrant cardamom, saffron, and nutmeg, with the bites of almonds, pistachios, and raisins takes the ice cream to the next level with these flavors. I adorn the ice cream with the Chikki (Cashew, Rose, and Cardamom Brittle, page 251), and I love the bits of crunch that I get with each bite. An ice cream maker is always worth the investment especially with the plethora of flavors that you can create from your own kitchen in no time and have an amazing ice cream experience!

INGREDIENTS

1½ cups (360 g) whole milk
2 tablespoons (16 g) milk powder
 cup (134 g) granulated sugar
2 tablespoons (41 g) corn syrup
1 teaspoon (2 g) ground cardamom
1 tablespoon (13 g) vanilla extract
1½ cups (300 g) heavy cream
½ cup Gajjar No Halvo (page 257)

GARNISH
1 cup Chikki (Cashew, Rose, and Cardamom Brittle, page 251), coarsely chopped

METHOD

To Make the Ice Cream Base

1. In a medium saucepan on medium heat, add the whole milk, milk powder, granulated sugar, corn syrup, and ground cardamom, and whisk continuously until the granulated sugar dissolves, and milk powder combines up to 3 to 4 minutes.

2. Turn off the stove and mix in the vanilla extract and heavy cream.

continued ➜

3. Let cool completely. Cover and refrigerate it for 6 hours.

4. Cool the ice cream container per the manufacturer's instructions, usually up to 24 hours in the freezer.

5. Pour all the contents of the ice cream base into the ice cream mixture. The Gajjar No Halvo should be at room temperature. Add the Gajjar No Halvo into the ice cream base, and whisk it to loosen the halvo. Churn the ice cream in the ice cream maker per the manufacturer's instructions.

6. Remove half of the ice cream into a loaf pan or any container with a spatula, and smoothen into a layer. Sprinkle half of the coarsely chopped brittle over the ice cream. Pour the remaining half of the ice cream into the container, spread it smooth with the spatula. Sprinkle the remaining coarsely chopped brittle on the top. Place the lid on the container, or if using a loaf pan, cover tightly with aluminum foil or you could use plastic wrap to stick to the ice cream to prevent freezer burn. Store in the freezer for 3 to 4 hours to set completely.

PRO TIP Ice cream can be made a week or two in advance and stored for up to 2 months.

Chai Masala Crème Brûlée
WITH CASHEW CARDAMOM SHORTBREAD

Serves 6; makes about 24 (2-inch or 5cm) round cookies

Crème Brûlée is a classic French dessert that is simple in ingredients, and easy to make. My first crème brûlée experience was a lavender crème brûlée that I had at the famous Michelin-star restaurant Girl and the Fig. I was blown away by the texture and the delicious floral taste of it! The texture was so smooth and pudding-like and it was gone within seconds! This was many years ago.

Here I have given this classic dessert an Indian twist with my Chai Masala (page 41). The Chai Masala gives the crème brûlée subtle spices that takes it to the next level. Paired with my Cashew Cardamom Shortbread, a recipe that I love, and some berries, it elevates this elegant dessert and makes it perfect for dinner parties. I whip it up quite often since it is so easy to prepare.

The shortbread recipe is more than what you require for the crème brûlée but I believe in making more to enjoy later. The richness from the ground up cashews and the floral sweet taste of cardamom make this shortbread irresistible!

INGREDIENTS

CASHEW CARDAMOM SHORTBREAD

⅓ cup (50 g) raw cashews

1 cup + 2 tablespoons (140 g) all-purpose flour

1 teaspoon (2 g) ground cardamom

½ teaspoon (3 g) salt

½ cup (1 stick; 113 g) unsalted butter, room temperature

½ cup (100 g) granulated sugar

1 teaspoon (4 g) vanilla extract

Additional flour for rolling

2 to 3 tablespoons finely chopped raw cashews

Edible gold leaf, for decoration, or edible gold paint and paint brush (kept aside specifically for painting on food)

CHAI MASALA CRÈME BRÛLÉE

2 cups (480 g) heavy cream

1 teaspoon (2 g) Chai Masala (page 41)

¼ teaspoon table salt

4 egg yolks, room temperature

⅓ cup (70 g) granulated sugar, plus 6 tablespoons (75 g) for the brûlée

1 teaspoon (4 g) vanilla extract

GARNISH

Fresh Raspberries or berries for garnish

Cashew Cardamom Shortbread

EQUIPMENT

Six 1-inch (2½ cm) deep, 4-inch (10 cm) round ramekins (4-ounce or 118 ml capacity each)

continued ➡

METHOD

To Make the Cashew Cardamom Shortbread

1. In a food processor, process the raw cashews using the stop-go motion on the processor to finely grind the cashews into a powder.

2. Combine the ground cashews, all-purpose flour, ground cardamom and salt in a small bowl and whisk to combine.

3. In the bowl of a stand mixer with a paddle attachment, add the butter and granulated sugar. Start on slow and mix the butter and sugar. Gradually increase the speed to high and mix for 2 to 3 minutes, until the mixture is off white and fluffy.

4. Add the vanilla extract and whisk to combine.

5. Add the flour mixture in two parts and mix to combine until you get a smooth dough. Do not overmix.

6. Wrap the dough in plastic wrap, form a disc, and keep it in the fridge for an hour for it to set.

7. Have two baking sheets ready with parchment paper.

8. On a clean surface, sprinkle extra flour. Remove the disc from the fridge and plastic wrap. Place it on the surface. Add extra flour on the top and gently roll it out into a flat dough about ¼ to ⅓ inch (½ cm to 1 cm) in thickness. Using a round cutter 2 inches (5 cm) wide, dip it in additional flour and start cutting out the rounds. Place them on the baking sheet with parchment paper. Dip the cutter in additional flour for every two to three cookies to prevent from sticking.

9. Once all the cookies are cut out, gather the remaining dough, and repeat the process of cutting out more cookies and place them on the baking sheet. Sprinkle a bit of the finely chopped cashews on each cookie and press gently to set.

10. Place the baking sheets in the freezer for 10 minutes.

11. Meanwhile preheat the oven to 350°F (175°C).

12. Remove the baking sheets from the freezer. Place them in the middle and bottom rack of the oven, and bake for 16 minutes. Switch the trays from middle to bottom and bottom to middle rack, half way through.

13. Let cool completely, about an hour.

14. Decorate with edible gold leaf or with a streak of edible gold paint. Store in an airtight container at room temperature for up to 2 weeks.

To Make the Chai Masala Crème Brûlée

1. In a medium pot or saucepan on medium to high heat, add the heavy cream, Chai Masala, and salt and whisk to combine. Bring to a simmer for about 3 to 4 minutes. Do not let it boil. Remove from the heat. Cover and steep for 8 to 10 minutes.

2. Meanwhile in a medium bowl, add the egg yolks and sugar and whisk vigorously in one direction for 2 to 3 minutes, until the yellow yolks take on a pale-yellow, ribbon-like smooth texture.

3. Add ¼ cup (60 ml) of the simmered cream mixture into the egg yolks to temper it, and whisk well to combine. Add this mixture into the cream mixture and whisk to combine and form the custard. Strain the custard via a fine sieve to remove any bits, and add it in a pourable cup or jar. Add the vanilla extract and whisk to combine.

4. Preheat the oven to 300°F (150°C). Boil about 2 cups (480 g) of water.

5. Place the ramekins on a baking sheet. Once the oven is preheated, place the baking sheet in the oven.

continued ➝

6. Slowly pour the custard mixture into the ramekins to the top.

7. Slowly pour the boiling water into the baking sheet, making sure to cover at least halfway up the ramekin. This water bath will ensure that the crème brûlée is baked evenly throughout.

8. Cook for 25 minutes. After 25 minutes, check to see if the custards are slightly jiggly. If they are, then they are done, and you can gently remove the baking sheet from the oven and remove the ramekins from the baking sheet. If they are very jiggly, almost runny, they are not done yet. Give it 2 to 3 more minutes and check again. Repeat until less jiggly and almost set.

9. Cool completely for 20 minutes.

10. Place the ramekins in the fridge to set for about 2 hours or more.

11. Just before serving, to brûlée the top, add about a tablespoon of granulated sugar on the top, spread it evenly, and then using a blow torch, torching the top evenly to form a nice caramelized top.

12. To serve, place a brûléed ramekin on a plate, add two Cashew Cardamom Shortbreads, and some raspberries to decorate.

PRO TIPS

1. The Cashew Cardamom Shortbread can be made a week in advance. Keep in the fridge and leave out for 20 minutes or so before rolling out.

2. Make a Thandai Crème Brûlée, using the Thandai Masala (page 38). It would flavor beautifully.

3. The crème brûlée can be kept in the fridge up to 2 days before serving, but do not torch the top until you are ready to serve.

4. If you do not have a blow torch, sprinkle sugar on each ramekin, set your oven on broil, and broil the ramekins (on a baking sheet) on the highest rack for about 2 minutes. Watch it carefully because you do not want to burn the sugar.

Mum's Famous Biscuits

Makes around 100 pressed biscuits

These biscuits have a story. These biscuits go back years, originating from Africa. They are called biscuits as the British call them—not cookies. My maternal grandma, or ba, moved to Uganda after she got married to my grandpa in 1948. She had to learn to cook by herself. She was 16 when she got married. She had an African helper, who also taught her how to bake. My ba had a small, white kitchen top oven. The helper taught Ba how to make these biscuits in her little oven, and Ba had these biscuits all the time in her kitchen for her family, and anyone who came over at odd hours (a very Indian thing to do.). All her daughters, including my mum, learned to make them too and it has become a tradition in all our homes to have these biscuits at all times. I love making them during Christmas and gifting them to friends in little packages.

My grandparents, along with their kids, migrated from Kampala, Uganda, to Mumbai in 1968 on a ship, because they were thrown out of the country. They had to take all their belongings with them. They brought their little white oven (a Siemens brand oven) with them as well. After Mum got married to my dad, the oven went to their house. That oven made all our birthday cakes, many tens of thousands of cookies, soufflés, and many other delicious bakes. That vintage white oven served my mum well. She used it up, until she had no energy to bake anymore in the early 2000s.

The biscuits were very popular among our family and friends. So, I had an idea. I told Mum that we should start selling them. I placed her advertisement in the papers and we started bulk producing the biscuits in the same little white oven. We made all these different flavors using the same base recipe, like cashews, cardamom, chocolate, and pistachios. and I would do the packaging for the bake sales. We got a ton of orders. That was Mum's first salary and it made her very happy. Those were fun and exciting times with my mum.

So, I am sharing one of my most favorite recipes with you! It is really simple to make, and a great one to share with your friends. My absolute favorite way to eat the biscuits is by dunking them in Masala Chai.

INGREDIENTS

4 cups minus 2 tablespoons (540 g)
   all-purpose flour

1 tablespoon + 1 teaspoon (7 g) ground ginger

1 teaspoon (4 g) baking soda

1 teaspoon (6 g) salt

1 cup (2 sticks; 226g) + 2 tablespoons (28g)
   unsalted butter, room temperature

1¼ cups (250 g) granulated sugar

1 tablespoon (13 g) vanilla extract

⅓ cup + 2 tablespoons (111 g) whole milk,
   room temperature

continued ➤

METHOD

1. In a medium bowl, combine the all-purpose flour, ground ginger, baking soda, and salt and whisk to combine.

2. In the bowl of a stand mixer, add the unsalted butter and granulated sugar, and, starting at a low speed, mix the ingredients. Increase the speed to high once you see the mixture combining and whisk on high speed for 2 to 3 minutes until the mixture is light and fluffy and off white in color.

3. Using a rubber spatula, clean the sides of the bowl to bring the butter mixture to the center. Add the vanilla extract and whisk on low to combine.

4. Slowly add the milk and whisk on low to combine.

5. Add the flour mixture in 2 batches, starting with the first batch, on low speed, to incorporate the mixture. Then add the second batch to incorporate it. Use a rubber spatula to get to any dry bits around the bowl and run the mixer again on low speed, then increase the speed to high to combine.

6. Let the dough rest for 15 minutes.

7. Preheat the oven to 400°F (200°C).

8. Follow the directions of the cookie press, make a log of a part of the biscuit dough, and pump the biscuits on a cookie baking sheet without parchment paper. The biscuits are buttery so they come right off after baking. See Pro Tip if you do not have a cookie press.

9. Bake the cookie sheet one at a time in the middle rack for about 14 minutes, until golden brown.

10. Remove it from the oven and cool for 10 minutes.

11. Repeat the process with the remaining biscuit dough and baking sheets.

12. Store in an airtight container for up to 2 weeks for maximum freshness.

PRO TIPS

1. You can switch the ginger spice with ground cardamom. Use 2 teaspoons freshly ground cardamom, since freshly ground cardamom is quite potent.

2. If you do not have a cookie press, you can roll out the biscuit dough into ¼- to ⅓-inch (½ to 1 cm) dough, using additional flour to roll out the dough. Use a fluted round cutter to cut out the biscuits and bake at the same temperature for around 12 minutes, until golden brown in color.

Mango Shrikhand Panna Cotta Tart
WITH A GINGERSNAP CRUST AND PISTACHIOS

Serves 8

Come mango season in the summer, Mum would use mangoes in every possible meal. We would have mangoes for breakfast, aam ras (thick, freshly pureed mango) with our thali lunch, mango milkshakes for an afternoon snack, and some form of mango at night, too. It would be a mango bonanza for two full months. Mangoes are only in season in the months of April and May in India, so they were a pricey commodity and quite expensive. My mum endlessly haggled with the mango wallas, as we would call them, to get a good price on the petis and petis (crates) of mangoes that she would buy to satisfy our mango cravings. The mango crates were filled with hay and the hay would drive my pet cat Sweety crazy! She would play with the hay and go absolutely nuts.

Shrikhand is a very popular Gujarati dessert, served at all get-togethers and weddings. It pairs especially well with puri. Shrikhand is typically made with Undhiyoo (page 184) and puri in the winter. I wanted to make an elevated dessert and that's how I came up with the idea to make Mango Shrikhand Panna Cotta Tart. It is essential to use full fat plain yogurt and whole milk for maximum creaminess and silky-smooth texture. The filling reminds of me of the hot Mumbai summers when Mum would make Mango Shrikhand for us, with the beautiful fragrance of floral cardamom and saffron, and the warm notes of nutmeg. Mango and ginger are a great pairing, so the base of the gingersnap crust pairs perfectly well with the silky smooth shrikhand filling in the tart. I love this tart and my kids love it too. It is so easy to make that it has become a regular in our home. It is definitely a showstopper for a party as well! I love how light it is in texture, and after a heavy Indian meal, this dessert feels quite light.

INGREDIENTS

GINGERSNAP CRUST
1 cup (250 g) crumbled gingersnap cookies
6 tablespoons (¾ stick; 85 g) unsalted butter, melted

MANGO SHRIKHAND PANNA COTTA FILLING
½ cup (130 g) mango puree
1 cup (220 g) full fat plain yogurt
1⅓ teaspoons (4 g) gelatin
1 cup (240 g) whole milk, room temperature
⅓ cup (75 g) granulated sugar
¼ teaspoon saffron
½ teaspoons (1 g) ground cardamom
Pinch of nutmeg

GARNISH
Fresh mango pieces
20 pistachios, very finely chopped
Crushed edible dried or fresh rose petals
Edible gold leaf

continued ➜

METHOD

To Make the Gingersnap Crust

1. In a food processor, add the gingersnap cookies. With the food processor on, bring the gingersnap cookies to a fine mixture.

2. Add the melted and cooled butter to the food processor and, while pulsing, bring the mixture together into a clump.

3. Preheat the oven to 350°F (175°C).

4. Empty the contents onto a 9-inch (23 cm) removable tart pan, and, with your fingers gently nudge the mixture to the edge of the pan, form an even layer throughout. Use a round measuring cup with a flat bottom to even out the layer throughout the bottom of the tart, and up against the edge of the tart to form a nice even layer.

5. Keep it in the fridge for 15 minutes.

6. Bake the crust in the oven for 10 minutes. Remove from the oven and let cool.

To Make the Mango Shrikhand Panna Cotta Filling

1. In a pourable bowl, add the mango puree and Greek yogurt. Whip it with a whisk until smooth.

2. Add the gelatin in a small bowl with ½ cup (120 g) of the milk and stir to mix. Set it aside for 3 to 4 minutes.

3. In a small saucepan on low heat, add the remaining milk, sugar, saffron, cardamom, and nutmeg and whisk to combine. Let it heat for 2 minutes until the sugar dissolves. Turn off the heat.

4. Add the gelatin-milk mixture into the warm milk mixture and stir to combine.

5. Add this mixture to the mango-yogurt mixture and whisk to make the mixture smooth. Gently pour the entire filling into the tart shell.

6. The panna cotta will take 4 hours and up to overnight to set and cool.

7. Garnish with mango pieces, finely chopped pistachios, rose petals, and edible gold on the top in whatever fashion that you desire, or garnish each slice before serving.

PRO TIPS

1. The panna cotta tart can be made the night before the day of serving. The crust will get soggy if left for too long.

2. You can garnish simply with finely chopped pistachios and almonds. You can even garnish it with whipped cream.

Fennel Pot de Crème
WITH SAFFRON, CARDAMOM, AND ROSE POACHED PEACHES

Makes six 4-ounce ramekins

Pot de crème is a classic French custard, which literally means "pot of cream," that dates back to the 17th century. It is a creamy custard that is set beautifully and delicately, and it literally melts in your mouth. The texture is smooth. Because of its richness, a little bit goes a long way.

I have created an Indian fusion version of this very famous French dessert. I steep the milk and heavy cream mixture with fennel seeds. The fennel seeds impart a delicate licorice flavor to the pot de crème that is sublime. Fennel seeds are a very popular spice in India. It is an excellent digestive after any meal, and a great mouth freshener as well. Fennel seeds help regulate constipation, indigestion, IBS, and more.

The dessert is decorated with poached peaches. Come summer, I go crazy for the seasonal fruits, especially stone fruits. My favorite is probably the peach. The peaches are utterly sweet, juicy, and slightly sour, making them a perfect snack. We go peach picking once in the season, as we have wonderful farms in the northeast, and pick up tons of peaches, which are used for jamming, shrubs, crisps, bars, lemonade, and more. Poached peaches themselves make an elegant dessert, served with a scoop of vanilla bean ice cream or simply a dollop of whipped cream. These peaches are poached in a mixture of saffron, cardamom, and rose water, making them delicate, elegant, and fragrant as well. Topped with a dollop of whipped cream and a garnish of pistachios and rose petals, this is the perfect Indian fusion dessert to serve your guests.

INGREDIENTS

FENNEL POT DE CRÈME

1 cup (240 g) heavy cream

1¼ cups (300 g) whole milk

6 tablespoons (78 g) granulated sugar

1 tablespoon (8 g) fennel seeds

4 egg yolks

Pinch of sea salt

2 teaspoons vanilla bean paste

SAFFRON, CARDAMOM, AND
ROSE POACHED PEACHES

1 cup (240 g) water

½ cup (100 g) granulated sugar

½ teaspoon saffron threads

Cardamom pods from 4 to 5 cardamoms

1 tablespoon (10 g) rose water

3 small, firm, ripe yellow peaches, halved
  lengthwise and pitted

WHIPPED CREAM

½ cup (120 g) heavy cream

2 tablespoons powdered sugar

½ teaspoon (2 g) vanilla extract

GARNISH

1 tablespoon coarsely chopped pistachios

1 to 2 dried edible rose buds

continued ➡

METHOD

To Make the Fennel Pot de Crème

1. Preheat the oven to 300°F (150°C). Place six ramekins on a baking sheet.

2. In a small saucepan on medium to low heat, add the heavy cream, whole milk and 3 tablespoons of granulated sugar with the fennel seeds. Heat the mixture but do not boil. It should take 2 to 3 minutes. Once heated, let the mixture steep with the heat switched off for 15 minutes.

3. In a medium bowl, add the egg yolks, remaining sugar, and salt, and whisk vigorously, until fluffy, frothy, and pale for about 2 minutes. Whisk in one direction continuously. It is a good arm workout.

4. Add the warm milk-cream mixture slowly into the egg mixture and keep whisking to combine. This process is called tempering to prevent the eggs from being cooked by bringing the eggs to the same temperature as the milk mixture.

5. Warm up the entire mixture on the stove for 2 minutes. Do not bring it a boil.

6. Strain the mixture through a fine sieve to remove any frothy bits or solids. The mixture should be smooth. Add the vanilla bean paste and whisk to combine. Equally distribute the mixture into the 6 ramekins. If there are frothy bubbles on the top, burst them with a toothpick. You want a smooth surface on each ramekin.

7. Boil at least 2 cups (480 g) of water to create a hot water bath for the baking sheet. Place the baking sheet with the ramekins in the preheated oven. Carefully pour the boiling water into the baking sheet, making sure to cover at least halfway up the ramekins. Bake for 40 minutes or until the tops are slightly jiggly when shaken.

8. Remove from the oven, and let sit on the baking sheet for 30 minutes. Remove ramekins from the tray and put it in the refrigerator to set for at least 3 to 4 hours.

To Make the Saffron, Cardamom, and Rose Poached Peaches

1. In a medium saucepan over medium-high heat, bring the water, granulated sugar, saffron, cardamom, and rose water to a boil; let boil for 1 minute. Set peaches flat in syrup. Reduce the heat to medium, and cook for 3 minutes. Gently turn the fruit over using a big spoon. Cook for 3 more minutes. Transfer to a plate and let them chill in the fridge for about 30 minutes up to a day.

2. With the remaining poaching liquid, heat it over medium-high heat and reduce it to about less than a cup (240 ml), for a total of 4 to 5 minutes. Transfer syrup to a jar, and store in the fridge for up to 2 weeks.

3. Before serving, gently remove the skin off the poached peaches.

To Make the Whipped Cream

In a medium bowl, add the heavy cream, powdered sugar, and vanilla extract. Using a balloon whisk, continuously whisk the mixture in one direction. It will start to thicken in a minute. Keep whisking and the whipped cream will have a good texture in a total of 2 minutes. You do not want to over-whip, or else the whipped cream will be too stiff. Keep it in the fridge until ready to serve.

To Assemble

Just before serving, top each pot de crème with a poached peach and drizzle 1 teaspoon of syrup. Add a tablespoon of the whipped cream on top. Garnish with chopped pistachios and dried rose petals.

 PRO TIP You can make the Fennel Pot de Crème and the poached peaches a day in advance..

Plum Kalakand Cake

Serves 10 to 12

Kalakand is a very delicious, fudgy Indian mithai/dessert made with sweetened milk solids or mawa and paneer, along with cardamom, saffron, and nuts. It is cut into squares, adorned with silver foil, and is available at the mithai shops or sweet shops in India. Mawa is made by slow cooking the milk for hours to remove all the moisture from the milk to form the milk solids, and that is used especially in North Indian mithais.

I use ricotta cheese, which is very similar to fresh paneer, along with the milk powder and condensed milk, to make a loose kalakand mixture, made fragrant with the freshly ground cardamom and nutmeg. The mixture in the cake batter, with whole pistachios and slivered almonds, adorned with beautiful in-season plum slices on the top, forms a wonderful teacake. The cake reminds me of mithaiwallas in India, with that soft texture, and the flavors from the kalakand in this cake. Since the cake is rich with condensed milk and ricotta cheese—a little bit goes a long way. The rose whipped cream adds a wonderful floral touch to the cake and makes for a lovely afternoon teatime treat.

INGREDIENTS

KALAKAND

¼ cup (37 g) milk powder

1¼ cups (310 g) ricotta cheese

1 cup (306 g) condensed milk

1½ teaspoons (3 g) freshly ground cardamom

¾ teaspoon (2 g) freshly grated nutmeg

CAKE BATTER

1½ cups (180 g) all-purpose flour

1 tablespoon (10 g) baking powder

1 teaspoon (6 g) table salt

½ cup (1 stick; 113 g) unsalted butter, room temperature

¾ cup (150 g) granulated sugar

2 eggs

2 teaspoons (8 g) vanilla extract

¼ cup (36 g) whole pistachios

¼ cup (25 g) slivered almonds

3 to 4 slightly crisp medium-sized plums, halved, pitted, and thinly sliced (about ¼ inch, 5 mm thick)

3 to 4 tablespoons (47 to 62 g) turbinado sugar

ROSE WHIPPED CREAM (OPTIONAL)

1½ cups (360 g) cold heavy whipping cream

½ cup (50 g) confectioners' sugar

1 teaspoon (4 g) vanilla extract

1 teaspoon rose water

GARNISH

2 to 3 tablespoons slivered pistachios

2 plums, cut into half and thinly sliced (about ¼ inch, 5 mm thick)

PRO TIPS

1. You can use pluots or cherries too instead of plums. I love the color and the sweet and tart flavor of plums in this cake.

2. The cake can be cut and stored in an airtight container for up to 2 days. It is a tea cake, so it is best served with tea or coffee.

continued ➤

METHOD

To Make the Kalakand

1. In a medium saucepan on medium to slightly high heat, add all the dairy ingredients. Using a rubber spatula, start stirring the mixture to combine. It will take 1 to 2 minutes for it to combine together.

2. Keep stirring with the rubber spatula for a total of 13 minutes. You have to keep stirring the mixture. It will simmer, then start to boil, then bubble up and finally subside. The moisture from the mixture will evaporate leaving a somewhat semi-solid mixture after a total of 13 minutes.

3. Remove from the heat. Add the cardamom and nutmeg and stir well to combine. Cool the mixture completely for half an hour.

4. You can remove it on a plate, and flatten it out to cool faster.

To Make the Cake

1. Preheat the oven to 350°F (175°C).

2. Grease a 9-inch (23 cm) springform pan with a removable bottom with cooking spray or you can apply butter all over the insides, and then sprinkle flour to coat the butter all over.

3. In a medium bowl, add the all-purpose flour, baking powder, and salt and whisk to combine.

4. In the bowl of a stand mixer with a paddle attachment, add the butter and granulated sugar and whisk at high speed for 2 to 3 minutes until pale and fluffy.

5. Using a rubber spatula, scrap the sides of the bowl to gather the contents in the center. Add the cooled kalakand mixture into the bowl and whisk to combine.

6. Slowly add one egg at a time. Whisk to combine. Add the vanilla extract and whisk to combine again.

7. Slowly add the flour mixture and, on slow speed, let the mixture combine. Do not overmix.

8. Fold in the pistachios and almonds. Add the cake batter to the springform pan. Using a small offset spatula, level out the cake batter.

9. Layer the thinly sliced plums in a pretty pattern on top of the cake. Sprinkle the top with turbinado sugar.

10. Bake the cake for 1 hour 15 minutes. Poke a knife or a toothpick in the middle to see if the cake is baked all the way through. If it comes out clean, the cake is ready. If not, leave it for 2 to 3 more minutes and check again. Turn off the oven and let it sit in the oven for 10 minutes.

11. Remove the cake and cool completely.

To Make the Rose Whipped Cream

1. In a medium to large bowl, add all the ingredients for the whipped cream, and, using a balloon whisk, whisk the cream all in one direction continuously with rapid movements for 2 minutes. It is an arm workout. After 2 minutes, if you see soft peaks on the whisk, you are done. If the mixture is still loose, whisk again for another minute with rapid movements, until you get soft peaks. A stand mixer can be used, but by using a balloon whisk, the texture of the whipped cream can be controlled to ensure that the whipped cream does not get over whipped.

2. Place it in a small serving bowl if you desire.

To Serve

1. Garnish the cake with slivered pistachios.

2. Serve a slice with some of the Rose Whipped Cream, if using, and plum slices.

Chocolate Chip and Toasted Almond Cookies

Makes about 28 to 30 (¼-cup scoop cookie dough ball) cookies; makes about 56 to 60 (2-tablespoon scoop cookie dough ball) small cookies

Every household requires a good chocolate chip cookie recipe. Who does not enjoy a warm, ooey-gooey Chocolate Chip and Toasted Almond Cookie right out of the oven that just melts in your mouth, with the slightly crisp edges and softness in the center, with the melty chocolate and bits of toasted almond pieces. I make these cookies very often for my family. I substitute the almonds for walnuts sometimes, sometimes plain toffee. It just depends on their mood. I usually freeze the cookie dough scoops (refer to Pro Tips), and that way we can enjoy cookies whenever we want to, because there is nothing like a warm fuzzy cookie to make you feel better. My kids have no patience to wait for the cookie to cool down. It is barely out of the oven and the cookies are already on their plates and silence fills the air for the next 2 minutes. Their fingers get smeared with the melty chocolate, which is the best part because you get to lick it all off! I make the smaller version of these cookies for the Chocolate and Almond Praline Ice Cream Sandwiches (page 282), which turn out sooo good! Try this recipe, because it is sure to be a hit!

INGREDIENTS

2 cups (240 g) all-purpose flour

1 cups (225 g) bread flour

2 teaspoons (10 g) baking soda

1 teaspoon (4 g) baking powder

2 teaspoons (12 g) table salt

2 teaspoons (5 g) ground cinnamon

1¼ cups (2½ sticks; 282 g) unsalted butter, room temperature

1 cup (200 g) packed light brown sugar

1¼ cups (250 g) granulated sugar

2 eggs, room temperature

1 tablespoon (13 g) vanilla extract

1 teaspoon (4 g) almond extract

8 ounces (227 g) bittersweet chocolate chunks or bittersweet chocolate chips (70% cocoa content)

8 ounces (227 g) semi-sweet chocolate chunks or semi-sweet chocolate chips (60% cocoa content)

1 cup (110 g) coarse (leaning towards fine) chopped toasted almonds

Flakey sea salt

METHOD

1. In a medium bowl combine the dry ingredients together, and whisk to combine.

2. In the bowl of a stand mixer with a paddle attachment, add the butter, brown sugar, and granulated sugar. Start the mixer on low speed, and gradually increase it to maximum speed, and let it mix for 3 minutes, until off-white and fluffy. Using a rubber spatula, clean the sides of the bowl and gather the mixture in the middle.

3. Add eggs one at a time and mix to combine.

4. Add the vanilla extract and almond extract and whisk to combine.

5. Add the flour mixture in two parts at slow speed so as not to splatter the flour everywhere. Mix until just combined.

continued ➝

6. Add the chocolate chunks or chocolate chips and the chopped toasted almonds and mix to combine, such that they are uniform in the cookie dough batter.

7. Using plastic wrap, add half the dough into the plastic wrap, seal it well to form a nice round dough ball.

8. Repeat Step 7 for the other half of the cookie dough.

9. Refrigerate for at least 3 hours, up to 24 hours.

10. Preheat the oven at 350°F (175°C).

11. Let the dough sit out for 10 minutes. Lay a baking sheet with parchment paper. Using a ¼-cup ice cream scooper, scoop out a ball, press it down to even out the scoop, and remove it on the parchment paper. Lay up to 6 cookie dough balls on each cookie sheet, placed at least 3 inches (7 cm) apart.

12. Place it in the middle rack of the oven for about 16 minutes in total. At about the 14-minute mark, remove the baking pan, and bang it on the counter 3 to 4 times for the cookies to spread slightly and settle. Place it back in the oven for 2 more minutes.

13. Once out of the oven, you can use a spatula to shape the cookie into a round shape by nudging it all around. Add a sprinkle of flakey sea salt on each cookie and place it on a wire rack to cool completely. Repeat for the other cookies.

PRO TIPS

1. If you do not want to bake off all the cookies at once, you can scoop out the cookies using the ¼-cup ice cream scoop, place it on the baking sheet with parchment paper, close to each other, and then place the sheet in the freezer for an hour. Remove the scoops and put them in a large ziplock bag. Store it in the freezer to have cookies at your disposal whenever you want.

2. You can place two baking sheets at a time in the oven, but it might require an additional minute or two of baking time. Keep checking on your cookies after 14 minutes to see if they are slightly brown on the edges and remove them accordingly.

3. Make smaller cookies by using a 2-tablespoon ice cream scooper. This works great for the Chocolate and Almond Praline Ice Cream Sandwiches (page 282).

Chocolate and Almond Praline Ice Cream Sandwiches

Makes about 14 to 15 small ice cream sandwiches

As kids, my brother and I would always look forward to Sundays. Sundays were special. It was ICE CREAM DAY! We had a couple of ice cream joints that we would go to as a family after dinner. Dad would take us all for a drive first, and then we would stop at one of the ice cream shops, get our favorite flavors, and devour our once-a-week ice cream with big smiles. One of those favorite places was called Naturals Ice Cream. They had a flavor called Choco Almond. Mum would also buy a tubful of the Choco Almond so we could enjoy it during the week as well. We did get a second ice cream scoop during the week, if she was in a good mood. It had toasty bites of almonds in it. India is a huge producer of almonds and is known for exporting the almonds as well. The flavor of those almonds are different and very tasty.

Inspired by our favorite flavor, I made a Chocolate and Almond Praline version of our childhood favorite, with almond praline pieces in it. I love a good crunch in ice creams and that is where my inspiration came from. The ice cream is decadent, and perhaps one of my favorite chocolate ice creams ever. Ice cream sandwiches are more fun to eat, especially when they are small and a manageable size like these ice cream sandwiches here. You can dunk them in dark chocolate to make them EXTRA! I usually make the Chocolate and Toasted Almond Cookies (page 279) and half of the cookie dough is used for making these ice cream sandwiches and half of the cookie dough is used for . . . eating the cookies! They are an instant hit with my clan and am sure they will be with your family too.

INGREDIENTS

ALMOND PRALINE
¾ cup (150 g) granulated sugar
¾ cup (90 g) toasted sliced almonds

CHOCOLATE AND ALMOND PRALINE ICE CREAM
1½ cups (300 g) whole milk
1½ cups (300 g) heavy cream
3 tablespoons (36 g) dark cocoa powder
¾ cup (150 g) granulated sugar
5 large egg yolks

2 teaspoons (8 g) vanilla extract
  or vanilla bean paste
¾ cup (125 g) semi-sweet chocolate chips
  (60% cocoa content)
¼ cup (60 g) whole milk
¾ teaspoon cayenne pepper

½ recipe Chocolate Chip and Toasted Almond
  Cookie Dough (page 279)

continued ➞

METHOD

To Make the Almond Praline

1. Line a quarter baking sheet with parchment paper.

2. In a small saucepan, cook sugar over moderate heat until melted, about 3 minutes. Let the sugar cook, without stirring, swirling the pan occasionally, just until a golden caramel color. Add almonds, stirring until coated well. This process happens very quickly, within a minute. Immediately pour mixture onto the baking sheet and, using a rubber spatula, spread it thin. Cool completely, about 30 minutes. Chop the praline into pieces with a sharp knife. Store in an airtight container until ready to use.

To Make the Chocolate and Almond Praline Ice Cream

1. Place a strainer over a medium bowl. Have a large bowl with ice water ready next to it.

2. In a medium saucepan on medium heat, add the whole milk, heavy cream, cocoa powder, and ½ cup (100 g) granulated sugar, and stir to combine. Stir until the temperature of the milk reaches about 175°F (80°C).

3. Meanwhile, whisk the egg yolks and remaining ¼ cup (50 g) sugar in a medium bowl until combined and pale yellow—whisk it vigorously. The mixture should be ribbon-like. Whisk half the warm milk mixture into the beaten yolks, ½ cup (120 ml) at a time, until combined.

4. Whisk the milk-yolk mixture into the warm milk in the saucepan; set the pan over medium heat and cook, stirring constantly with a wooden spoon, until steam appears, foam subsides, and the mixture is slightly thickened or the temperature is up to 180 to 185°F (82 to 85°C). (Do not boil the mixture or the eggs will curdle.)

5. Immediately strain the custard into the medium bowl, and then set it in the ice bath; cool the custard to room temperature, stirring it occasionally to help it cool. Once cooled, add the vanilla extract and stir.

6. Meanwhile, while the custard is cooling, in a small double boiler, melt the chocolate chips, whole milk, and cayenne pepper, until it is a smooth mixture. Slowly add the chocolate mixture into the custard and whisk to combine, until well incorporated.

7. Cover and refrigerate for at least 6 hours or up to 24 hours.

8. Line an 8-by-13-inch (20-by-33 cm) baking pan with parchment paper. You can spray it with cooking spray, and then line the paper so it adheres to the pan properly.

9. Once, the custard is ready, pour the custard into the ice cream machine and churn, following the manufacturer's instructions, until the mixture resembles soft-serve ice cream, about 25 minutes. Transfer half the ice cream into the prepared pan and spread it with a small offset spatula. Sprinkle the almond praline on top of the ice cream. Then add the remaining ice cream on the top and again flatten the entire surface with the small offset spatula. Press plastic wrap on the surface, and freeze the ice cream until firm, at least 4 hours.

To Bake the Sandwich Cookies

1. Preheat the oven to 350°F (175°C).

2. Remove the dough from the fridge. Let sit for 10 minutes. On two baking sheets with parchment paper, take a 2-tablespoon ice cream scoop of packed dough, and remove it onto the baking sheet. Add about 8 to 10 per baking sheet. Keep a 2-inch (5 cm) gap between the cookies.

3. Place them into the oven in the bottom and middle rack, and bake for about 12 to 13 minutes. Rotate the pans and switch racks halfway through to bake the cookies evenly. You do not want them baked all the way. Remove and bang them on the surface of the counter two to three times to flatten them slightly. Using a spatula, nudge the cookie from all sides to round them. Cool for 10 minutes on the baking sheets. Transfer them onto a wire rack and cool completely for about 30 minutes.

4. Repeat the process for the remaining cookie dough. You will get about 28 to 30 small cookies.

5. Store them in an airtight container until the ice cream is set and you are ready to fill the cookies.

6. Keep a baking sheet with parchment paper on the side ready to keep the assembled ice cream sandwiches.

7. Remove the set ice cream from the freezer. Use an offset spatula to loosen the ice cream from the edges between the paper and the baking sheet. Using the parchment paper as flaps, remove the ice cream slab from the tray, and set it on a board. Using a 2¼-inch (5½ cm) round cutter, cut off a round of ice cream. Invert half the cookies so that the flat side is facing upwards. Using a small offset spatula, gently remove the ice cream round from the slab and place it on the flat surface of the cookie. Gently place a same size cookie on the top of the ice cream and press it gently to adhere to the ice cream. Place the assembled ice cream sandwich on the baking sheet on the side.

8. Repeat for the other ice cream rounds. This process has to be quick. If the ice cream starts to melt, place the ice cream slab back into the baking sheet and into the freezer for an hour and make the ice cream sandwiches once the ice cream is set again. Place the assembled ice cream sandwiches in the freezer again for an hour to set.

9. You will have some leftover ice cream, which you can put in an airtight container, or a deli container. Store it in the freezer to enjoy later.

PRO TIPS

1. For the cookies to keep their round shape, as soon as you remove them from the oven, shape them in a round shape with a spatula, by nudging the edges to make a round shape, so that all the cookies are as even as possible. You can also use a large round cookie cutter and scoot the cookie around to coax the perfect round shape.

2. Make mini sandwiches by making mini cookies with a 1-tablespoon ice cream scoop and the same size of the ice cream round as well.

3. Once the ice creams sandwiches are set, you can store them in an airtight container and place them in the freezer to preserve their freshness. It will keep in the freezer for 2 weeks (if it even lasts that long!).

Plum, Cardamom, and Chaat Masala Granita

Serves 8

Granita reminds me of golas in Mumbai. Gola is essentially shaved ice on a stick, loaded with overly sweetened artificial syrup, and served in a glass that has more syrup to slurp on. It is dangerously delicious and addictive and not good for you. But as kids we loved it. My favorite flavor was Kala Khatta, which is made with java plums, rock salt, and chaat masala. The syrup is a deep purple from an artificial color they add to it. It is irresistible, I must say. Gola is served by street vendors on the roadside and their carts are always flocked with people. They have a machine that shaves the ice really quickly, and it reminds me of shaved ice in Hawaii.

Java plums are not available in California, or at least I have never seen them. I used plums to make a more clean, organic version of this very popular street food and added ground cardamom and chaat masala to it, which gives it the slight salty and savory taste, along with the floral notes from the ground cardamom and vanilla extract. This granita is addictive and is perfect in the summer months when it is much needed to cool down from the heat and the humidity. Granitas are the Italian version of the Indian gola, but made with fruit pulp rather than artificial flavors. I love their simplicity, and how easy it is to whip them up!

INGREDIENTS

2 pounds plums, pitted, chopped into 1-inch (2½ cm) pieces
1 cup (200 g) granulated sugar
2 cups (480 g) water
2 tablespoons (30 g) lemon juice
1 teaspoon (2 g) chaat masala
1 teaspoon (2 g) ground cardamom
1 teaspoon vanilla extract

GARNISH
Mint sprigs
Plum slices

METHOD

1. In a medium saucepan on medium heat, combine plums, sugar, 1 cup (240 g) of the water, lemon juice, chaat masala, and cardamom and stir to combine. Cover with a lid partially and let it simmer for 15 minutes in all. Stir occasionally. After 15 minutes, remove from the heat. Cover the saucepan, and let cool completely.

2. Puree the entire mixture and strain through a sieve over a medium bowl. Add the remaining 1 cup (240 g) of water and vanilla extract and whisk to combine.

3. Pour the mixture into a 9-by-13-inch (20-by-33 cm) baking pan, and put it into the freezer for 2 hours.

4. Using a fork, scrape the entire surface, and continue scraping through the mixture to loosen it up into ice particles.

5. Repeat the scraping process three times, every 45 minutes, for a total of 2 hours 15 minutes.

6. The granita is ready to eat. Serve in glasses with a sprig of mint for garnish and some plum slices if you wish.

PRO TIP The granita will keep in the freezer, in an airtight container, for up to 2 weeks.

Mini Maple Sandwich Cookies
WITH PEAR AND SPICE BUTTERCREAM

Makes about 28 to 30 sandwich cookies

I developed this recipe a few years ago for my blog. I love mini desserts, mini cookies, mini anything! They are a joy to eat and especially make for a great party dessert. When I was developing jam recipes for Jam Lab, I loved showcasing how to use the jams beyond toast. One of my favorite ways to use jams is in buttercream. A plain vanilla buttercream can be elevated by using jam to flavor it and give it a bit of oomph!

These Mini Maple Sandwich Cookies are made with pure maple syrup, and warm fall spices like nutmeg and cinnamon. The buttercream filling has Pear and Chai Masala Jam (page 35), and provides a wonderfully subtle sweetness and flavor to the buttercream, elevating this cookie to the next level! These cookies have always been a hit with family and friends, and are a must bake in the fall, especially with its cute shape.

INGREDIENTS

MAPLE COOKIES

½ cup (1 stick; 113 g) unsalted butter, softened

¼ cup (50 g) packed light brown sugar

¼ cup (80 g) good quality maple syrup

1 large egg yolk

1¼ cups (150 g) all-purpose flour

½ cup (48 g) almond flour

½ teaspoon (1 g) freshly ground nutmeg

½ teaspoon (1.3 g) ground cinnamon

½ teaspoon (3 g) salt

BUTTERCREAM FILLING

4 tablespoons (½ stick; 56 g) unsalted butter, softened

¼ teaspoons (1.5 g) salt

1 cup (140 g) powdered sugar or more for consistency

1 tablespoon heaped Pear and Chai Masala Jam (page 35)

1 teaspoon (4 g) vanilla extract

EQUIPMENT

Maple Leaf Cookie Cutter

Pastry bag

Quarter-inch round piping tip

METHOD

1. In the bowl of a stand mixer, cream together butter and brown sugar until light and fluffy for 2 to 3 minutes. Add the maple syrup and egg yolk until mixture is combined well.

2. Sift together the flours, nutmeg, cinnamon, and salt in a medium bowl. Whisk to combine.

3. Slowly add the flour mixture into the stand mixer at low speed, and fold in thoroughly. Do not over mix. Chill dough, wrapped in plastic wrap, until firm, about 2 hours.

4. Preheat the oven to 350°F (175°C).

5. Divide the dough in half and keep one half chilled. Lightly flour the other half on a lightly floured surface gently pound with a rolling pin to soften. Roll out the dough to about ⅛-inch-

continued ➤

thick (⅓ cm) and with a floured maple leaf cookie cutter cut out cookies, chilling scraps. Arrange cookies on a baking sheet lined with parchment paper.

6. Repeat Step 5 with the remaining half of the dough and stamp out all the cookies and place them on the baking sheet. Collect all the scraps, form into a ball, wrap in the plastic wrap and chill them in the fridge for 15 minutes.

7. Remove the dough from the fridge, roll it out on a floured surface, and stamp out more cookies with the maple leaf cookie cutter. Arrange cookies on a baking sheet lined with parchment paper.

8. Bake cookies in the middle of the oven until edges are golden, about 13 minutes, and transfer to a wire rack to cool.

To Make the Buttercream Filling

While the cookies are resting, in a medium to large bowl, add the butter, salt, and powdered sugar, beating with a hand mixer on low until incorporated. Add the jam and vanilla extract and mix on high for 1 minute. Put the icing in a ziplock bag, with a ¼-inch (½ cm) round tip.

To Assemble

1. Apply the icing on the back of one cookie, cover with another cookie to make the sandwich cookies.

2. They can be kept at room temperature for up to 3 days for maximum freshness.

PRO TIPS

1. Substitute the almond flour with all-purpose flour.

2. Make the cookies on one day and add the buttercream the next day for assembly.

Peacock Macarons

WITH APRICOT SAFFRON JAM BUTTERCREAM AND CHOPPED PISTACHIOS

Makes about 28 macarons

A peacock has a deep significance for the Indian culture. A peacock symbolizes harmony, peace, beauty, good luck and joy. The peacock has been a part of India mythology for generations. Lord Krishna wore a peacock feather on his crown. Lakshmi, who is the goddess of wealth and purity, is also symbolized by the peacock. Peacock is the national bird of India. The first rains are also synonymous with a dancing peacock. The sight of this majestic bird spreading his feathers majestically and dancing away is the most magical sight you will ever see. It brings shivers down my spine. The times when I have seen a peacock spread its feathers is a sight I will never forget.

Macarons are one of those iconic French desserts that I have been making for a very long time! Macarons are delicate, fragile, beautiful and one of those desserts that, when mastered, you feel ecstatic to have achieved it! They are difficult and do take time to get the hang of. Hence, I have given you all the tips and tricks, measurements, and proper instructions to get them right. It took me several tries to really perfect them every single time. These Peacock Macarons are not only very pretty to look at, but the delicately flavored Apricot and Saffron Jam Buttercream, along with the bite from the chopped pistachios, really takes these macarons to next level fusion. You can taste the floral saffron, along with the fruity apricots and bite from the nuts. Make them to impress your family and friends, or give them as gifts for a special occasion.

INGREDIENTS

MACARON SHELL

7 ounces (198 g) confectioners' sugar

4 ounces (113 g) almond flour

3 large or 4 medium (4 ounces) egg whites, room temperature

Pinch of cream of tartar

3.5 ounces (100 g) granulated sugar

1 teaspoon vanilla extract

4 to 5 drops Americolor Blue Sheen food gel color (more to get a deeper blue)

4 to 5 drops Americolor Navy Blue food gel color (more to get a deeper blue)

Smidge of Americolor Black food gel color (to get the dark blue color)

EQUIPMENT

16-inch (40 cm) pastry bag

⅓ inch (1 cm) round tip

FOR DECORATING THE MACARON SHELLS

Fine brushes (used only for edible painting)

Americolor Green Sheen

Americolor Teal

Americolor Lavender Sheen

Americolor Violet

Americolor Gold Sheen

continued ➤

BUTTERCREAM FROSTING

6 tablespoons (¾ stick; 85 g) unsalted butter, room temperature

2 cups (240 g) confectioners' sugar

2 tablespoons Apricot and Saffron Jam (page 49)

1 teaspoon vanilla extract

¼ teaspoon salt

1 to 2 tablespoons whole milk, room temperature

Drop of Americolor Orange food gel color

2 tablespoons (15 g) finely chopped pistachios

METHOD

To Make the Macaron Shell

1. In a bowl of a food processor fitted with a metal blade, pulse 4 ounces of the confectioners' sugar with the almond flour until a fine powder is formed. Transfer mixture to a mixing bowl and mix the remaining confectioners' sugar. Using a fine sieve, sift mixture four to five times into a large bowl. Set aside. This process is important, do not cut this step short!

2. Make the meringue: In a bowl of a stand mixer fitted with a whisk attachment, whip whites and cream of tartar on medium speed until foamy for about 2 minutes. Gradually add granulated sugar. Once all the sugar is incorporated and the mixture is thick, scrape down the sides of the bowl, add the vanilla extract and the food colors and increase the speed to high, whipping until firm and glossy peaks form, at least 4 to 5 minutes. When you remove the whisk attachment and turn it upside down, the meringue should form in between a soft and firm peak. Whip for another minute if the meringue is still loose.

3. To complete the macaronnage, add the almond flour mixture, one-third at a time, over the egg white mixture, and fold using a large spatula until just combined. Take in the batter with your spatula and press it against the bowl in the same motion to remove the air from the batter. This step is very important and you keep whipping it in the same direction, and

pressing against the bowl, until you get a ribbon-like flow. You should be able to make a figure 8 easily with the batter, when the spatula is raised a bit above the batter. If you overmix the batter will be too runny. It should flow like lava, slowly but form ribbons. The ribbons should settle into the batter, at a slow count of 20. That is the consistency you are looking for. STOP RIGHT THERE!

4. Transfer the batter to a pastry bag filled with a ⅓-inch (1 cm) plain round tip. The best way to do this is to put the pastry bag in a tall and wide glass jar, open it wide enough and pour the batter in.

5. Keep three baking sheets with a silicone mat (with the Macaron template) ready. Pipe 1¼-inch (3 cm) rounds on the silicone mats on the baking sheets to help get the round shape. You can use a macaron template to help guide the shape of the macarons. Hold the tray with both hands on either side and bang each sheet on the work surface to release trapped air. Do this step at least 10 to 15 times. The batter will spread and the rounds will become slightly bigger. If there is a bubble, use a toothpick to poke and fill up gently.

6. Let stand at room temperature for 45 minutes at the minimum. Check for a slight crust to form on the macaron. The macarons should not stick to your finger when lightly touched.

7. While the macarons are resting, preheat the oven to 310°F (155°C).

8. After the rest time, bake one sheet at a time, on the middle rack of the oven, rotating halfway through, until macarons are crisp and firm, about 15 to 16 minutes.

9. Allow macarons to cool on the baking sheets for 30 minutes and transfer to a wire rack to cool completely before filling.

continued ➤

To Decorate the Macaron Shells

1. Keep 4 small bowls ready. In bowl 1, add 2 drops each of Americolor Green Sheen and Teal food gel. In bowl 2, add 2 drops each of Americolor Lavender Sheen and Violet. In bowl 3, add Americolor Sheen Green. In bowl 4, add 5 to 6 drops of the Americolor Gold Sheen.

2. Use separate paint brushes for each bowl and mix the individual colors in the individual bowls.

3. Pair the macarons to match the shape. On half of the macarons, using bowl 1: paint a green circle, keeping a ¼-inch (½ cm) gap from the rim and paint inside. It does not have to be perfect but paint it completely. Let dry completely.

4. Next paint a purple circle with bowl 2, inside the green circle, leaving a small gap to show the green. Let dry completely.

5. Next paint a light green circle inside the purple circle, with bowl 3. Let dry completely.

6. Paint a gold circle with bowl 4 around the outer rim of the green circle, but do not complete the circle, depicting the feathers of a peacock. Let dry completely. Repeat the gold circle to accentuate it. Let it dry again.

To Make the Apricot and Saffron Jam Buttercream Filling

1. In a stand mixer fitted with a paddle attachment, add the butter and salt and whip until light and creamy, about a minute.

2. Add the confectioners' sugar, Apricot and Saffron Jam, vanilla extract, 1 drop of the orange food gel color and 1 tablespoon of milk to the whipped butter and mix until the ingredients are well combined and the mixture is smooth, 1 to 1½ minutes, starting at low speed (so that the sugar does not fly everywhere.) and gradually increasing the speed to high. Use a 12-inch (30 cm) pastry bag with a ¼-inch (½ cm) round tip to fill the buttercream filling. Use a bench scraper to scrape down the buttercream in the pastry bag.

To Assemble

1. Pipe on the flat side of one macaron, leaving ¼ inch (5 mm) from the outer rim. Sprinkle a bit of the fine pistachio crumbs on top of the buttercream. Use a same-sized painted macaron shell to cover the buttercream filling.

2. This can be kept at room temperature for a day. Afterwards, store in an airtight container, in the fridge for up to 3 to 4 days for maximum freshness.

3. Remove about half an hour before eating, so the buttercream comes to room temperature.

1. Whip the meringue thoroughly. The best way to check after 5 minutes of whipping is to remove the whisk, stir the meringue vigorously, and turn it upside down. The meringue should stay firm like a peak with a slight bend.

2. You can use parchment paper instead of the silicone mats. The macarons come out even and perfectly round with the silicone mats. If you use parchment paper, place a macaron template underneath the parchment paper. Seal the parchment paper onto the baking sheet by dabbing a bit of the macaron batter on all the 4 corners, and seal it onto the baking sheet so that the paper does not move especially when you are piping the macarons on top of the parchment paper.

3. When using the pastry bag to pipe the macarons, hold it absolutely vertical, and center to the holes on the template and slightly above it. Do not touch the mat to pipe it. You need to squeeze just a tad bit to release the batter onto the mat.

4. Do not over mix the batter or else it will be too runny, and your macaron shells will be flat. Do not under mix either, or else your macarons will not form a proper shell and you will not have a smooth texture. Plus, they will take longer to dry out before placing into the oven.

5. DO NOT remove the shells off the parchment paper as soon as the tray comes out of the oven, or else you will break the shell. Wait for 30 minutes at least for it to cool down.

6. It is very important that you follow the recipe exactly and by weight to get the best results. Read the instructions carefully a few times to understand the process before attempting macarons.

7. You can keep the shells covered with a paper towel and complete the buttercream and assembly the next day as well. The shells will keep for a couple of days.

Coffee Cardamom Mini Cheesecakes

Makes 12 two-inch diameter mini cheesecakes

Coffee and cardamom is a very classic Indian combination that just works together. As a teenager, like any other, I loved hanging out with my friends. Who is family at that point?! I would typically be hanging out at some friend's house perpetually every other day, and the mom of one friend in particular made the BEST cold coffee. At some point, we started hanging out at her place more often, just so that we could have aunty's cold coffee. She would use the Indian Nescafe—the instant coffee granules—and put loads of ice, sugar, whole milk, and cardamom.

When I came up with this Coffee Cardamom Mini Cheesecake, I was thinking of my friend's mom, and the countless days and stay overs we had at her place. I use a chocolate cookie base with ground ginger, giving it a bit of earthiness. The cream cheese filling has ground cardamom in it for the floral notes, along with the instant coffee, and mind you, I use the Indian Nescafe too! I love mini desserts, as they can be served at a party, make for pretty presentations, and there is no wastage, as they are so small and not heavy at all. This recipe is eggless, comes together fairly quickly, and stores well in the fridge for a few days. One of my favorite recipes and I hope they will be your favorite too.

INGREDIENTS

BASE

90 grams chocolate cookies

2 tablespoons (25 g) granulated sugar

Pinch of salt

1 teaspoon (1.75 g) ground ginger

4 tablespoons (½ stick; 56 g) unsalted butter, melted and cooled

COFFEE CARDAMOM CHEESECAKE FILLING

1 tablespoon (15 g) water

1 tablespoon (8 g) cornstarch

¼ cup (57 g) Greek yogurt

⅓ cup (80 g) heavy cream

1 teaspoon vanilla extract

1 tablespoon (15 g) lemon juice

2 teaspoons (4 g) instant coffee

1 teaspoon (2 g) ground cardamom

12 ounces cream cheese (340 g), room temperature

⅓ cup + 1 tablespoon (84 g) granulated sugar

STABLE WHIPPED CREAM

¾ cup (180 g) heavy whipping cream

3 tablespoons (24 g) confectioners' sugar

1 tablespoon (8 g) milk powder

½ teaspoon vanilla extract

DECORATION

Chocolate sprinkles

Chocolate covered espresso beans (optional)

Edible gold leaf

EQUIPMENT

Twelve 2-inch (5 cm) mini cheesecake pan

12-inch (30 cm) pastry bag

¼-inch (½ cm) round tip

continued ➡

METHOD

To Make the Base

1. Preheat the oven to 350°F (175°C).

2. Using a food processor, add the chocolate cookies, granulated sugar, a pinch of salt, and the ground ginger and process until it forms a powder, about a minute.

3. Add the melted butter and mix again until combined.

4. Put about a heapful tablespoon in each of the 12 cavities of the cheesecake pan. Distribute it equally. Using the tablespoon, press the mixture down to seal it tight.

5. Place the pan into the oven for 10 minutes for it to set. Remove and let cool.

To Make the Coffee Cardamom Cheesecake Filling

1. In a small bowl, add the water and cornstarch, mix until well combined, and set aside.

2. In a medium bowl, add the Greek yogurt, heavy cream, vanilla extract, lemon juice, instant coffee, and ground cardamom, combine well until smooth and set it aside.

3. In the bowl of a stand mixture with a paddle attachment, add cream cheese and whip for a minute, until it softens. Add the granulated sugar and whip again for 30 to 60 seconds until well combined. Add the Greek yogurt mixture into the cream cheese, and whip again for a minute. Using a rubber spatula, scrape the batter off the sides of the bowl into the center. Add the cornstarch mixture as well, and whisk again to combine, until well incorporated.

4. Distribute the mixture evenly among all 12 cavities of the cheesecake pan. Tap it gently for the mixture to even out.

5. Place it into the preheated oven for 16 to 18 minutes. Do not overbake, or else the cheesecake will crack and will not have the creamy texture when ready to eat. It should be slightly jiggly in the center.

6. Remove from the oven and cool completely.

7. Put the cheesecake pan into the fridge for 2 hours for it to set further and get cold.

8. Release the cheesecake by lightly running a warm sharp knife around each cavity. Remove them gently from the bottom of the cheesecake pan by pushing on the removable bottom, so as not to break the mini cheesecakes. Place them on a plate.

To Make the Stable Whipped Cream

1. In a medium to large bowl, add the heavy whipping cream, powdered sugar, milk powder, and vanilla extract. Using a handheld mixture, whip for 1 to 2 minutes until you get stiff peaks. In the pastry bag, cut the end off and put in the piping tip. Secure it. Open up the bag, and place it into a tall glass. Add the whipped cream into the piping bag. Slowly twist the top, push down the whipped cream. Test with the piping bag how you want to decorate your mini cheesecakes.

2. Or simply place the piping bag at a 90-degree angle above the mini cheesecake, and pipe rounds around the mini cheesecake. Lower the pressure as you come up slightly to get a fine tip on top of the cheesecake. Decorate with a few chocolate sprinkles, optional chocolate-covered espresso bean, and a bit of edible gold leaf on each cheesecake on the whipped cream. Serve cold.

PRO TIPS

1. The mini cheesecakes can be made 2 to 3 days in advance, and stored in an airtight container in the fridge.

2. Remove from the fridge 15 minutes before serving. I like them slightly cold. They taste great with warm coffee..

Masala Chai Tiramisu

WITH ROSE MASCARPONE, WHIPPED CREAM, AND PISTACHIO SPRINKLE

Serves 10 to 12

Tiramisu is an Italian coffee-based dessert made with ladyfingers (long biscuits) that are dipped in coffee and layered with an egg-based mascarpone mixture, and finally sprinkled with cocoa powder. The word tiramisu means to "pick me up" and it does wake you up after having a piece of this really creamy and delicious dessert.

Tiramisu was my mum's absolute favorite! For her birthday every year, she would enjoy an Italian meal, ending the night with a slice of heaven. After her passing, we still celebrate her birthday with a slice of tiramisu, because it would make her the happiest.

My masi Chandon (my mum's sister) makes the most wonderful tiramisu. She lives in Wales, and whenever we visit, we always get to eat her famous eggless tiramisu, which is always a treat! No trip to England is complete without her tiramisu. She uses an eggless sponge cake as the base and I use that recipe here.

In honor of Mum's love for tiramisu and masala chai, here is a Masala Chai Tiramisu with an eggless sponge cake that has been soaked in my Masala Chai Concentrate (page 319), It is then covered with a rose flavored whipped mascarpone, pistachio powder, and topped with another layer of sponge and mascarpone. Finally, it is covered with blobs of whipped cream, and covered with a pistachio powder, adorned with edible dried rose buds and edible gold leaf to make it extra special. This tiramisu is filled with so much flavor, and yet it is beautifully delicate. It will be the star of any party! Watch the faces of your guests, as their eyes open wide when they taste this very unique tiramisu!

INGREDIENTS

EGGLESS SPONGE CAKE

2¾ cups + 1 tablespoon (340 g) all-purpose flour

2 tablespoons (16 g) cornstarch

3 teaspoons (12 g) baking powder

1 teaspoon (4.8 g) baking soda

2 teaspoons (4 g) Chai Masala (page 41)

½ teaspoon (3 g) table salt

½ cup (1 stick; 113 g) + 6 tablespoons (¾ stick; 85 g) unsalted butter, at room temperature

1¼ cups (250 g) granulated sugar

½ cup (114 g) Greek yogurt, room temperature

1 tablespoon (10 g) vanilla extract

1¼ cups (300 g) whole milk, room temperature

1¼ cups (10 ounces or 296 ml) Masala Chai Concentrate (page 319)

ROSE WHIPPED MASCARPONE

1 cup (240 g) cold heavy whipping cream

¾ cup (90 g) confectioners' sugar or powdered sugar

1 teaspoon (4 g) vanilla extract

1½ tubs (12 ounces or 340 g) cold mascarpone cheese

1 teaspoon rose water

continued ➡

STABLE WHIPPED CREAM

1¼ cups (300 g) cold heavy whipping cream

⅓ cup (40 g) confectioners' sugar or powdered sugar

1 teaspoon (4 g) vanilla extract

1 tablespoon (8 g) milk powder

GARNISH

½ cup (65 g) whole raw pistachios, (bright pistachios)

Edible gold leaf

Edible dried rose petals

EQUIPMENT

16-inch (40 cm) pastry bag

½-inch (1¼ cm) round tip

METHOD

To Make the Eggless Sponge Cake

1. Preheat the oven to 350°F (175°C). Prepare a 9-by-13-inch (23-by-33 cm) baking pan by using cooking spray all over the inside. Add parchment paper, such that it has an overhang on either side of the length of the pan. That way it is easy to remove the cake once cooled. Spray the parchment paper as well with the cooking spray. Set it aside.

2. In a medium bowl, add the all-purpose flour, corn starch, baking powder, baking soda, salt, and Chai Masala, and whisk to combine.

3. In the bowl of a stand mixer with a paddle attachment, add the butter and granulated sugar. Start off slow and increase the speed to high, and mix for 2 to 3 minutes, until light and fluffy, and the color has turned a pale yellow.

4. Add the Greek yogurt and vanilla extract and whisk to combine. Scrape the sides of the bowl and whisk to combine again.

5. Alternating the flour mixture and the whole milk, add it in two iterations, and whisk to combine after adding the flour mixture, then whisk to combine after adding the whole milk,

and repeat the process one more time for the remaining flour mixture and milk. Do not over mix the batter.

6. Add the batter into the pan. Level it off with a small offset spatula. Place it into the middle rack of the oven and bake for about 50 to 60 minutes, or until the cake tester comes out clean from the middle of the cake.

7. Once baked, let cool for 30 minutes. Using the parchment paper overhang, remove it from the pan, and let it completely cool.

To Make the Rose Whipped Mascarpone

1. In the bowl of a stand mixer with a whisk attachment, add the heavy cream, powdered sugar, and vanilla extract. Start off slow, and change to high speed, and whisk for 1 to 2 minutes, until you get soft peaks. Do not over whip, or else the cream will curdle.

2. Add the mascarpone and rose water. Whisk for about 30 seconds to a minute to combine. The mixture should be silky smooth.

To Make the Stable Whipped Cream

1. In the bowl of a stand mixer with a whisk attachment, add the heavy cream, powdered sugar, vanilla extract, and milk powder. Start off slow, and change to high speed, and whisk for 1 to 2 minutes, until you get slightly stiff peaks. Do not over whip, or else the cream will curdle.

2. In a pastry bag, cut off the end and add the round piping tip. Secure it. Add the bag into a tall glass and widen it, so that it is easier to put in the whipped cream. Using a rubber spatula, add the whipped cream into the pastry bag. Remove the bag from the glass, push the cream down, twist the top, and secure with a clip. Set it aside.

continued ➤

To Assemble

1. In a high-speed blender, process the pistachios to grind them as fine as possible. Do not over grind it, as the oils from the nuts will release.

2. Get the pan you want to use to assemble the tiramisu in. I have used a 9.5-inch (24 cm) square baking pan to assemble the tiramisu.

3. Use cooking spray to spray the inside of the pan.

4. Cut the cake horizontally into half, using a serrated knife. Cut out the cake size that would fit into the pan.

5. Add one layer of the cake into the pan. Drizzle about 5 ounces (148 ml) of the Chai Masala Concentrate all over the cake, such that the cake soaks it up nicely. Or use a pastry brush to dab the entire cake with the Masala Chai Concentrate, until the 5 ounces (148 ml) are used up.

6. Add half of the Rose Whipped Mascarpone onto the cake. Using a small offset spatula, gently spread it across the cake and even out the layer.

7. Using a fine to medium sieve, add half of the finely chopped pistachios into the sieve, and sprinkle all over the layer.

8. Add another layer of the cake on top of the pistachio layer. Drizzle the remaining Chai Masala Concentrate all over the cake, such that the cake soaks it up nicely. (There will be some cake remaining if you use a 9.5-by-9.5-inch pan to bake in, which you can simply snack on.)

9. Add half of the Rose Whipped Mascarpone onto the cake. Using a small offset spatula, gently spread it across the cake and even out the layer.

10. Using the whipped cream in the pastry bag, keeping it perpendicular to the tiramisu, start piping the whipped cream in an even pattern of round dots, all over the layer.

11. Let the tiramisu set overnight.

12. Next day, before serving, using a fine to medium sieve, add the remaining half of the finely chopped pistachios into the sieve, and sprinkle all over the layer. If you have coarse pistachios left in the sieve, grind them again in the blender, and sprinkle the extra over the whipped cream.

13. Decorate with edible gold leaf and dried rose petals on top of the tiramisu.

PRO TIPS

1. The tiramisu can be made 2 days in advance. Decorate the final pistachio layer, edible gold leaf, and dried rose petals just before serving to maintain the brightness of the pistachios and decorative items.

2. To serve, cut clean layers using a sharp knife. Use a pie server or a thin wide silicone spatula, to scoop out the layers onto small plates.

3. Make individually sized portions in small ramekins or glasses as an alternative to serving.

4. Add a dash of rum or brandy in the Masala Chai Concentrate to give the cake a bit of a kick as well.

Eggless Chocolate Fudge Cake

Serves 12 to 14

My mother was famous for her baked goods, and especially her cakes. Many friends, relatives, and acquaintances have enjoyed her cakes. She made pineapple upside-down cakes, fruit cakes, pineapple cakes with whipped cream frosting—she was a pro. Her eggless chocolate fudge cake made appearances at most of our birthday parties, year after year. My friends looked forward to it; sometimes they would ask my her to make it for their special occasions too, and my mum would happily oblige. It was her specialty after all! Her chocolate cake was moist, fudgy, heavenly, and decadent in every possible way. She did not do any decorations, no frills, no fuss. It was simple with frosting, and that's it. We loved it that way, and we always wanted more of it.

I adapted my mother's recipe to make it my own. I know she would still be proud of it! The cake layers in India are somehow smaller, so I made my cake layers a bit thicker. The chocolate frosting is definitely more fudgy.

The cake is like a warm hug on a cold winter day. My precious kids are very fond of this cake, and now this is how they remember their grandma—as the grandma who loved to bake and spread joy through her bakes.

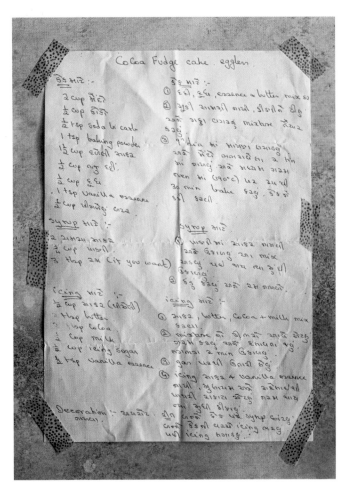

continued ➔

INGREDIENTS

EGGLESS CHOCOLATE CAKE

2½ cups (300 g) all-purpose flour

½ cup (38 g) unsweetened dark cocoa (100% cacao)

2 teaspoons (8 g) baking powder

½ teaspoon (4 g) baking soda

½ teaspoon (3 g) table salt

1 tablespoon (3 g) instant coffee, ground into a powder

1 cup (2 sticks; 226 g) unsalted butter, melted

1¼ cups (250 g) granulated sugar

2 teaspoons (8 g) vanilla extract

½ cup (113 g) Greek yogurt

1 cup (240 g) whole milk

CAKE SYRUP

2 tablespoons (30 g) water

2 tablespoons (25 g) granulated sugar

3 tablespoons (42 g) good quality rum

CHOCOLATE FUDGE FROSTING

½ cup (1 stick; 113 g) + 2 tablespoons (28 g) unsalted butter, room temperature

1 cup (76 g) unsweetened cocoa (100% cacao)

½ teaspoon (3 g) table salt

cup (227 g) whole milk, room temperature

6 to 7 cups (720 to 840 g) sifted confectioners' sugar

1 teaspoon (4 g) vanilla extract

CHOCOLATE GANACHE DRIP

1 cup (142 g) dark chocolate chips (60% cocoa)

½ cup (120 g) heavy cream

CHOCOLATE BUTTERCREAM

½ cup (1 stick; 113 g) unsalted butter, room temperature

½ teaspoon (3 g) table salt

1 tablespoon sifted unsweetened cocoa (100% cacao)

2 cups (240 g) sifted confectioners' sugar

1 teaspoon (4 g) vanilla extract

2 to 3 tablespoons whole milk or heavy cream

DECORATIONS

Food gel coloring: chocolate brown, black

Edible decorations like shimmering stars, gold/silver decoration (optional)

EQUIPMENT

Two 8-inch (20 cm) cake pans

Rotating cake stand

Bench scraper

Eight-inch cardboard cake disc

Pastry brush

Three 12-inch (30 cm) pastry bags

Wilton 1M tip

Ateco 863–star tip

Ateco 865–star tip

METHOD

To Make the Eggless Chocolate Cake:

1. Preheat the oven to 350°F (175°C). Prepare two 8-inch cake pans by spraying with cooking spray and putting in the parchment paper. Spray again with the cooking spray inside the pan. Set it aside.

2. In a medium bowl, sift the all-purpose flour, unsweetened dark cocoa, baking powder, baking soda, salt, and instant coffee powder through a medium sieve or sifter.

3. In a bowl of a stand mixer with a paddle attachment, add the melted butter and sugar, and start mixing on low speed. Gradually increase the speed to high and mix for 2 minutes.

4. Add the vanilla extract and Greek yogurt and mix again until combined.

5. Slowly add half the flour mixture, alternating with half the milk. Mix to combine. Do not over mix. Repeat by adding the remaining flour mixture again and then the milk. Mix again to combine.

continued ➞

6. Bake in the middle rack of the oven for about 25 to 30 minutes, until the cake tester comes out clean.

7. Let rest in the cake pan for 20 minutes. Gently turn the pan over and remove the cake. Cool completely on a wire rack for another 15 minutes.

8. Cover each cake layer with plastic wrap and place in the fridge for 3 to 4 hours or preferably overnight.

To Make the Cake Syrup

In a small saucepan on medium heat, add the water and granulated sugar. Stir occasionally until the sugar dissolves, about 3 minutes. Add the rum and set it aside.

To Make the Chocolate Fudge Frosting

1. In a medium saucepan on medium to low heat, add the unsalted butter and melt it. Add the cocoa powder and salt and start mixing it with a rubber spatula. Add ⅓ cup (80 g) whole milk to the mixture and mix to combine. Remove from the heat.

2. Add the mixture to the bowl of a stand mixer with a whisk attachment. Start whisking the mixture, starting off slow, and increasing the speed to high for 1 minute.

3. Add the confectioners' sugar (start with 6 cups or 720 g) and whisk on slow for a minute. Add the remainder of the milk and vanilla extract. Using a rubber spatula, clean up the sides to put the mixture in the center of the bowl. Whisk on high speed for 5 to 7 minutes. The chocolate fudge frosting should be a fluffy, creamy, and thick but spreadable consistency. If it is a bit runny, add ½ cup (57 g) of confectioners' sugar at a time up to 1 cup and whisk again for 1 to 2 minutes until the frosting is fluffy and creamy in consistency.

To Frost the Cake

1. Start with the crumb coat. On a rotating cake stand, add a smidge of frosting for the cardboard cake disc to adhere. Apply a smidge of frosting on the middle of the disc.

2. Remove the cold cakes from the fridge and discard the plastic wrap. Invert one cake and place on the disc so the flat side of the cake is facing up.

3. Using a pastry brush, brush the top of the cake with the cake syrup. Spread half of the cake syrup on the top.

4. Using an ice cream scoop, add about 5 scoops of the chocolate fudge frosting on the top for ensuring an even layer of frosting between the cake layers.

5. With a small offset spatula, spread the fudge frosting until the edge of the cake. Ensure that the frosting layer is smooth and even all over the cake.

6. Place the second cake layer, again inverted, with the flat side facing up, aligning exactly with the frosted bottom layer.

7. Press it gently from the top to stick to the frosting.

8. Using a pastry brush, brush the top of the cake with the cake syrup. Spread the remaining cake syrup on the top.

9. With the small offset spatula, apply the frosting on top of the layer to form an even layer.

10. Using the small offset spatula, start spreading the frosting on the sides of the cake, from top to bottom in one area, spread to even it out and then move to the next vertical area of the cake and spread the frosting. Repeat the process, such that the entire cake is covered in the frosting. It will not look good, or perfect. You want the frosting to cover every part of the

cake. Spread it evenly all around the cake with the small offset spatula to even out as much as possible. Do not mess with it too much since this is just the crumb coat of the cake, which ensures that the crumbs stay intact.

11. You will have chocolate fudge frosting left, which you will use to even out the cake layer after it rests in the fridge.

12. Place the cake in the fridge for an hour.

13. Remove the cake from the fridge. Place a glass with hot water next to you along with a clean kitchen towel.

14. Using a small offset spatula, spread the fudge frosting around the cake to even out as much as possible.

15. Dip the spatula in the hot water, and wipe it with the towel and then, with it being perpendicular to the rotating cake stand, smoothen the side of the cake lightly to remove any excess frosting as you rotate the cake stand. Keep repeating the process of dipping the spatula in hot water, cleaning with the towel and smoothening the cake frosting on the outside and fussing with the cake. This process takes about 15 minutes to get a very smooth layer. You will get the hang of it as you work with the spatula and the cake. If there are slight cracks you can smoothen them out by adding a bit of frosting and filling it in with the spatula.

To Make the Chocolate Ganache Drip

1. In a bowl, add the chocolate chips and set it aside.

2. Microwave the heavy cream for 1 minute and 15 seconds. Pour the hot heavy cream on top of the chocolate chips, cover with a lid, and let it sit for 4 to 5 minutes.

3. Remove the cover and stir with a small rubber spatula. Keep stirring—it will eventually come together, the chocolate will melt, and the ganache will look silky and smooth. It takes 3 minutes to stir and get to the silky-smooth texture.

4. Using a spoon or a squeeze bottle, gently pour a bit at a time on the edge of the cake to gently drip down the cake. Repeat at ⅓ inch (1 cm) intervals, to get drips all around the cake. Pour the ganache slowly to get a nice drip on the side of the cake, or else the drip will go all the way down to the bottom of the cake and will look messy.

5. Apply ganache using a large spoon on top of the cake. Use a small offset spatula to spread it to create an even layer on top of the cake.

6. Place the cake back in the fridge to firm up for 20 minutes.

To Make the Chocolate Buttercream

1. In the bowl of a stand mixer, add the butter, salt, and cocoa powder, and whisk on high speed for 1 minute.

2. Add the confectioners' sugar, 2 tablespoons of whole milk or heavy cream, and vanilla extract, and start whisking on slow. Increase the speed gradually to high, so as not to splatter all the sugar. Whisk on high for 1 minute. The buttercream should be fluffy and creamy. If it is still stiff, add one more tablespoon of whole milk or heavy cream and whisk to combine.

3. Set up two bowls and add ¾ cup (180 ml) of the buttercream into each bowl. You can keep the same colors for all the buttercreams, or use different shades of brown for all three buttercreams using the chocolate brown color and a slight black to create a darker brown for one buttercream, and then use the chocolate brown to create a different shade of brown for the second buttercream. Keep the third butter-

continued ➡

cream as is. One buttercream will be used to pipe rosettes with the 1M Wilton Tip. The second will be used to pipe using the Ateco 863-star tip. The third will be used to pipe using the Ateco 865-star tip. If using colors, use separate mini rubber spatulas to stir each buttercream in order to incorporate the color completely.

4. Fill the three pastry bags with the three piping tips: the Wilton 1M tip, Ateco 863, Ateco 865, or create a similar star tip by cutting the end of the pastry bag. The tips should be tightly fit into the pastry bag.

5. Fill the most amount of buttercream in the 1M tip pastry bag. Using a bench scraper, scrape the buttercream down to the bottom. Twist the top and seal it with a clip. Repeat the same with the other two buttercreams: Fill it and push it down with the bench scraper. Twist the top and seal it with a clip.

To Decorate the Cake

1. Remove the cake from the fridge. Start piping rosettes, keeping the piping bag at 90 degrees to the cake, using the 1M tip piping bag. Use your creativity to pipe the rosettes and the star tip buttercream all around the cake or simply be whimsical.

2. You can put glitter on the top, or star shimmers, or gold and silver sprinkles. Make this cake your own using your creativity.

PRO TIPS

1. You could simply stop the decoration at the chocolate fudge frosting, and make swirls with the fudge frosting and keep it simple.

2. The cake should be removed half an hour before serving for the best moist, soft, fudgy cake possible.

3. The cake can be made ahead and kept in the fridge for up to 2 days. Finish off the frosting, ganache drip, and buttercream decoration, all in one day.

4. The cake can be cut into slices, and stored in an airtight container, for up to 2 weeks.

5. For placing the buttercream into the piping bag, the best method is to take a tall glass, place the piping bag in it, open it as wide as possible, and then, using a rubber spatula, put the buttercream inside. Then close the bag and push it down with your hands. Use a bench scraper, to clean the bag from the top and push the buttercream all together.

6. Practice piping the buttercream on a plate first to get a hang of it, and then continue piping on the cake.

Drinks

Tea, though ridiculed by those who are naturally coarse in their nervous sensibilities, . . . will always be the favorite beverage of the intellectual.

—Thomas de Quincey

Beverages are an essential part of our daily lives. We start our day with a hot beverage—in my case, it is Aadhu Masala Chai (page 315). It is the most calming and therapeutic moment of my day. The whiff of the spices and loose black tea brewing together is magical, and it sets the mood for the entire day. As kids, we grew up with Haldar Nu Doodh (page 328), or golden milk, as the rest of the world calls it. It is an ancient medicinal drink that was part of our routine when we were sick. My mother would not allow any further activity unless she saw an empty glass. Masala Chaas (page 335), which is essentially savory lassi, is a digestive, best had after a meal. It helps to cool down the spices that you have eaten through your foods. The Peach, Mint, and Cardamom Lassi (page 327) is a derivative of the humble lassi that my mother made in the hot and humid months in Mumbai. She also made Kachi Keri Nu Sharbat (Raw Mango and Fennel Concentrate/Syrup, page 330), a thirst quencher that hydrates your body during the hottest months of the year. All these drinks that I grew up with have medicinal properties in some form or another, and are good for you, even with a little bit of sugar in them. They were carried forward through generations, from my great-grandmothers to grandmothers to my mother.

Cocktails, on the other hand, are ice breakers, conversation starters, mood lifters. They bring people together in the most unprecedented times. Cocktails in moderation bring joy and fun to any party. My husband and I are not big drinkers but we do enjoy the occasional cocktail, especially a fruity one like his favorite Blood Orange and Rosemary Bourbon Cocktail (page 312), and his favorite spirit cachaça, which I used in the Kumquat and Ginger Caipirinha (page 316), both of which use seasonal California produce and make a wonderful Friday night drink to bring on the weekend. The Kachi Keri Margarita (page 332) is my fusion take on margaritas, using Kachi Keri Nu Sharbat, which is absolutely refreshing. End a spicy Indian meal with my Thandai Cocktail (page 336), which is my take on a dessert cocktail. Be sure to take small sips of this exquisite cocktail, after dinner, with deep conversations to end a wonderful night on a high note.

Blood Orange and Rosemary Bourbon Cocktail

Make 2 cocktails

When I started my jam business, I would come up with tons of recipes for jams to demonstrate their versatility. One of my absolute favorite creations has been the Blood Orange and Rosemary Marmalade (page 33). When I first made this marmalade, people didn't know what to expect. I gave small samples to my friends and colleagues to try and I can happily say that everyone loved this marmalade. It is not bitter like traditional marmalades and is delicious on buttered toast.

Jam is fun to use in cocktails. My husband is a huge fan of bourbon, and citrus and bourbon are a match made in heaven! I first made this drink five years ago during the Oscars and Raj raved about it! We have been making it for every Oscar season since. It is perfect for the winter season, with fresh citrus notes and warming bourbon.

INGREDIENTS

¼ cup (50 g) granulated sugar, for sugar rim

Square cubes of ice (to keep the cocktail cold)

1 rosemary sprig, plus 2 rosemary sprigs for garnish

2 tablespoons Blood Orange and Rosemary Marmalade (page 33)

4 ounces (120 ml) freshly squeezed blood orange juice

2 ounces (60 ml) freshly squeezed lime juice

3 ounces (90 ml) bourbon

1.5 ounces (45 ml) Cointreau

Ice

Splash of club soda in each glass

GARNISH

Blood orange slices from 1 small blood orange

METHOD

1. Place 2 glasses in the freezer for 10 minutes.

2. Add a square ice cube into each glass.

3. In a cocktail shaker, add the rosemary sprig and the marmalade. Muddle the rosemary with the marmalade. Add the blood orange juice, lime juice, bourbon, Cointreau, and 6 to 7 cubes of ice. Shake vigorously for 30 seconds. Divide the cocktail between the 2 glasses.

4. Add a splash of club soda on top of each drink. Stir to combine. Add a sprig of rosemary and 2 slices of blood oranges in the cocktail. It is ready to sip!

PRO TIP

Replace the blood orange and rosemary with 1 tablespoon rosemary simple syrup. To make, combine ½ cup (100 g) granulated sugar and ½ cup (120 g) water in a small saucepan over medium heat. Stir until the sugar has dissolved and then add 2 rosemary sprigs. Stir for another 2 minutes, turn off the heat, and let steep for 10 minutes. Strain and store syrup in a glass jar in the fridge for up to 2 weeks.

PRO TIPS

1. Once the black tea and chai masala is brewed, you can strain the mixture into a cup and add warm nut milk to the mixture for a Vegan Masala Chai.

2. Add fresh lemongrass to the chai to give it a wonderful aroma.

3. A tip from my Aunt Ranju: Add saffron to make a Royal Aadhu Masala Chai.

Aadhu Masala Chai (Ginger Masala Chai)

Makes one 10-ounce (300 ml) serving

Where did masala chai originate? Chai has a long reigning history in India. Black tea was brought to India by the British in the 1900s, when the British India Tea Association planted tea plantations in Assam, India. They were trying to promote black tea and make it popular, but due to how expensive it was, masalas were added to keep the cost down along with milk and sugar (which was already how the British had their English Tea). This became the drink of choice and it became more popular as time went by. The tea that is made in India is called CTC, which is a processing method that means to cut, tear, and curl, where huge cylindrical rollers with sharp teeth take care of the process. It results in a richer brewed black tea.

While in school and college, I would drink a lot of masala chai to keep myself awake till the wee hours, due to the caffeine content in black tea, and the spices are refreshing in the chai. As college-going kids, we had a lot of chai from the local street vendors too called "chai wallahs." They called the chai half cutting or full cutting, which means half glass or a full glass. They are typically served in small glasses. The chai wallahs would even bring the chai up to our classrooms if we told them when and at what time. What fun!

I learned how to make masala chai from my mum when I was 9. It became my job to make it for guests that would frequent our home. Every home has its own way of making masala chai: my grandma's chai is different from mine, which is funny considering my grandma taught my mum, and my mum taught me.

Masala chai is a welcome drink served with biscuits, cookies, or a savory snack. It breaks the ice and warms up conversations. It is also had after meals, especially lunch, as a digestive because of all the spices that go into it. Gujaratis tend to add a lot of ginger in the masala chai and hence it is called Aadhu Masala Chai.

INGREDIENTS

1½ cups (360 g) water
2 teaspoons loose black tea or 2 black tea bags
1 tablespoon (12 g) brown sugar
½ leveled teaspoon Chai Masala (page 41)
½ cup (120 g) 2% milk
1 teaspoon freshly grated ginger

METHOD

1. In a medium pot on medium heat, add the water, black tea, brown sugar, and Chai Masala. Brew for about 4 minutes until it starts to boil. Add the milk and grated ginger, and let it come to a boil again in about 3 minutes. Once the boil comes to the surface of the pot, lower the heat immediately. Increase the heat and bring to a boil once again (a second boil). Let it boil for 30 seconds or so and then remove from the heat.

2. Using a fine mesh strainer over a cup, strain the masala chai into the cup. Your piping hot chai is ready.

Kumquat and Ginger Caipirinha

Makes 1 cocktail

When Raj and I started dating, I learned a lot about different cultures and foods from him. Being from India and coming to the United States exposed me to a lot of different things but the Bay Area is still contained in terms of different cultures. Los Angeles is very diverse in terms of people from all over the world. It is a melting pot of cultures. My husband, who grew up in LA, was exposed to it. The more I got to know him, the more I realized how intelligent and well-read he was about art, culture, fashion, religion, technology, history, and geography—basically any topic! It was fascinating to listen to him rattle off about different subjects, and it made conversation with him that much fun and easy as we always had a lot to talk about and discuss. To date, there has never been a dull moment, and it's been 16 years together.

So, it was through one of our conversations during the initial dates, that I found out about his love for Caipirinha, and how he devoured the drink. Caipirinha is a Brazilian cocktail made with cachaça, lime, sugar, and ice. The cachaça is made with raw sugarcane, and it has quite a wonderful aroma. It was only apt that I make a drink with cachaça for my partner in crime. This drink is made with the candied syrup used in the Kumquat and Black Sesame Bundt Cake (page 240). The additional syrup can be used to make this amazing, refreshing cocktail with kumquats. I dare you to have just one—it's that good!

INGREDIENTS

3 to 4 kumquats, each sliced into 4 horizontally

½ teaspoon freshly grated ginger

1 ounce (30 ml) lime juice

3 ounces (90 ml) cachaça (Brazilian rum)

1½ ounces (45 ml) Simple Kumquat and Ginger Syrup (page 240)

1 cup (150 g) ice

GARNISH

Mint leaves

1 kumquat, sliced into 4 horizontally

METHOD

1. In a cocktail shaker, add the kumquat and ginger and muddle it with a muddler for 10 seconds. Add the lime juice, cachaça, simple syrup, and ice. Close the cocktail shaker and mix for 20 to 30 seconds vigorously.

2. Empty all the contents with the ice into an old-fashioned glass. Garnish with the mint leaves and additional sliced kumquats on a cocktail stick. Cheers!

Iced Masala Chai Latte
WITH LAVENDER FOAM

Makes two 8-ounce (240 ml) servings

Many moons ago, on one of our biannual trips to wine country, we stumbled upon a quaint coffee shop in an outdoor mall that had a lavender chai latte. I instantly loved it and, believe it or not, I ordered a second after finishing the first cup pretty quickly! I loved this latte instantly! The lavender flavor is not overpowering, just enough to de-stress and calm you.

I have re-created this drink by making a Masala Chai Concentrate that you can store in the fridge for up to a week. The milk is steeped with dried edible lavender and then foamed and gently poured on top of the chai. In the words of my daughter who loves this latte, "If you make this every day, I will be calm for the entire day!" It always lifts her mood.

INGREDIENTS

2½ cups (600 g) water
1 tablespoon (5 g) loose English black tea
⅓ cup (75 g) granulated sugar
1 tablespoon (4 g) Chai Masala (page 41)
1 cup (240 g) whole milk
1 tablespoon culinary-grade dried lavender
Ice cubes

GARNISH
Dried lavender

METHOD

To Make the Masala Chai Concentrate

1. In a medium saucepan over medium to high heat, combine the water, loose black tea, sugar, and Chai Masala. Let it come to a boil, about 2 minutes. Once it starts boiling, boil for about 3 minutes. Remove from the heat and cool, about 15 minutes.

2. Strain the mixture through a fine sieve into a pourable bowl, and pour it into a sealable glass jar. Store it in the fridge to cool for about 2 hours.

To Make the Lavender Foam

In a small saucepan on medium heat, add the milk and lavender. Bring it to a slight boil, about 2 minutes. Remove from the heat. Cover the saucepan and steep the mixture for 15 minutes. Strain the mixture through a fine sieve into a glass. Cool in the fridge for about an hour.

To Make the Iced Masala Chai Latte

1. Use a milk frother to froth the lavender milk to create a foam. You can even use a frother band or your blender to create the milk foam.

2. Pour about a cup of the cold Masala Chai Concentrate into a glass, along with 2 ice cubes.

3. Pour the lavender foam slowly into the glass, by keeping the glass at an angle of 60° so that it does not disturb the masala chai layer.

4. Garnish with a few dried lavender on the top. Mix with a spoon before having the drink.

 PRO TIP You can make it vegan by using plant-based milk.

Plum and Fennel Sparkling Lemonade

Makes 8 servings

Five years ago, we planted a lemon shrub in the backyard. It took three years for the young tree to bear fruit. When we finally started seeing lemons on the tree, lemonade became a norm, be it winter, spring, summer, or fall. We use the lemons and seasonal fruit to create all different flavors. My kids and I, with my daughter's friends, had a lemonade stand one summer as well. The money we collected was donated to a local animal shelter.

Living in California, we are fortunate to have bounty of fruits growing within a 50-mile radius of our home, which makes it conducive for farmers to bring the fresh fruit from farm to market in no time. This plays a huge part in how it enhances the flavor of the fruit in the final product. Plums are abundantly available in the summer and fall and they do make a wonderful combination with fennel and thyme in this lemonade. Growing up in Mumbai, my mum would make fennel seed sugar water for us in the hot months of the year to cool us down. Fennel seeds have a lot of medicinal properties. It helps to cool you down in the hot weather, it reduces flatulence and indigestion, and it is used as a massage oil for joint pains.

This lemonade is a perfect coolant in the summer months and very tasty! We fill a huge pitcher with the lemonade and love taking it to any summer party!

INGREDIENTS

1¼ cups (250 g) granulated sugar

3¾ cups (780 g) water

2 tablespoons (14 g) fennel seeds

8 sprigs of thyme

3 to 4 ripe plums, can be slightly soft too, plus more for garnish

¾ cup (170 g) freshly squeezed lemon juice

2 cups (300 g) ice

One 33.8-ounce (1 L) bottle of soda water or seltzer

METHOD

1. Make the simple syrup: In a small saucepan on medium heat, add the sugar, 1¼ cups (300 g) of the water, fennel seeds, and thyme. Stir it to combine. Bring it to a slight boil, approximately 3 minutes. The sugar will completely dissolve. Once boiled for a minute, remove from the heat, cover the saucepan, and steep the mixture for 10 minutes.

2. Cut the plums into slices, remove the seeds, and puree the plums, along with the skin, in a high-speed blender to form a smooth puree.

3. Add the steeped simple syrup into a small pourable bowl. Mix the plum puree into the syrup and mix to combine. Strain the mixture through a medium sieve to discard any solids. Next strain the mixture again through a fine sieve so that you get a smooth liquid that is perfect for a lemonade. Straining the mixture through the fine sieve may take some time but it is so worth it.

4. In a large jug or pitcher, combine the mixture, along with lemon juice, the remaining 2 cups (480 g) of the water, and ice, and stir until well blended. Chill it until ready to serve.

5. When ready to serve, add the bottle of soda water or seltzer and serve with plum slices.

PRO TIP

Use the same base recipe and change up the fruit and whole spice to make your own lemonade combination like strawberries and black pepper or peach and mint.

PRO TIPS

1. The discarded fruit can be used to make a smoothie. Remove the whole star anise before using the fruit.

2. Puree the discarded fruit and add it to a waffle batter for additional fruity taste.

Nectarine, Star Anise, and Ginger Shrub

Makes about 2½ cups (600 ml)

Nectarines are fruity, sweet, and sour, and available only in the summer months going into fall. They get ever so slightly soft as you let them sit out for 2 to 3 days, for maximum flavor. We love using nectarines on waffles, in smoothies, in summer Panzanella salads, pies, and tarts to name a few. I eagerly wait for the summer months to enjoy the stone fruits.

One of the flavors that I sold on my Etsy store was nectarine and star anise jam. It was not popular. Along with the main order, I would send the customers a 2-ounce bottle of a flavor that I feel they would enjoy. The feedback received, once they tried the sample, was always so heartwarming! Food can be tricky. It may sound good, it may look good, but you can never know and trust it until you taste it, and that's when you know something is delicious!

The warmth and licorice flavor of star anise complements the fruity, tart notes of nectarine really well. I make a refreshing shrub, using this combination, along with ginger. Shrubs are essentially fruit, sugar, and vinegar together. Vinegar aids in digestion and is a great health tonic, so although shrubs have sugar, they aid in gut health. We love this shrub with sparkling water and some ice, or it works great in a cocktail too as I am going to show you in the next recipe.

INGREDIENTS

1 cup nectarines, pitted and chopped into tiny pieces (2 to 3 nectarines is about 200 g)

4 whole star anise

2 inches (5 cm) ginger

1 cup (200 g) granulated sugar

1 cup (240 g) apple cider vinegar

METHOD

1. In a large bowl, combine the finely chopped nectarines, and its juices along with the star anise, freshly grated ginger (with the ginger juices), and the granulated sugar and mix with a rubber spatula to combine.

2. Cover with plastic wrap and set it aside in a cool place in the kitchen for 2 hours. After 2 hours, using the spatula, combine the sugars and the fruit again. The sugar will completely dissolve.

3. Repeat Step 2. Let it set again for 2 hours and again stir the mixture until the sugar is dissolved.

4. Store the covered bowl in the fridge for 24 hours.

5. Add the apple cider vinegar into the mixture and stir to combine. Store in an airtight container in the fridge for about 2 days for the flavors to merge.

6. After 2 days, using a medium sieve over a medium bowl, strain the mixture through the sieve. Using a rubber spatula, press onto the fruit to release as much juices as possible. Discard the solids.

7. The shrub is ready to use. It takes 3 days from start to finish to get the flavors to blend. Pour about 1 to 2 ounces (30 to 60 ml) in a glass along with 6 ounces (180 ml) of sparkling water and ice. You have a delicious cooling drink ready for you.

Nectarine Shrub and Gin Cocktail

Makes 2 cocktails

Shrubs are wonderful and refreshing and they carry a lot of benefits because of the apple cider vinegar and spices in the shrubs. The vinegar and the spices aid in digestion, help with liver health, and several other benefits, making it good for you. The latest trend has been to add shrubs to cocktails, giving them a beautifully distinct flavor. I have been making a lot of shrubs the past couple of years, and I love the versatility of this delicious drink. The Nectarine, Star Anise, and Ginger Shrub (page 323), along with a tad bit of ginger and lemon juice, and a good-quality gin makes for a refreshing cocktail to sip on those Friday evenings, relaxing the nerves and sliding into the weekend. The ginger juice gives a warm fuzzy feeling inside, which I love. You can use any liquor you fancy to create your own cocktails with the shrub.

INGREDIENTS

Ice

3 ounces (90 ml) gin

2 ounces (60 ml) Nectarine, Star Anise, and Ginger Shrub (page 323)

¼ teaspoons fresh ginger juice

2 teaspoons lemon juice

4 ounces (120 ml) club soda, chilled

GARNISH
Whole star anise

Few tiny cubes of nectarine

Drop of grenadine

METHOD

1. In a cocktail shaker, add the ice, gin, shrub, ginger juice, lemon juice, and club soda and stir for a minute to combine and get cold.

2. Using a cocktail strainer, pour the cocktail into cups. Garnish with star anise, a few of the nectarine cubes, and a drop of grenadine, stir, and serve cold. Cheers!

Peach, Mint, and Cardamom Lassi

Makes 2 servings

The sultry, balmy, humid, hot summers in Mumbai are something I do not miss at all! Showers would happen three times a day. It was unbearable! Perspiration was a real thing, compared to the dry California weather. Lassi was dessert many days, especially in the summers. What is lassi? It is a drink made with yogurt, water, and ice. It can be sweet or salty. I love both. The sweet one is usually sweetened with sugar and cardamom. Mum would make fruity sweet lassis and plain sweet lassis depending upon her mood. The fruity lassis were seasonal. Mango season would mean mango lassis, strawberry season would mean strawberry lassis. And other times we would simply have plain ones.

Lassi is a cooling drink for the body, especially from an Ayurveda perspective. It helps with digestion and bloating as well. Just like Mum, I love using seasonal fruits in my lassi, especially with all the summer California produce. My favorite combination is peach, mint, and cardamom. It is fruity, fresh, and floral, just the way I like it. It is my preferred drink of the summer!

INGREDIENTS

MINT SIMPLE SYRUP
¼ cup (50 g) granulated sugar
¼ cup (60 g) water, plus 1¼ cups (300 g) cold water
10 to 12 mint leaves

2 ripe peaches, washed and cut into cubes
1 cup (220 g) Greek yogurt
½ teaspoon (1 g) freshly ground cardamom
4 to 5 ice cubes

METHOD

1. In a small saucepan on medium heat, add the sugar, ¼ cup (60 g) of water, and mint leaves. Let the sugar dissolve and the mixture come to a simmer for a total of 3 to 4 minutes. Remove from the heat. The mint leaves will steep in the mixture for the next 10 minutes. Let it cool completely and then strain to remove the mint leaves.

2. In a high-speed blender, add the peaches, Greek yogurt, 1¼ cups (300g) of the cold water, cardamom, mint simple syrup, and ice and blend completely for 1 to 2 minutes.

3. Serve in 2 glasses over more ice if desired. Drink immediately and enjoy.

Haldar Nu Doodh (Turmeric Milk)

Makes 1 serving

Haldar Nu Doodh has become extremely popular all around the globe, widely known as "Golden Milk," and has its origins in India. Turmeric, the key ingredient in this drink, has been used in the Vedic culture of India for around 4,000 years. Turmeric is primarily grown in India and 80 percent of it is consumed in India. Per Ayurveda, the benefits of this spice are innumerable. It helps with anti-inflammation, digestion problems, asthma issues, colds, coughs, sore throats, pains, and more, all in moderation. It is widely used in Indian cooking and forms a huge part to give the food color and flavor.

Turmeric is a fantastic antiseptic and helps with open bruises and cuts. Whenever we would scrape ourselves as kids, while riding our bikes or playing outside on the concrete roads, Mum would immediately wash the wound and put a bit of turmeric to stop the blood from oozing. It would heal in a couple of days.

As a kid, I hated Haldar Nu Doodh. Whenever I had a cold or a cough, I had to have it. I would close my nose and quickly drink it, with my mum standing next to me closely watching. But it worked wonders and I would recover faster. As I grew older, I realized and appreciated this drink more than ever. When I moved to the United States and was all alone here without family, there were times I really missed her and her tips, tricks, and remedies. Over phone calls, I would ask her for the best remedies when I was sick, and it helped me recover faster.

Ginger and ghee help to smoothen out a scratchy throat. Ghee is also required since curcumin, which is the main active component found in turmeric, requires a fat to make the curcumin soluble. Jaggery is used to sweeten it to make it palatable. I add cardamom and cinnamon to the drink for added flavor. I use the same practices that my mother taught to me with my kids. It is the circle of life.

INGREDIENTS

1½ cups (180 g) whole milk, 2% milk, or plant-based milk

10 grams jaggery or honey

½ teaspoon ground turmeric

¼ to ½ teaspoon ground ginger

¼ teaspoon ground cinnamon

¼ teaspoon ground cardamom

¼ teaspoon black pepper

1 teaspoon ghee or coconut oil

METHOD

1. In a small saucepan on medium-low heat, add all the ingredients. Use a whisk to combine. Simmer the mixture for 5 minutes.

2. Strain the mixture through a fine sieve into a cup. Sip slowly and enjoy the soothing effects of Haldar Nu Doodh.

PRO TIP

My mother would make a paste of ground ginger, ground turmeric, pinch of black pepper, and jaggery and make small balls out of it, which are fantastic to cure sore throats.

Kachi Keri Nu Sharbat (Raw Mango and Fennel Concentrate/Syrup)

Makes about one 32-ounce (1 L) jar

Aam Panna or Kachi Keri Nu Sharbat is a very popular Indian drink in the summer months. Kachi keri means green or raw mango, sharbat means a cooling drink. It has cooling properties because of the raw mango pulp in it. It helps to replenish from severe heat and dehydration. It is good for digestion because of the mint, cumin, and fennel, which help to relieve stomach-related issues.

We grew up drinking a lot of this sharbat in the 100% humidity Indian summers, which were wretched, sweaty, and dehydrating. We would step out of the house and our clothes would be drenched with sweat. Luckily, we lived by the coast in Mumbai, so the high levels of humidity helped with the dehydration to a certain extent. Aam panna was the much-needed thirst quencher. Mum would get the concentrate from the grocery store. She did not make it at home. I learned how to make this from a friend's mum who would make it at home. I would watch aunty, playing close attention to the aromas of the green mango and spices that went into it!

Summers in California are dry, so you feel dehydrated pretty quickly. Hence, I started making my own concentrate at home a few years ago. I store it in the fridge, and drink it with cold water, and a couple of ice cubes. Absolutely refreshing!

INGREDIENTS

1 pound (453 g) raw or green mangoes (approximately 2 mangoes)

2 cups (480 g) water

1 teaspoon (2 g) cumin seeds

½ teaspoon (1.2 g) whole black pepper

½ cup washed and packed mint

2 cups (400 g) granulated sugar

½ to ¾ teaspoon (3 to 4 g) rock salt or black salt

1 tablespoon (6 g) fennel seeds

1 tablespoon (15 g) lemon juice

METHOD

1. Peel the skin of the green mangoes using a peeler or a knife. Remove the flesh of the mango and set them aside. Try to remove as much flesh as you can with a sharp knife by getting as close to the seed in the middle as you can. Dice into 1-inch (2½ cm) cubes.

2. In a medium saucepan on medium heat, add the mango cubes and 1 cup (240 g) of the water. Add the lid and cook for 15 minutes. Keep stirring occasionally and mush the mango flesh with a masher.

3. Meanwhile, toast the cumin seeds and black pepper by putting them in a small skillet on medium heat, and toast for 3 minutes. Stir while toasting the seeds so that they do not burn. Cool after toasting.

4. In a coffee or spice grinder, grind the cumin and whole black pepper to a powder.

5. After the mangoes are cooked down in 15 minutes, remove from the heat. Add the mint, cover, and let sit for 5 minutes.

6. In a high-speed blender, add the mango flesh and mint to make a fine pulp.

7. Next, using the same medium saucepan, add the mango-mint pulp, additional 1 cup water, sugar, cumin-black pepper powder, rock salt, and fennel seeds. On medium heat, start cooking the pulp-sugar mixture to form a concentrate. Cook this mixture for about 15 minutes in total, stirring occasionally so as not to burn the mixture.

8. Cool the mixture for 5 minutes. Strain through a fine to medium sieve to get a smooth concentrate. Add the lemon juice and mix.

9. Using a funnel, add the concentrate to a bottle, and refrigerate it for up to a month.

PRO TIP

Rock salt gives this concentrate its distinct flavor, but if you do not have it, you can use sea salt.

Kachi Keri Margarita

Makes 2 cocktails

After caipirinhas, margaritas are Raj's second favorite cocktail. We make all different kinds of margaritas depending upon the seasonal fruit. While my personal favorite is a blood orange margarita, this Kachi Keri Margarita has become a close second.

Kachi Keri Nu Sharbat (page 330) is a raw mango and fennel syrup or concentrate that I make in the summer months when the heat is unbearable. A glass with the syrup, along with water and some ice cubes, really helps to cool my insides and takes me back to the hot summers of Bombay, reminiscing about all the sharbat I had as a kid! This syrup makes the flavor base of a wonderful lip-smacking margarita that my husband has slowly grown to like. Since I have the syrup in the fridge at all times, the margaritas are simple to whip up in no time!

INGREDIENTS

1 lime, cut into half to rub the rim

2 teaspoons (8 g) granulated sugar

Lots of ice

4 ounces (120 ml) good-quality tequila

2 ounces (60 ml) triple sec

2 ounces (60 ml) fresh lime juice

2 to 3 ounces (60 to 90 ml) Kachi Keri Nu Sharbat (page 330)

GARNISH

Ice, for the glass

Whole lime slices

Mint

METHOD

1. Prepare the glasses. Rub the rim of the glass with half a lime. On a plate, distribute the sugar. Invert the glass and dip it in the sugar, making sure to coat the entire rim. Repeat with the second glass.

2. Add ice in the glasses three-quarters of the way.

3. In a cocktail shaker, fill it one-third of the way with ice. Add the tequila, triple sec, lime juice, and Kachi Keri Nu Sharbat. Close the cocktail shaker and shake continuously and vigorously for 20 to 25 seconds.

4. Pour the margarita equally into each glass.

5. Garnish with a lime wheel and lots of mint.

PRO TIP Add ½ teaspoon of rock salt to the sugar for the rim to give is a slight sweet-salty rim.

Masala Chaas
(Masala Buttermilk/Savory Lassi)

Makes two 8-ounce (240 ml) servings

Masala Chaas, or buttermilk, is a cooling drink consumed in different forms in India. It is essentially made with yogurt, spices such as rock salt, black pepper, and freshly ground roasted cumin, and aromatics such as ginger and cilantro. I like adding green chilis to it as well to make a spicy buttermilk, and it turns out really good. Mumbai has a very humid climate, and to survive in that climate, you need cooling drinks all the time. Masala Chaas was one of them, and we had it with every lunchtime meal. We had tiffinwallas or dabbawallas that came to school, who would deliver baskets with tiffins in it, filled with hot food from home, that Mum had prepared. She would always pack Masala Chaas for us in a thermos, and I would pour it in the stainless steel glasses for my brother and I.

Masala Chaas has a lot of benefits. The drink is cooling for the body, and helps to calm the stomach after a spicy meal. The spices, such as ginger, black pepper, and cumin, help to aid digestion. It also aids sleep, and you will surely feel sleepy after that glass of cold chaas! This drink helps in dehydration as well because of the yogurt and the salt in it. Enjoy it after a heavy Indian meal or have it as is during hot summer days and you will feel 100 percent refreshed after that glass of cold Masala Chaas.

INGREDIENTS

1¾ cup (170 g) Greek yogurt

1 cup (240 g) water

5 to 6 ice cubes

¾ teaspoon rock salt

½ teaspoon black pepper

½ teaspoon freshly ground roasted cumin

1 teaspoon freshly grated ginger

2 tablespoons chopped cilantro

1 tablespoon chopped mint

METHOD

Add all the ingredients in a high-speed blender and blend until it's fully incorporated. Pour into 2 glasses. Enjoy it cold.

PRO TIP This is best made fresh and enjoyed with a spicy meal to cool off the spiciness.

Thandai Cocktail

Makes 4 cocktails

Bhaang is a natural alcohol prepared from cannabis. It has been used for thousands of years in foods and drink preparations in India. In fact, it is added to the traditional Thandai drink that is consumed during the spring festival of Holi—the Festival of Colors. It is a very customary drink served to adults at big events/parties during the Holi Festival, when people of all ages, no matter what caste or creed, gather together, wearing light-colored clothes and throw color at each other in celebration of the onset of spring, which means harvest time for the farmers.

Growing up in Mumbai, my family and I would gather with our friends in our neighborhood and we would play Holi, throwing color, chasing each other, and trying to get each other wet with water balloons! It was a lot of fun—a day when you simply got messy and mum would not tell us anything, even if the house got dirty. Those were really fun days that I cherish, and the memories are etched in my mind.

The Holi Thandai drink inspired me to make a Thandai Cocktail with oat milk. I love the texture of oat milk, and how creamy it is. It is naturally quite light, and oat milk, along with the Thandai Masala (page 38) and sugar turns out quite wonderful by itself. The mixture, when combined with the almond liqueur and brandy, makes for a, smooth dessert cocktail, and a lovely, delicate finish to an Indian meal. Tiny sips of this drink over a good conversation with good friends is how I envision this cocktail. Super easy to make and a perfect way to end a laughter filled night!

INGREDIENTS

2 cups (490 g) oat milk

3 tablespoons (21 g) Thandai Masala (page 38)

3 tablespoons (37.5 g) granulated sugar

2 ounces (60 ml) almond liqueur, plus 1 tablespoon for the rim

3 tablespoons finely chopped pistachios

1 tablespoon (12.5 g) granulated sugar

2 ounces (60 ml) brandy

Ice for the cocktail shaker, and some for the glass

GARNISH

Rose petals

METHOD

1. In a small to medium saucepan on medium heat, add the oat milk, Thandai Masala, and granulated sugar and whisk to combine. Simmer for 5 to 6 minutes, stirring occasionally to pick up the flavors of the Thandai Masala. Remove from the heat. Cover the saucepan and steep for 20 minutes.

2. Strain the mixture through a fine sieve into a small container. Using a small rubber spatula, press against the sieve to gather all the flavors from the leftover masala and strain any liquid through the sieve. Mixture should be cool, at room temperature.

continued ➡

3. Prepare 4 glasses. On two separate small plates, add 1 tablespoon almond liquor to one plate, and add the finely chopped pistachios and granulated sugar to the other plate. Mix to combine.

4. Invert the glass, first onto the plate with the liquor to wet the rim. Transfer the glass into the second plate with the pistachio-sugar mixture and coat the rim again. Add 2 to 3 ice cubes in the glass and set aside.

5. In a cocktail shaker, add the oat milk-Thandai mixture, almond liqueur, brandy, and lots of ice. Close the shaker tightly, and shake for 20 to 25 seconds vigorously.

6. Pour evenly into the glasses with a strainer on the cocktail shaker.

7. Decorate with rose petals in each glass and serve chilled.

PRO TIPS

1. The oat milk-Thandai mixture can be made 2 to 3 days in advance. Simply prepare the cocktail when ready to serve.

2. The Thandai drink can be made non-alcoholic. Skip the step of adding the alcohol. Continue with all the remaining steps and serve.

Accompaniments and Snacks

Accompaniments are like sidekicks, without which a main meal is incomplete. Every Indian main meal has a counterpart, which is an essential part of the meal. For example, breads, pulao, biryani, rice, or raita make up the side dishes, which are required with the main curry or daals or vegetable dish on your dinner table.

As kids, we knew when there were puri being made in the kitchen because of that very alluring smell of frying. We would run to the kitchen to eat the hot puri off the stove. Puri were made on special occasions and we would get excited to eat them. I am sharing the Spinach Puri (page 342), which my kids have grown to love now, and the scene repeats itself, with them running to get dibs on the first puri. It is indeed amazing how life comes full circle, and there are so many déjà vu moments.

Rotli, thepla, and paratha are the humblest meals in all Gujarati homes. They are the first breads I learned to make from my mother at a tender age of 9. I remember making different states of India while trying my hand at rolling the rotli. It took me a while to get them round. But after much practice, I got the hang of it. I am sharing my childhood recipes with you and hopefully you can get the rotli round much faster than I did!

I am also sharing a couple of my favorite North Indian breads that are not typical of a Gujarati kitchen, but are widely known in all parts of the world and enjoyed with a few of the mains in this book, like my soft and fluffy Butter Garlic Naan (page 357), and the Wild Mushroom and Green Garlic Kulcha (page 351), which we love as is, hot off the stove! Vegetable Pulao (page 369) is my ba or grandmother's recipe, which she makes every time there is kadhi. I love this pulao plain with yogurt, or with my Fajeto (Mango Kadhi or Mango Yogurt Soup, page 208).

You'll find other accompaniments, such as Saffron Aioli (page 379) and Fried Curry Leaf and Toasted Cumin Aioli (page 370), which are great with the appetizers in this book.

Snacks are to Gujaratis what wine is to Americans. Gujaratis cannot live without their snacks. Snacks make up the accompaniment for teatime, usually around 4 p.m., when a hot cup of masala chai is essential to carry forward with the second part of the day. Snacks were always prevalent in our home. And my mother made a lot of them. My brother and I fought over the last bits of any snack that our mum made. We got back from school at 4 p.m. and there were always some fresh or dried snacks available for us to munch on before we got on with our homework. Panzanella with Vaghareli Sourdough Bread (page 389) is a twist on the classic Vaghareli bread that was one of my most favorite afterschool snacks. It is not a surprise that my twist has become a hit with my kids now! Chevdo, or a dried crunchy mix, was a must in the house. There would be fried chevdo at home, but my Cornflakes Chevdo (page 363) is a derivative of Mum's sekelo poha chevdo or roasted flat rice chevdo, and it is really addictive! It makes for a great homemade gift as well. Other snacks, such as Masala Mixed Nuts (page 383) or Masala Potato Chips (page 375), are perfect bites to have with a cocktail or wine.

This chapter has some of my favorite accompaniments and snacks. They have become a part of my kitchen and my family, and I hope they will become a part of yours, too.

Spinach Puri

Makes 24 (4- to 5-inch, 10 to 13 cm) round puri

Puri are deep fried dough, usually made from whole wheat flour or all-purpose flour and eaten with any curry. Puri is an essential part of a fancy home cooked meal. They were special occasion treats. If we had some guests over for lunch or dinner, or my father's business associates over, puri were made as part of an elaborate Gujarati meal called Thali. Thali consists of various vegetarian dishes, curries, daal, rice, some savory snacks, an Indian sweet dish, and hot puri. No fancy Indian meal is complete without these iconic fried beauties!

There are many kinds of puri in our Gujarati culture. We have plain ones, masala (page 360), spinach (as per this recipe.), jaggery (sweet puri), and paratha (which are double the size of the puri slit with two lines in the middle). The puri are green because of the spinach and cilantro in them. They taste amazing as is, or with the Bateta Nu Shaak (Potato Curry, page 181). These are a huge hit with my kids. Another popular way of eating puri is also with shrikand, which is essentially sweetened yogurt spiced with cardamom, saffron, and nutmeg, and garnished with almonds and pistachios. The combination is any kid's favorite meal.

INGREDIENTS

2 cups (480 g) water

3 cups (80 g) packed spinach

½ cup (20 g) packed cilantro

330 grams whole wheat flour

½ teaspoon (3 g) table salt

1 teaspoon (2 g) freshly grated ginger

3 tablespoons (28 g) vegetable oil

½ teaspoon (1 g) cumin seeds

½ teaspoon (1 g) carom seeds or ajwain

Oil for frying

METHOD

1. In a medium pot over medium heat, add the water and bring to a simmer for about 2 minutes. Add the washed spinach and cilantro for 2 to 3 minutes until it has all wilted. Strain the spinach and cilantro through a medium mesh strainer, reserving the water to bind the dough. Put the greens in a food processor to make a green pulp.

2. In a large bowl, add the flour, salt, ginger, green pulp, 2 tablespoons oil, cumin, and carom seeds, and mix. Slowly add ¾ cup (180 g) of the reserved water to the dough and combine. The dough should NOT be sticky, but pliable at the same time. If the dough is sticky, add about 2 to 3 tablespoons of flour at a time and knead the dough to come to a pliable consistency. If the dough is too dry and you are unable to bind all the dry dough, add 1 tablespoon more of the reserved water at a time. Keep kneading for

continued ➡

3 minutes. Add 1 tablespoon more vegetable oil on the surface to make it soft and pliable. Cover the bowl with plastic wrap and set it aside.

3. In a medium to large pot, add oil for frying on medium to high heat, and bring it to 350°F—measure using a fryer thermometer. Keep a plate with paper towel to soak up excess oil.

4. Make small balls of the dough, weighing about 25 grams each. Roll them between the palm of your hands to make a round ball and then flatten them gently. Keep them aside.

5. Using a rolling pin and a rolling board/marble slab, roll each ball out round into about a 4- to 5-inch (10 to 13 cm) diameter circle to make the puri. The trick is to first roll out the dough in a circular motion and then uniformly around the edges, and keep turning the flat dough to get an even and uniform round circle.

6. You can roll one by one and fry them, or I like to roll out a few at a time (four or five), set them aside on a plate, and then fry them all, before rolling out the next batch.

7. Once your oil is ready, add each puri into the oil. With a spider skimmer, tap the puri gently to make it rise—it will start puffing up immediately, about 20 seconds. Turn the puri to cook the other side for 10 to 15 seconds. Remove it from the oil and place it on the paper towel. It will be slightly brown with small bubbles on the top.

8. Roll out the other puri, and fry them two at a time. Your piping hot Spinach Puri are ready to eat.

PRO TIPS

1. Use a tortilla press to make the puri or roll them out with a rolling pin, like you do pastry dough.

2. Fried foods can sometimes cause acidity and indigestion, and one way to prevent it is to use carom seeds in the dough, which helps with better digestion of fried foods. That's why these puri have carom seeds in them.

3. To get puffy puri, it is important to roll them out evenly and uniformly, and one way to do so is to first roll on the dough in a circular motion to increase the size, and then roll around the edges one side at a time, and to keep the shape perfectly round. It requires practice, and you get better as you practice more.

4. Puri are fantastic with aam ras or mango puree. It is a must try!

Plain Rotli

Makes about 25 (6-inch, 15 cm) rotli

What is rotli? Rotli, or roti, is the most basic, simple bread, eaten in many parts of India, made from three ingredients: whole wheat flour, water, and oil. It is unleavened flatbread that goes well with practically any curry or Indian-spiced vegetable. It is a vessel for carrying all the spiced foods and it complements the spicy curries. Consisting of carbohydrates, it gives us energy. It is the essential part of any Indian household, especially Gujaratis. Rotli is made as part of every meal, along with vegetable or shaak, lentils or daal, and rice. It completes an Indian thali.

I have the fondest memories of standing on a stool when I was 9, making rotli with my mum in the kitchen with her rolling pin and her marble round board. She would cook the rotli on the tawa or the flat pan, and then place it on an open flame to make it puff up, all with her bare hands, and I would be amazed at her skills! "Mommy how do you do that?!" To date, I am unable to do so. I use tongs. Making rotli with my mum was my favorite pastime. I would make all these different shapes, which would not puff up and she would still go ahead, cook and eat them!. Such was the immense patience in her, which of course I lack when it comes to my kids. I know a lot of Indian readers will relate to my story, since rotli is one of the first breads that we learn as kids.

A smear of ghee on the hot rotli with the spiced vegetables and daal is the kind of comfort food that I crave, especially when I would miss home and miss my mum after being in this country. It would take me back to my mum's kitchen, standing next to her, watching her do her magic, cooking meals day in and day out for our family without a snitch of complaining, and always with that beautiful smile on her face.

I hope you will give these rotli a try. Once you get the hang of it, you will see how fast it goes, and there is nothing more comforting than fresh, hot, homemade rotli as a healthy delicious meal accompaniment.

INGREDIENTS

340 grams whole wheat flour, plus extra for rolling out the dough

1 cup (240 g) warm water

2 teaspoons (9 g) vegetable oil

½ cup (90 g) ghee

EQUIPMENT

Round rolling board (marble board)

Rolling pin

Flat tongs

Wire gauze or rotli grill

Flat pan for the rotli

continued ➤

METHOD

1. In a large bowl, add the whole wheat flour and add the warm water slowly, ½ cup (120 g) at a time, mixing with your fingers to bind the dough together. Add all the water and combine the dry flour from the sides of the bowl into the middle to bind the dough. Keep mixing it until it comes together, about 3 to 4 minutes. Add the vegetable oil and massage the dough with your hand, moving it around inside the bowl, to collect all the dry bits together until the bowl appears clean. Keep kneading for 2 to 3 minutes. The dough is ready when you press a finger into the dough and it bounces back slightly. If the dough is sticky (depending upon the flour brand you use), add 2 tablespoons extra flour at a time, knead again to ensure that it is pliable and cohesive, and not sticky.

2. Let the dough rest, covered with a kitchen towel for half an hour, for the gluten to develop.

3. Divide the dough into 25 pieces, each piece about 25 grams.

4. Roll each piece between the palm of your hands into a small round ball and flatten it ever so slightly, and keep it in the bowl. Repeat for all the other pieces. You will get 25 discs of dough, ready to be rolled out into rotli. Keep them covered with a kitchen towel to prevent from drying out.

5. Keep the marble board and rolling pin handy. Place a bowl with the extra flour next to your board as well. On the stove at medium heat, heat up the flat pan. On the other side of the stove, turn on the heat, and have the rotli grill (wire gauze) ready. Keep a plate on the side to place the cooked rotli.

6. Take a piece of the flat disc, drench it in the extra flour, and place it on the rolling board. Using the rolling pin, flatten the dough slightly and, using very even pressure on both the palms of your hands and consistent movement, keep moving the rolling pin, to flatten out the dough.

Sprinkle extra flour if the dough sticks ever so slightly to the board. The movement should be fluid and consistent to roll out the dough thin enough into a 6-inch (15 cm) round disc.

7. After it is about 4 inches round, I apply even pressure on the outside of each disc and keep moving the disc to make all the sides evenly round on the outside. This ensures that the rotli will puff up when you place it on the stove. This comes with a bit of practice but once you get it, it is an elated feeling.

8. Place the rotli on the flat pan, and cook for about 45 seconds. Turn to the other side using the tongs and cook for about 5 seconds. Using your tongs, place the rotli on the rotli grill on the second stove and turn up the heat to high. It will slowly puff up. Once it is puffed, turn the rotli using your tongs and let it char on the second side.

9. Place the cooked rotli on the plate on the side, and smear with a teaspoon of ghee.

10. Repeat Steps 6, 7, 8, and 9, until you get a whole stack of rotli. Eat immediately or store them wrapped up in an aluminum foil, in the fridge, up to 3 days.

PRO TIPS

1. The recipe is in grams because it forms the best dough for rotli with the amount of flour to water ratio.

2. Practice makes perfect! Keep playing with your first few pieces of dough to get a feel of the dough. It takes practice but you WILL get it.

3. The rotli stay fresh for up to 3 days in the fridge, covered in aluminum foil. To eat them, simply warm in the microwave, one rotli at a time, for about 15 seconds.

Masala Popcorn
WITH PEANUTS AND CARAMEL

Serves 4 to 6

My younger brother and I went to the same school. We would meet during our short breaks by the school entrance to get a snack. There was a vendor who would sell peanuts, potato chips, and masala popcorn for one rupee each. My brother would either get the peanuts or potato chips, and I would get my favorite masala popcorn. This was an almost daily ritual that I loved. He has the ability to finish a pretty decent bag of peanuts in one seating!

This creation is a riff on both our love of peanuts and masala popcorn, and I brought them together in a cluster with caramel, because everything that I make has a smidge of sweet, salty, and spicy. Masala popcorn by itself is highly addictive and my kids love it so much that I make it quite often for movie night. But ever since I made the masala popcorn with peanuts and caramel, it's become THE snack for movie night! The recipe is super simple and comes together in 30 minutes.

INGREDIENTS

1½ teaspoons (3 g) ground turmeric

¼ to 1 teaspoon (2 g) red chili powder, depending on how spicy you like it

2 teaspoons (12 g) table salt

2 tablespoons (26 g) granulated sugar

4 tablespoons (54 g) vegetable oil

1 cup (192 g) popcorn kernels

1½ cups (150 g) roasted peanuts

CARAMEL

½ cup (1 stick; 113 g) unsalted butter

1 cup (200 g) light brown sugar

⅓ cup (100 g) corn syrup

1 teaspoon Maldon salt

1 teaspoon (4 g) vanilla extract

METHOD

To Make the Popcorn

1. In a small bowl, add the spices, salt and sugar and mix to combine.

2. In a large deep nonstick saucepan or Dutch oven, add the oil on medium heat. Once the oil is hot after about 2 to 3 minutes, add about 3 to 4 popcorn kernels, and close with the lid. After 2 minutes, you will hear the popcorn pop. At this point, turn off the heat. Remove the popped kernels.

3. Add all the remaining popcorn kernels. Add the spices and sauté to mix well. Place the lid back onto the saucepan. Turn on the heat tro medium to high heat for a minute. Now, lower the heat to medium. The kernels will start popping in 2 minutes or so; continue popping for 30 seconds. At that point, shake the pot a couple of times, holding the lid with both hands to stir the kernels around with the spices.

continued ➡

4. Kernels will keep popping, until the sound subsides. At this point, remove from the heat. Let sit for 2 minutes as it will be very hot.

5. Remove all the popped corn into a big bowl, making sure that the unpopped kernels are left behind in the pan. Keep the peanuts handy by the side.

6. Line two half baking sheets with parchment paper. Adhere the parchment paper, by using a bit of cooking spray on all four corners of the baking sheet, and then putting the parchment paper on top.

7. Distribute the popcorn evenly between the two baking sheets and spread evenly. Distribute the peanuts between the baking sheets and evenly spread.

8. Preheat the oven to 250°F (120°C).

To Make the Caramel

1. Meanwhile, prepare the caramel. In a medium saucepan, add the butter, light brown sugar, and corn syrup. On medium heat, mix it with a rubber spatula and bring the mixture to a boil. Boil for about 4 minutes without touch-ing it, and your caramel is done. Turn off the stove, add the Maldon salt and vanilla extract and mix.

2. Immediately pour half of the caramel on the popcorn on the first baking sheet. Use two rubber spatulas to mix well. This process has to be fast, since the caramel will solidify. Spread it out as soon as possible on the baking sheet and smooth it out with the rubber spatula.

3. Repeat Step 2 with the remaining caramel on the second baking sheet.

4. Place the baking sheets on the medium and bottom rack. Bake the mixture for 15 minutes. The popcorn will become crunchy.

5. Remove and let cool for 20 minutes. Break off clusters and store it in an airtight container for up to 5 days, if it lasts!

 PRO TIP Skip the caramel and the peanuts and just enjoy the spicy popcorn.

Wild Mushroom and Green Garlic Kulcha

Makes six (5½- to 6-inches, 12 to 15 cm) kulcha

A few years ago, when I was visiting my family in Mumbai, we went to a fine-dining restaurant called Masala Library, owned by the very famous late Chef Jiggs Kalra. The restaurant has a great concept of fusion foods, and the menu is wonderfully constructed with ingenious creativity. You can see the effort that has been put into each dish and in the meticulous preparation and service as well. It was an overall fantastic experience that I will always remember. They had a mushroom kulcha that I thoroughly enjoyed and I wanted to recreate it with the amazing California produce from the farmers' market.

Green garlic is an underrated allium that has so much flavor and fragrance without being too potent like garlic cloves. So, I came up with a filling, using beautiful wild mushrooms like shiitake and oyster mushrooms (that are organically sold at my local farmers' market), and the green garlic with Indian spices. You can always substitute the wild mushrooms with button mushrooms, and the green garlic with four to five cloves of garlic cloves. The filling is delicious and gives a wonderful aroma to the kulcha. The kulcha dough is fluffy and forms the perfect bed to scoop up raita and curries. I change up the curries every so often to make it a meal to remember.

INGREDIENTS

KULCHA

300 grams all-purpose flour
1 teaspoon (4 g) baking powder
1 teaspoon (5 g) baking soda
1 teaspoon (12 g) table salt
1 teaspoon (4 g) granulated sugar
2 tablespoons (38 g) Greek yogurt
3 tablespoons (42 g) melted butter
½ cup (120 g) warm water

FILLING

1 tablespoon (13 g) olive oil
2 tablespoons (28 g) unsalted butter
2½ heaping cups (170 g) wild mushrooms such as shiitake, oyster, crimini, etc, finely chopped
1 cup (80 g) finely chopped green garlic

½ teaspoon (6 g) table salt
½ teaspoon (1 g) chaat masala
½ teaspoon (1 g) amchur (dried mango powder)
½ teaspoon (1 g) ground turmeric
½ teaspoon (1 g) garam masala
⅓ cup (15 g) finely chopped cilantro

TOPPING

¼ cup (20 g) finely chopped green garlic
¼ cup (12 g) finely chopped cilantro
2 tablespoons (20 g) onion seeds (kalonji)
Oil, for rolling out dough
4 tablespoons (½ stick; 56 g) butter, melted

continued ➡

PRO TIPS

1. Kulcha are best eaten with cucumber raita and chole masala.

2. The stuffed kulcha can also be eaten with any of the curries like the Bateta Nu Shaak (page 181) or the Vegetable Koftas in Tomato Cashew Curry (page 198).

METHOD

To Make the Kulcha Dough

1. In a large bowl, add the all-purpose flour, baking powder, baking soda, salt, and sugar, and whisk to combine. Add the Greek yogurt and melted butter, and combine with a spatula or a fork.

2. Add the warm water, and bring the dough together with your hands. Keep massaging the dough until it all comes together and looks smooth. Knead the dough for 2 to 3 more minutes to round it out, and smoothen out the edges. Use a slightly wet and clean kitchen towel, and cover the dough. Let rest for 1½ hours.

To Make the Filling

1. Meanwhile, let's make the filling. In a medium nonstick pan on medium to high heat, add the olive oil, and butter and melt the butter. Add the mushrooms, green garlic, salt, and all the spices and sauté ever so often. Cook the mixture for 5 to 7 minutes. It will reduce considerably. Add the cilantro and sauté for 2 more minutes. Remove from the heat.

2. Remove the mixture into a bowl and let cool completely.

To Make the Stuffed Kulcha

1. Divide the dough into six equal portions, each portion about 95 g, or weigh your dough and divide by six, to get an exact amount of dough.

2. Round up each piece of dough between the palm of your hands, where one hand has clockwise motion and the other hand has a counterclockwise motion to form an exact round. Repeat for the remaining five pieces.

3. Cover with the wet kitchen towel and rest for an hour.

4. Heat a medium nonstick skillet or cast-iron skillet on medium to high heat.

5. Take one dough ball, and on a wooden surface or marble surface, pat it with a little bit of oil to form a flat surface that is about 4 inches in diameter.

6. Add about 2 tablespoons of the filling into the center, collect the dough overhang to cover the filling properly, twist the top of the dough to seal, and pat it flat between the palms of your hands to flatten.

7. Using a drop of oil, pat the flattened dough on the surface with the tips of your fingers, as well as the heel of your hand to extend the dough into a round shape about 5½ to 6 inches in diameter.

8. Add another drop of oil and spread it on the top of the flattened dough. Sprinkle a bit of the green garlic, cilantro, and onion seeds on the top and press it gently with your fingers to adhere to the dough.

9. Lift the dough gently off the surface, brush the bottom layer of the kulcha with water, and place on the hot pan. The water creates steam that helps to create the layers for the kulcha. Cook for about 2 minutes on each side.

10. Once both sides are cooked, apply melted butter with a pastry brush, on top of the toppings and place it on a plate.

11. Repeat the process for the remaining five pieces of dough. Your kulcha are ready to eat.

Triangle Paratha

Makes 15 paratha

Paratha are essentially layered flatbread made with whole wheat flour, water, and oil or ghee, and sometimes spiced with red chili powder. They are pretty filling for breakfast, lunch, or dinner, and can be eaten simply with spiced mango pickle and masala chai but they are very tasty by themselves spiced with salt and red chili powder. They are layered, rolled, put on a hot pan and cooked with a bit of oil or ghee, which makes it hearty and filling. Paratha go well with any type of curry as well.

Mum would make these Triangle Paratha that we would have with a restaurant style curry. This was the next unleavened bread that I learned to make after rotli and I found that it was fun and easy. The fun part about these paratha are that they look like wobbly triangles. They do not have to be the perfect round shape that we otherwise strive for with other Indian flatbreads, making it a bit easier than the quintessential rotli. They are ever so slightly thicker than the rotli and go well with a thick daal as well. Paratha keep well for a few days in the fridge. Try your hand at making these fun wobbly triangles. Trust me—it makes for a fun experience!

INGREDIENTS

300 grams whole wheat flour, plus extra for rolling out the dough

1 cup (240 g) warm water

2 tablespoons (28 g) vegetable oil

1½ tablespoons (26 g) table salt

1 tablespoon (8 g) Kashmiri red chili powder

3 tablespoons (42 g) vegetable oil

Oil, for shallow frying the paratha

METHOD

1. In a large bowl, add the whole wheat flour and the warm water slowly, ½ cup (120 g) at a time, mixing with your fingers to bind the dough together. Add all the water and combine the dry flour from the sides of the bowl into the middle to bind the dough. Keep mixing it until it comes together, about 3 to 4 minutes. Add the vegetable oil and massage the dough with your hand, moving it around inside the bowl to collect all the dry bits together until the bowl appears clean. Keep kneading for 2 to 3 minutes. The dough is ready when you press a finger into the dough and it bounces back slightly. If the dough is sticky (depending upon the flour brand you use), add 2 tablespoons extra flour at a time and knead again to ensure that it is pliable and cohesive, and not sticky.

2. Let the dough rest, covered with a kitchen towel for half an hour, for the gluten to develop.

3. Divide the dough into 15 pieces, each piece about 35 g.

4. Roll each piece between the palm of your hands into a small round ball and flatten it ever so slightly, and keep it in the bowl. Repeat for all the other pieces. You will get 15 discs of dough, ready to be rolled out into paratha. Keep them covered with a kitchen towel to prevent from drying out.

5. Keep the marble board and rolling pin handy. Place a bowl with the extra flour next to your board as well. On the stove at medium heat,

continued ➡

heat the flat nonstick skillet. Keep a plate on the side to place the cooked paratha.

6. Take a piece of the flat disc, drench it in the extra flour, and place it on the rolling board. Using the rolling pin, flatten the dough slightly and, using very even pressure on the palms of your hands and consistent movement, keep moving the rolling pin to flatten out the dough to a small 4-inch (10 cm) circle. Add ½ a teaspoon of oil and sprinkle a pinch each of salt and red chili powder in the center. Using your index and middle finger tips, smear the oil, salt, and chili powder in a circular motion and spread it to about a 2-inch-wide (5 cm) circle.

7. Fold the circle into half and then a quarter. Press it with your palm and start rolling it evenly to form a rough triangle paratha. Make sure to roll out the pointed edges and also all the sides to even out the paratha. Roll it to about 6 inches diameter.

8. Place the paratha on the flat pan, add about 2 teaspoons of oil around the paratha and cook for about 45 seconds. It will start to bubble on the top. Turn to the other side using a flat spatula and cook for about another 30 to 40 seconds, pressing gently with the flat spatula, until there are brown spots on the bottom of the paratha.

9. Place the cooked paratha on the plate on the side.

10. Repeat Steps 6, 7, 8, and 9, until you get a whole stack of paratha.

PRO TIPS

1. The recipe is in grams because this makes the accurate amount of dough and forms the best dough for the paratha with the amount of flour to water ratio.

2. Practice makes perfect! Keep playing with your first few pieces of dough to get a feel of the dough and to be able to move your rolling pin around on the dough.

3. The paratha stay fresh for up to 3 days in the fridge, covered in aluminum foil. To eat them, simply warm each paratha at a time in the microwave for about 15 seconds.

4. The paratha are best eaten with any kind of curry in this book.

Butter Garlic Naan

Makes about 10 naan

Naan is a leavened Indian flatbread found at every Indian restaurant and that people cannot get enough of. Naan originated from Persia in different forms. There is a lot of similarity between Indian and Persian spices, lentils, and breads.

India has many kinds of breads from the different regions and cuisines around the country. Naan is popular in Northern India, along with its famous cousin, roomali roti. Roomali roti is made with maida or all-purpose flour, and is a thin translucent roti that is stretched by throwing it in the air and cooked on a dome-shaped oven that is very hot.

Naan is made with all-purpose flour or a mix of all purpose and whole wheat flour, and active dry yeast. It gets its flavor from yogurt and softness from whole milk. It can be made using baking powder and baking soda as well, but I do like the flavor that is developed with the yeast. The bread process is pretty simple, with few ingredients. Traditionally naan is cooked in a tandoor or a clay oven, with hot coal burning inside, which gives the naan its signature char on top from all the air pockets formed due to the yeast. The way we try to mimic the tandoor and char is by using a tawa griddle. You brush water on the back of the naan and stick this to the tawa. If the naan sticks to the tawa, you can actually turn the entire tawa, and get the char marks on the naan by bringing it close to the gas flame, if you have a gas stove. The alternative is to simply use tongs and let it go directly on the gas stove to get the char marks.If you do not have a gas stove, you can cook the naan on a griddle, turning with tongs until you see brown or black spots appearing. The Maldon salt in the end gives it that final touch of flavor, taking it to the next level.

My kids and Raj love Butter Garlic Naan. I make it with a combination of all-purpose flour and whole wheat flour. I use them to make the Breakfast Naan Pizza (page 81) or the Tandoori Vegetable Wrap (page 205), which are both very popular at home.

INGREDIENTS

⅓ cup (80 g) warm water (105°F), plus more as needed for binding and brushing the dough

1 tablespoon (12.5 g) granulated sugar

1 envelope (7 g) active dry yeast

3 cups (450 g) all-purpose flour, plus extra for rolling out the dough

1 cup (145 g) whole wheat flour

2 teaspoons (12 g) salt

¾ cup (184 g) whole milk

½ cup (125 g) Greek yogurt

3 cloves garlic, grated

Vegetable oil

8 to 10 cloves garlic

⅓ cup finely chopped cilantro

1 tablespoon (10 g) onion seeds (kalonji or charnushka; optional)

4 tablespoons (½ stick; 56 g) melted butter

Maldon flaky salt

continued ➝

METHOD

1. In a small bowl, stir together the warm water, sugar, and yeast. Let it sit for 10 minutes. It should be foamy by then. If the yeast is not foamy, your yeast is not good and you should start with fresh yeast.

2. In a large mixing bowl, whisk together the flours and salt. Add the milk, yogurt, garlic, and yeast mixture. Mix the dough with both hands to bring it together into a dough. Add water 1 tablespoon at a time, up to ¼ cup (60 g), if need to help bind the dough. On a floured board, knead the dough for about 10 minutes, until it is smooth in texture. Oil the same mixing bowl, add the dough, cover with a tea towel or plastic wrap, and let it rest for 2 hours. It needs to be in a warm place at about 80°F (27°C). I keep it in the oven with the oven light on. Let the dough rise until doubled in size.

3. On a lightly floured board, knead the dough for 3 to 4 minutes to develop elasticity from the gluten. Divide the dough into 10 equal pieces, about 100 grams in weight, and roll them into balls. Place on parchment paper and cover with a tea towel for 10 minutes.

4. Heat a flat griddle, nonstick skillet, or cast-iron skillet on the stove on medium-high heat. Keep a pastry brush and a bowl with ¼ cup (60 ml) water handy next to the stove. Sprinkle some flour on the board. Remove one ball of dough, keeping the others covered. Starting from the center, roll out the ball of dough into an oblong shape about 8 inches (20 cm) long and 5 to 6 inches (12 to 15 cm) wide from the center. Grate one garlic clove on the dough and spread it with your fingers. Sprinkle 1 teaspoon chopped cilantro on top and press it lightly with your hands. Sprinkle about ¼ teaspoon onion seeds on top. Use the rolling pin to press the toppings lightly onto the dough. Turn the topping side of the naan onto your palm and gently brush water with the pastry brush on the back side of the naan.

5. Lay the wet side down onto the griddle and let it puff up undisturbed for up to 2 minutes. You will see air pockets form on the surface. If you have a gas stove, use tongs and flip the naan, placing it directly onto the gas burner. Let it cook for 10 seconds. Rotate it on the burner to cook different parts of the naan for another 10 seconds in total. You are looking to char the top of the naan to give it that signature charred taste and to cook the top too. If you do not have a gas stove, use tongs to flip the naan to the other side and cook on the griddle for another 30 seconds or so, to char the top.

6. Lightly brush the topping side of each naan with melted butter and remove it from the griddle. Sprinkle with Maldon flaky salt.

7. Repeat the same with all the naan, and they are ready to eat.

PRO TIPS

1. Make sure the water temperature is not more than 110°F, or it will kill the yeast.

2. If the dough does not rise and double in size, either the place where it was kept is not warm enough and you need to leave it for a longer time, or the yeast was not good and did not activate.

3. The naan can be stored in the fridge, wrapped in aluminum foil for up to a week.

Masala Puri

Makes about 30 (4-inch, 10 cm) puri

School vacation time in the Mumbai summer is the month of May, which is also peak mango season in India. As kids that meant a lot of things—constant playing with friends in our building compound, meeting school friends and having them over for stay overs, beach fun with family and friends, vacations, lots of mango desserts and ice creams, and indulgent foods made by our mother like the quintessential combination of Masala Puri with the Bateta Nu Shaak (page 181) and Mango Shrikhand . This would be our Sunday lunch sometimes, and we knew what meal this was going to be as soon as we could smell the fragrance of something being fried in oil. The anticipation was real and we would wait patiently for the puri to be fried, so that we could start eating it first with the Mango Shrikhand, almost like having an appetizer first! And then move on to the main course with the Bateta Nu Shaak.

These puri are really very easy. You simply mix all the ingredients in a bowl, knead the dough, make small balls, roll it out, and fry them. The spices are minimal and give the best flavor to these puri. Mum would always make extra puri so we could have it with masala chai the next day as breakfast. The combination of the Masala Puri with the chai is something that you have to taste yourself to understand what I am talking about. It is a taste of the sensory with the salty and slightly spicy puri with the sweet chai. This takes me right back home to Juhu, picturing my mum and I sitting on the sofa, bantering together and having our puri and chai for breakfast.

INGREDIENTS

330 grams whole wheat flour, plus extra for rolling out the dough

½ teaspoon (1 g) carom seeds or ajwain

½ teaspoon (1 g) cumin seeds

1 teaspoon (2 g) ground turmeric

¾ teaspoon (1.5 g) red chili powder

1¼ teaspoons (7 g) table salt

Pinch of asafoetida

2 tablespoons (28 g) vegetable oil

1 cup (240 g) warm water, plus more for binding the dough as needed

METHOD

1. In a large bowl, add the flour, carom seeds, cumin seeds, turmeric, red chili powder, salt, asafoetida, and oil and mix. Slowly add the water and bind the dough with your hand. The dough should not be sticky, and should be pliable at the same time. If the dough is too dry and you are unable to bind all the dry dough, add 1 tablespoon more water at a time and bind. Knead for 3 minutes. If the dough is too sticky, add about a tablespoon of flour at a time, until soft and pliable. Roll it into a ball. Cover the bowl with plastic wrap. Set it aside.

continued ➡

2. In a medium to large pot, add oil for frying on medium to high heat, heat it to 350°F (175°C), measuring with a fryer thermometer. Place a plate with the paper towel, to soak up excess oil, on the side.

3. Make small balls of the dough, weighing about 20 grams each. Roll them between the palm of your hands to make a round ball. Keep them aside. Set aside a small bowl with extra flour in it.

4. Using a rolling pin and a rolling board/marble slab, first flatten the dough ball gently between the palm of your hands. Then cover it with excess flour and roll each ball out round into about a 4-inch (10 cm) diameter circle to make the puri. The trick is to roll around the edges, and keep turning the flat dough, to get an even and uniform round circle.

5. You can roll one by one and fry them, or I like to roll out a few at a time (four or five), and then fry them all, before rolling out the next batch.

6. Once your oil is ready, add each puri into the oil. With a spider skimmer, tap the puri gently to make it rise, it will start puffing up immediately, within 10 seconds. Turn the puri to cook the other side for 10 to 15 seconds. Remove it from the oil and place it on the paper towel. It will be slightly brown with small bubbles on the top.

7. Roll out the other puri, and fry them two at a time. Your piping hot puri are ready to eat.

PRO TIPS

1. Use a tortilla press to make the puri or roll them out with a rolling pin, like you do pastry dough.

2. Fried foods can sometimes cause acidity and indigestion, and one way to prevent it is to use carom seeds in the dough, which helps with better digestion of fried foods. That's why these puri have carom seeds in them.

3. To get puffy puri, it is important to roll them out evenly and uniformly, and one way to do so is to roll around the edges one side at a time, and to keep the shape perfectly round. It requires practice, and you get better as you practice more.

Cornflakes Chevdo

Makes one 32-ounce (1 L) jar

Chevdo can be best described as a fried dry snack made with various different ingredients like puffed rice or flattened rice or chickpea flour crunchies as the base, and then tossed with various nuts and dried fruit, a couple of herbs like curry leaves, cilantro leaves, and dry Indian spices. Together, it makes a delicious, addictive snack that is absolutely hard to put away once you have a bite of it! Chevdo highlights the Gujarati palate of sweet, sour, spicy, and salty in one bite. It is a constant in Gujarati households, and has been popularized in Mumbai. There are countless varieties found in the Indian snack stores. I promise you that your eyes will pop out looking at the many options available. Whenever I return from a trip to India, one bag is at least half full with the different chevdos and farsan available there. You just do not get certain varieties in the US Indian grocery stores.

We grew up eating chevdo sometimes as breakfast with masala chai, or sometimes as a tea time snack around 4 p.m. Gujaratis associate chai with snacks. Both are inseparable and you cannot have one without the other. Chevdo was a constant in our home. Mum would make about 1 kilogram or 2 pounds of the chevdo and, of course, gift some to family and friends. She was famous for her chevdo. I learned how to make the fried flattened rice chevdo from her. She would also make a low-calorie roasted corn flakes chevdo, which is actually my favorite. When I left to come to America in 1999, she packed a lot of different homemade snacks, one of them being this Cornflakes Chevdo. My kids love it too. Rishan frequently helps me make it because it is really easy to put together.

INGREDIENTS

½ teaspoon (1 g) Kashmiri red chili powder

½ teaspoon (1 g) ground turmeric

½ to ¾ teaspoon (4 g) table salt

1 teaspoon (3 g) powdered sugar

1 teaspoon (2 g) mustard seeds

⅓ cup (48 g) raw peanuts

⅓ cup (50 g) raw broken cashew nuts

¼ cup (48 g) roasted bengal dal or dalia (optional)

¼ cup (40 g) golden raisins

10 curry leaves

1 green chili, horizontally cut into 4 pieces

¼ cup cilantro leaves (washed, and dried between paper towels)

3 cups (90 g) cereal corn flakes

⅛ teaspoon citric acid (optional)

3 tablespoons (40 g) vegetable oil

¼ cup (15 g) toasted coconut strips

continued ➜

METHOD

1. Keep all the ingredients ready to go in small bowls, because the process goes very quickly. For the spices like Kashmiri red chili powder, turmeric, salt, and powdered sugar, add it into a small bowl and whisk to combine.

2. In a large wok on medium heat, add the oil. Let it heat up for a minute. Add the mustard seeds and wait for them to splatter. Once they start popping, you can add the peanuts, cashews, and roasted bengal gram dal and sauté with a wooden spoon for 2 minutes. Add the golden raisins and sauté for a minute. Reduce the heat to low for the next step.

3. Next add the curry leaves and green chilis in a cleared area of the wok. It will splatter because of the water content in the leaves, so be careful. Once they start to wilt in a few seconds, add the cilantro leaves. The oil will splatter here too so be careful. Once the cilantro leaves start to wilt in a few seconds, move on to the next step.

4. Add all the spices and sauté again for 30 seconds.

5. Next add the corn flakes and sprinkle of citric acid and mix everything thoroughly to coat the corn flakes with all the spices for 2 minutes. Remove from the heat. Add the coconut strips and mix again.

6. Cool the mixture for an hour in the wok.

7. Store in an airtight container for up to 1 week for maximum freshness.

PRO TIP Citric acid gives the chevdo that slight sour taste but you can omit it if you do not have it or find it.

Radish Mint Cumin Raita

Makes about 2 cups (about 500 g)

Raita is a yogurt dip or a sauce, typically made with raw vegetables, or sometimes even fruit, along with a few spices. Raita is the best accompaniment to any Indian meal, as it acts as a fantastic coolant to cool your throat down after eating a spice laden-meal.

I remember those meals where Mum would make fruit raita, with the different in season fruits, and chaat masala to spice it up. The combination of the salty, sweet, and the luxurious texture of the yogurt (dahi) was absolutely delicious on the palate. We would have raita as an after-school snack sometimes, especially on those hot summer days where the heat was simply unbearable.

I love radishes. It is an acquired taste. California farmers' markets are always abundant with different kinds of radishes. I love eating them just like that—sliced with a squeeze of lemon on it. I love the spicy, peppery taste and that, combined with yogurt, some mint, and freshly toasted and ground cumin in this raita here is absolutely divine! It is the perfect accompaniment to any of the main dishes, along with some Butter Garlic Naan (page 357), and you have a wonderful meal right there.

INGREDIENTS

1 teaspoon freshly roasted cumin seeds (see Pro Tip)

1½ cups (315 g) Greek yogurt

2 small radishes (80 to 90 g), finely grated (along with the liquid from the radish)

2 to 4 tablespoons water

1 teaspoon (6 g) table salt

1 teaspoon (4 g) granulated sugar

1 grated garlic clove

1 tablespoon finely chopped mint

1 tablespoon finely chopped cilantro

GARNISH

1 small (40 g) finely grated radish

Mint leaves

METHOD

1. In a coffee or spice grinder, grind freshly roasted cumin seeds to a coarse texture.

2. Whisk the Greek yogurt and water until the texture is smooth. Add all the remaining ingredients and mix to combine. Radishes contain a lot of water, which gives the raita a fluid consistency.

3. If the texture is a bit thick, you can add 2 tablespoons of water at a time to mix to get the right consistency.

4. Garnish with more finely grated radish and mint leaves.

PRO TIPS

1. To roast the cumin seeds, place them on a small skillet on medium-low heat. Stir occasionally for 2 to 3 minutes, until you get the aromas. Remove from the heat.

2. Raita is best served cold.

Vegetable Pulao

Serves 6

When plain rice is boring, pulao always comes to the rescue! As a kid, I didn't mind rice, but I really wanted some variety, and that's when Mum would make pulao. It is a dish that my ba (grandma) makes quite often, even to this day. Her pulao is very tasty, and when I make this Vegetable Pulao, it reminds me of Ba.

Pulao is an easy way to make the rice tasty by adding a few whole spices, a couple vegetables like green peas and carrots and letting it cook for a quick 20 minutes until it is fluffy and ready to eat. My favorite way to eat pulao is with Gujarati kadhi or a yogurt-based soup, which is absolutely delicious and one of my all-time favorite dishes.

INGREDIENTS

1 cup (185 g) basmati rice or long grain rice

3 cups (720 g) water

2 tablespoons (28 g) vegetable oil

2 teaspoons (4 g) cumin seeds

1 bay leaf (optional)

3 cardamom pods, crushed lightly

3 cloves

½ cup (85 g) green peas

1 small (50 g) carrot, diced into small pieces

2 cups (480 g) water

1 teaspoon (6 g) table salt

¼ cup finely chopped cilantro

METHOD

1. In a medium bowl, rinse the basmati rice by rubbing it with your hands under the water, draining the water, and repeating the process three or four times until the water drains clear.

2. Once the rice is clean, add 1 cup (240 g) of the water and let them soak for 30 minutes.

3. In a medium pot over medium heat, add the oil. After the oil has heated up for a minute, add the cumin seeds. Once it starts splattering after 30 seconds, add the bay leaf, cardamom pods, and cloves, and sauté for 15 seconds.

4. Drain the water from the rice, add the soaked rice into the pot, and sauté for a minute.

5. Add the green peas and carrots and sauté for a minute.

6. Add the remaining 2 cups (480 g) of water and salt, mix it around. Cover the lid, reduce the heat to medium, and cook the rice for 15 minutes.

7. After 15 minutes into the process, fluff up the rice with a fork, and cook for 5 more minutes for a total of 20 minutes of cooking.

8. Remove from the heat. Remove the lid, fluff up the rice, garnish with cilantro, and gently mix it into the rice. It is ready to serve.

PRO TIPS

1. Rinsing the rice is very important because it helps to remove the additional starch from the surface of the rice. The additional starch is what makes the rice clumpy.

2. Soaking the rice is very important for a soft and fluffy texture.

Fried Curry Leaf and Toasted Cumin Aioli

Makes about 1 cup (about 180 g)

Aioli is usually made out of garlic, salt, egg yolks, and olive oil, and is popular in the Mediterranean countries of Italy, Spain, and France. It is usually eaten with seafood. This dip is versatile and can be used with various flavor pairings to create a dynamic dip for any appetizer. I have used Indian flavors in this aioli to make a very delicious dip, with flavors of coarse roasted cumin and fried curry leaves in it. It gives the aioli a lovely aroma and texture from the fried curry leaf along with the earthiness of the roasted cumin.

INGREDIENTS

2 tablespoons (29 g) vegetable oil to fry

6 to 8 curry leaves

¾ cup (160 g) mayonnaise

1 garlic clove

1 tablespoon (15 g) lemon juice

½ teaspoon (1 g) roasted coarsely pounded cumin

¼ teaspoon black pepper

½ teaspoon (3 g) table salt

PRO TIPS

1. To roast the cumin seeds, place them on a small skillet on medium low heat. Stir occasionally for 2 to 3 minutes, until you get the aromas. Remove from the heat.

2. The aioli can be stored in an airtight container for up to a week.

METHOD

1. In a small frying pan on medium heat, add the vegetable oil to fry. After a minute, once the oil is heated, add the curry leaves. Make sure the curry leaves are patted dry with a paper towel. Be careful when you add them as the oil may splatter. It will fry up very quickly within a minute so keep a watch on it. Once they look shriveled, the curry leaves are fried and ready. Place it on the side onto a small plate with a paper towel.

2. In a medium bowl, add the mayonnaise. Grate in the garlic. Add the lemon juice, cumin, black pepper, and salt. Add 3 to 4 curry leaves lightly crushed with your fingers into the mixture and whisk to combine.

3. Garnish with the remaining fried curry leaves.

Roasted Tomato and Dried Pasilla Chili Salsa

Makes about 1 ½ to 2 cups

Our family loves Mexican food. But what's not to love? Mexican food is very similar to Indian food in many ways, such as our love for using our chilis in our foods to bring out the various spice levels. We love using different vegetables and colorful produce in our dishes. We have rotli and they have tortillas, which form the foundation of many of our dishes. Both cuisines have so many vegetarian options, and many more such similarities.

I love learning about Mexican culture, with its close proximity to California and the influence of Mexican food in California's culture. The influence is clearly present and we are lucky to have good authentic Mexican restaurants around us to experience and learn from. A few years ago, I took a couple cooking classes in Mexico, and it was fun learning straight from the chef. The experience was wonderful and I highly recommend taking cooking classes in any country that you visit, because you learn a lot about the people, the food, and the culture, and it makes for a memorable experience, one that you will never forget! It was the first time I had a Jamaica Agua Fresca, which is essentially a Hibiscus Lime Drink. It was really refreshing in the Mexican summer. One of the things we learned was to make different salsas from scratch, and I am sharing a tweaked recipe here with you all.

This Roasted Tomato and Dried Pasilla Chili Salsa will become a family favorite— I guarantee you! It is packed with a flavor punch, and has all the amazing flavors that remind you of the beautiful country of Mexico. I love those dried chilis—they are readily available at grocery stores and I always keep them in my pantry. Make this salsa, along with tortilla chips on the side, and watch your family and friends devour them!

INGREDIENTS

4 to 5 small to medium (300 to 320 g) tomatoes

½ medium (80 to 100 g) red onion, coarsely chopped into chunks

3 garlic cloves

1 jalapeño

2 dried pasilla chili

2 tablespoons (27 g) extra virgin olive oil

1 tablespoon apple cider vinegar

2 teaspoons (8 g) Maldon salt

½ teaspoon (1 g) black pepper

¼ cup tightly packed cilantro

Juice of 1 lime

METHOD

1. In a medium cast-iron skillet, or skillet, on medium to high heat, add the whole tomatoes, red onion, garlic cloves, jalapeño, and dried pasilla chili. Let it sit for 2 minutes. It will start charring. Using tongs, turn each vegetable individually to char all sides. Garlic and the pasilla chili will char faster, and it will be done in 5 minutes. You will start smelling the smokiness of the chili and the garlic. Remove the garlic and pasilla chili after 5 minutes into a medium bowl.

continued ➝

2. Keep turning the jalapeño, onions, and tomatoes, charring them equally on all sides. The tomatoes will start bursting and the juices will come out, but that's okay—keep turning and charring them. Remove the charred tomatoes and onions after 12 minutes into the medium bowl and cover with plastic wrap or aluminum foil to retain the heat and continue the cooking process.

3. Keep turning the jalapeño for another 3 minutes, for a total of 15 minutes from the start. Turn off the heat, remove the jalapeño and place it into the bowl, and keep it tightly covered for 10 minutes.

4. In a food processor, add all the charred ingredients, extra virgin olive oil, apple cider vinegar, salt, pepper and cilantro and process in bursts to keep slight bits and pieces in it. It will take about 1 to 2 minutes to process it.

5. Remove it into a bowl, add the lime juice, and stir to combine. You can store it in an airtight container, in the fridge for up to a week.

PRO TIPS

1. Dried chilis are available easily at grocery stores in the international aisle. You can even replace the pasilla chili with dried guajillo chili.

2. Deseed the pasilla chili and jalapeño, if you do not like the salsa to be spicy.

Masala Potato Chips

Serves about 4

Masala Potato Chips are an ode to my dear brother, whose love for potato chips knows no bounds! All our food-related memories involve him having potato chips. Our mum would give us 2 or 3 rupees each for us to spend a few times each week, for a snack from a tiny stall outside our school. It was a treat for us. He would get either peanuts or Masala Potato Chips, and I would always get the masala popcorn. As we grew into teenagers, we would have long chats, listening to American music on the radio till the wee hours of the night. He would get his Masala Potato Chips into the room and munch on them, while I had my masala popcorn. He could finish a huge bagful of those chips in one sitting! He also found a life partner who loves potato chips as much as he does, and they are surely going to pass it onto my niece—their daughter—as well.

These Masala Potato Chips are highly addictive, I must tell you. They are really very simple to make, and they turn out crisp and tasty with all the spices, especially enjoyed with some beer on a Friday evening after a long work week. My kids often ask me to make these, and I make them not as often as they would like, because they do get eaten in one sitting! You can easily switch up the spices to your preference. There is nothing like homemade chips, especially when you know what you are putting into them. No preservatives—pure ingredients and pure fun.

INGREDIENTS

450 grams Yukon gold white potatoes

Oil for frying

¾ teaspoon (4.5 g) table salt

¾ teaspoon red Kashmiri chili powder

¾ teaspoon chaat masala

METHOD

1. Using a mandoline, thinly slice the potatoes as thin as possible. They should not be paper thin, but just thin enough. No need to peel the skin.

2. Place the potatoes in a large bowl with cold water, and using both hands, rub the slices to remove as much starch as possible. Set it aside for 5 minutes. Drain off the water completely.

3. Place two kitchen towels side by side and remove each slice and lay each on the towel. Cover with two more towels and dab lightly to dry them out.

4. In a large wok or pot, add oil about halfway through, on high heat. Let the temperature of the oil come to 350°F (175°C). It will take about 6 to 8 minutes for the oil to heat up properly.

continued ⟶

Set aside a baking sheet with a wire baking rack on top to drain off the excess oil.

5. Test the oil by adding one slice of potato. If it rises up immediately and browns nicely within a minute, the oil is ready.

6. Add a few slices at a time. Do not overcrowd the pan. If you add more, it will bring down the temperature of the oil. There will be a lot of bubbles on the surface but it will calm down. Cook on each side for about 1½ minutes. Flip the slices after 1½ minutes and cook for another 1½ minutes, or until they are slightly brown in color.

7. Using a spider skimmer, remove the chips and place them on the baking wire rack.

8. Repeat Steps 6 and 7 until all the chips are cooked.

9. Place the chips in a large bowl. Add half the spices and toss the bowl to coat the chips well. Add the remaining spices and toss the bowl again to coat the chips well. Toss it a few times to ensure all chips are somewhat evenly coated. Some may have more masala than the others.

10. Enjoy them fresh or store in an airtight container, outside on the kitchen counter.

PRO TIPS

1. It is important that each batch cooks well and the oil is always hot at the temperature of 350°F (175°C). Otherwise, there is a chance that the chips may turn out soggy. If the oil is not hot enough after frying a batch, wait for the temperature to rise up again to 350°F (175°C).

2. Add a bit of sugar if you would like or change up the masalas too.

3. Toss the Masala Potato Chips in the Frankie Masala (page 235) to make Frankie Masala Chips.

Saffron Aioli

Makes about 1 cup (about 180 g)

This aioli uses saffron as a component. Saffron comes from a flower called saffron crocus. Saffron is the stigma and style of the flower, and has to be hand-picked gently and dried, which is why it is an expensive spice. Always get the authentic version to get the best color and flavor of the spice. The spice can be used in a sweet or a savory dish. My favorite way to use it is in desserts, of course, but I love how this spice works in an aioli, and is one of my most favorite ways to use it. The aioli gets a wonderful subtle fragrance and a pretty orange hue from the saffron. It goes fantastic with many appetizers, and would be great with baked potatoes, or the Masala Smashed Potatoes (page 116), or in this case, I have used this aioli with the Aloo Tikki Arancini (page 148), and it makes for a perfect pairing!

INGREDIENTS

1 teaspoon warm milk

¼ teaspoon saffron threads

¾ cup (160 g) mayonnaise

1 garlic clove

1 tablespoon (15 g) lemon juice

¼ teaspoon black pepper

½ teaspoon (3 g) table salt

METHOD

1. In a small bowl, add the warm milk and saffron, and let it sit for a minute. The color and fragrance of the saffron will come through.

2. In a medium bowl, add the mayonnaise. Grate in the garlic. Add the lemon juice, saffron-milk mixture, black pepper, and salt. Whisk to combine.

PRO TIPS

1. The aioli can be made 1 to 2 days in advance.

2. The aioli can be stored in an airtight container for up to a week.

Vagharela Bhaat (Turmeric Rice)

Serves 4

Day-old rice can be used in many ways. Since it is dried up, and retains less moisture, it makes for an absolutely delicious fried rice or it can be used in burritos, burgers, or soups. Different cultures make fried rice in different ways. All the Asian countries have their own way of making fried rice, with ingredients specific to their region; for example, kimchi fried rice is specific to Korea and so on. Latin American countries have their own version of fried rice.

Folks from Gujarat have our own version as well. We love to temper anything and make it a dish. If there is leftover rotli, we will use tempering spices and add the leftover rotli to it to make vaghareli rotli. And when there is leftover rice, we use the tempering spices, add the day-old rice, and make it Vagharela Bhaat, which essentially means tempered rice. I grew up eating this dish very often because we had leftover rice almost every other day, and it was easy to make and very delicious—you cannot resist it! It literally takes less than 5 minutes to put this dish together. It is best served with plain cold yogurt and some Lemon Pickle (page 59). That is my favorite way to eat it. When I was recipe testing to get the measurements correct, I had my kids try the dish and they both loved it. There are very few ingredients in this dish and it is the simplicity that I love the most!

INGREDIENTS

1 tablespoon (13 g) vegetable oil

4 to 5 fresh curry leaves

1 teaspoon (3 g) mustard seeds

½ teaspoon (1 g) cumin seeds

½ teaspoon (1 g) ground turmeric

⅓ teaspoon (1 g) red chili powder

3 cups (360 g) cooked day-old rice

½ teaspoon (3 g) table salt

GARNISH

2 tablespoons finely chopped cilantro

Cold plain yogurt

Lemon Pickle (page 59)

METHOD

1. In a medium pot on medium heat, add the vegetable oil. Once it is hot after a minute, add the curry leaves, mustard seeds, cumin seeds, ground turmeric, and red chili powder. Temper the spices for 1 minute. Then add the cooked rice and mix it well for 1 minute until it looks uniform with all the spices. Sprinkle in the salt and mix again. Cook for 2 to 3 minutes, stirring occasionally.

2. Plate the Vagharela Bhaat and garnish with the cilantro. Eat with some cold plain yogurt and Lemon Pickle.

Masala Mixed Nuts

Makes about 3½ to 4 cups

Masala nuts are readily available at all grocery stores in India and they have many different varieties, It is pretty incredible to see! The snack market in India really thrives because of its varieties and the ease it takes to carry them on public transportation for a quick bite. Masala nuts are a part and parcel of every Indian household, Indian party, and Indian gathering. Light and deep conversations, belly-holding laughter, beers and whiskeys, card games like Rummy and Teen Patti—it all happens around this iconic snack. No party is complete without them. Inspired by this really addictive snack, I created the Masala Mixed Nuts with walnuts, almonds, cashews, pistachios, and peanuts in the mix. I have fond memories of my parents throwing parties at home, or going to our family friend's home for a party. Our parents would gather around with their friends over a few games of cards, drinks, and the masala nuts, while the kids hung out, and they had their own virgin drinks and snacks to enjoy. Those were certainly fun times that I deeply cherish.

This snack comes together quickly. After mixing the nuts with the spices, the rest is done in the oven and requires some roasting time for the nuts to catch the flavor profile and crisp up, for maximum flavor, crunch, and nuttiness. It makes for a good after-school snack, and keep the kids satiated up until dinnertime, with all its protein content.

INGREDIENTS

½ cup (56 g) raw walnuts

½ cup (75 g) raw almonds

1 cup (150 g) raw cashews

½ cup (75 g) raw pistachios

1 cup (130 g) raw peanuts, with skin

3 tablespoons (42 g) vegetable oil

¾ teaspoon (2 g) amchur (dried mango powder)

1½ teaspoons (9 g) table salt

1 teaspoon (1 g) Kashmiri red chili powder

1 ¼ teaspoons granulated sugar

1 teaspoon (2 g) chaat masala

1 teaspoon (2 g) black pepper

½ teaspoon (1 g) ground turmeric

METHOD

1. In a large bowl, combine the nuts.

2. In a small saucepan over medium to low heat, add the oil. Let the oil heat up for about 30 seconds. Add all the spices and sauté for 30 seconds.

3. Add this mixture into the nuts, and, using a rubber spatula, stir to combine and make sure all the nuts are thoroughly coated with the masala mixture.

4. Preheat the oven to 300°F (150°C).

5. In a quarter sheet pan, add the nuts. Spread them evenly with the rubber spatula.

6. Place the sheet in the middle rack of the oven for a total of 35 minutes. Remove in 15-minute intervals to mix them around and spread them again evenly.

7. Remove after 35 minutes, and let cool completely.

8. Store in an airtight container in a cool place for up to 2 weeks.

Methi Laccha Thepla

Makes 12 (6½- to 7-inch, 16 to 18 cm) thepla

Fenugreek, or methi as it's called in the Gujarati language, is a leafy green that is ever so slightly bitter in taste. It has a distinct taste, with fantastic nutritious properties. It is great for balancing cholesterol, helps with digestive problems, and aides breastfeeding mothers with milk production. Methi is used a lot in Gujarati cuisine to make wonderful flavored dishes. The bitterness is balanced with other spices that are added to any dish with methi.

Gujaratis make a flatbread called thepla, which comprises a vegetable, in this case methi or fenugreek, along with a range of dry and a few whole spices, to make a dough that is really flavorful by itself once cooked. Thepla are shaped round and thin, and cooked with a little bit of oil. They are soft in texture, due to the addition of yogurt. This is our travel food. I have memories of tons of trips and vacations that we took as kids, where my mum would make at least 50-plus thepla that saved us if we had issues finding any decent food. Thepla invariably were finished within 2 to 3 days, because they would work as a perfect afternoon snack. When I left for the United States to study for my masters, I didn't know anyone in this country. I came to the university, all by myself, and had to look for an apartment and roommates within the first week. Mum's thepla came to the rescue.

Laccha paratha is a kind of paratha that is made in the northern states of India. Laccha literally means a ring. The paratha is flaky and has these beautiful rings of dough that are formed by making a fan fold of the dough, and then rolling it out round and thin. They are then cooked on the stove with some oil, and once done, they are crushed from the sides, between the palms of your hands, ever so slightly to show off their flakiness. I combined my love for methi thepla and laccha paratha to make Methi Laccha Thepla. They are flavorful with a punch—delicious and flaky, and make for a perfect breakfast, main, or a snack.

INGREDIENTS

210 grams whole wheat flour, plus extra for rolling out the dough

150 grams all-purpose flour

2 teaspoons (12 g) table salt

1 teaspoon (3 g) ground turmeric

1 teaspoon red chili powder

1 teaspoon cumin seeds

¾ teaspoon carom seeds or ajwain

1 tablespoon sesame seeds

2 teaspoons (8 g) light brown sugar

2 garlic cloves

1 inch (2½ cm) ginger

1 green chili

¾ to 1 cup (50 g) tightly packed, finely chopped methi (fenugreek leaves), thoroughly washed

2 tablespoons finely chopped cilantro

¼ cup (57 g) Greek yogurt

1 tablespoon (13.3 g) + 1 to 2 teaspoons vegetable oil

¾ cup (180 g) warm water

⅓ cup (80 g) vegetable oil or ghee, for smearing on the thepla while rolling

⅓ cup (80 g) vegetable oil, for cooking the thepla

continued →

METHOD

To Make the Dough

1. In a large bowl, add the whole wheat flour, all-purpose flour, salt, turmeric, chili powder, cumin seeds, carom seeds, sesame seeds, and light brown sugar, and mix to combine.

2. In a mini food processor, add the garlic, ginger, and green chili and grind to make a paste.

3. Add the paste, along with the fenugreek and cilantro, Greek yogurt, and 1 tablespoon vegetable oil. Mix with a spatula, or one hand to combine. It will be a coarse texture.

4. Add the water slowly to bind the mixture. Start off with ½ cup (120 g) water and then increase the quantity as required. Using your hand, bind the dough with the water, collecting all the mixture from the sides of the bowl, and bringing it to the middle. Knead the dough until well combined. The dough should be pliable. There should be no dry bits left. Add more water 1 tablespoon at a time as required. The process takes about 4 to 5 minutes. You have to keep collecting the mixture from the side and get any dry bits into the dough. Combine until you get a smooth texture on the outside and the dough feels soft.

5. Use 1 to 2 tablespoons of the vegetable oil to massage the dough on the work surface until the dough feels really smooth.

6. Place the dough back into the bowl and cover it with a damp cloth and let rest for 30 minutes.

To Make the Methi Laccha Thepla

1. Divide the dough into 12 portions, 54 to 55 grams each. Place a bowl of extra flour and a bowl with ¼ cup (40 g) vegetable oil on the side.

2. Roll each dough into a round ball, between the palms of your hands and flatten it slightly.

3. Dip the flattened round ball of dough in a bowl of extra flour on the side, coating it generously. Place it on the rolling board. Press it slightly with your fingers and roll it into a 6-inch (15 cm) round thepla. It will be thin, less than ⅛ inch (¼ cm) in height. Rolling is a technique, and it comes with practice. Place your hands on either side of the rolling pin, and gently apply pressure, alternating the pressure on either side of your hands and roll the dough in a continuous motion. It should be rhythmic. If you need extra flour, sprinkle it to make the rolling easier on you.

4. Once the thepla is about 6 inches (15 cm) round, dab your middle 3 fingers in oil or ghee and smear it on the flattened dough, to cover it entirely. Sprinkle some flour on the top. From the farthest top end, make a fan fold, horizontally toward you, by folding it about ¾ inch (2 cm) thick. Once it is completely folded, you will get a thin strip. Elongate it a little by stretching both the sides from either end. Turn the entire strip at 90 degrees, such that you can see all the folds. From the left end, start forming a snail shell pattern, like a spiral, till it forms a round. Tuck the end underneath the spiral. Press to flatten the dough.

5. Dip the flattened dough in extra flour on either side, and start rolling it again with the rolling pin on the board. Sprinkle additional flour if required to ease out the rolling action. Roll into a round shape by placing your hands on either side of the rolling pin, and gently apply pressure, alternating the pressure on either side of your hands and roll the dough in a continuous motion. Roll until you get about a 6½- to 7-inch-wide (16 to 18 cm) thepla.

6. Repeat Steps 3 to 5 for the remaining thepla.

7. Heat a medium, shallow, nonstick frying pan on medium-high heat for about 2 to 3 minutes.

8. Gently place a rolled thepla into the pan. Add about 1½ teaspoons of vegetable oil on the top. Smear it with a flat spatula, turn the thepla, and add another 1 teaspoon of vegetable oil and smear it again to coat the thepla. Turn it again. Cook on that side by gently pressing on the thepla, for about 1 to 1½ minutes, until slightly charred.

9. Turn the thepla, and gently press it to cook the other side for another minute.

10. Set it to the side on a plate.

11. Using your bare hands, crush the thepla gently from both sides, to sort of release the layers of dough, and reveal its flakiness.

12. Repeat Steps 7 to 11 for the remaining thepla.

13. Enjoy while they are still warm, with some Bateta Nu Shaak (page 181) and yogurt and delicious Lemon Pickle (page 59).

PRO TIPS

1. Fenugreek is usually available at Indian grocery stores.

2. If you do not have fenugreek, you can substitute the same amount of spinach.

3. Wrap the leftover thepla in aluminum foil and store in the fridge for up to 2 days. Warm each in the microwave for about 30 seconds before serving.

Panzanella

WITH VAGHARELI SOURDOUGH BREAD, HEIRLOOM TOMATOES, AND PEACHES

Serves 8

One of our after-school snacks was this very delicious vaghareli bread. Vaghar essentially means to temper spices, so vaghareli bread translates to tempered bread. Leftover bread gets the refined treatment with vaghar, making it really tasty by sautéing onions and curry leaves, then adding the necessary spices and the leftover bread cut into pieces. It is all sautéed together so the bread gets a slightly crispy oily crust, with fragrance from the spices, and crystallization from the sugar. The final garnish is lots of cilantro.

There would be a freshly made snack every single day waiting for us at 4 p.m. There would be chaat, ranging from bhel to sev puri to papdi chaat to vegetable chutney sandwiches and this vaghareli bread, to name a few. We were very lucky kids.

Panzanella is a very popular Italian salad, made with sourdough bread, paired with fresh tomatoes, basil, and a red wine vinaigrette that soaks into the crusty bread to make it slightly moist and delicious. I took one of my favorite snacks from my childhood and one of my favorite Italian salads from adulthood and transformed them into a Panzanella with Vaghareli Sourdough Bread. Tossed with heirloom tomatoes and peaches, and dressed up with a curry lime vinaigrette, this salad/snack is uber delicious and one that has gained popularity with my family, here in the United States. It is the perfect amalgamation of the two places I have lived: Mumbai and California. It makes me happy that I can bring a part of my childhood into my kids' childhood too, a dish that they will remember when they grow up.

INGREDIENTS

¼ cup (40 g) vegetable oil

Pinch of asafoetida

1½ teaspoons mustard seeds

1 medium (180 g) red onion, finely diced

1½ teaspoons ground turmeric

1 teaspoon red chili powder

2 teaspoons (12 g) table salt

2 teaspoons granulated sugar

450 grams sourdough bread,
    cut into 1-inch (2½ cm) pieces

CURRY LIME VINAIGRETTE

¼ cup (40 g) extra virgin olive oil

12 to 15 fresh curry leaves

1 green chili (1 more if you like it spicy),
    split into half

1 tablespoon honey

2 tablespoons lime juice

½ teaspoon salt

1 teaspoon black pepper

2 large (350 to 400 g) heirloom tomatoes,
    cut into ¾-inch pieces

2 medium (300 g) peaches, cut into ¾-inch pieces

¼ cup finely chopped cilantro, plus extra for garnish

continued ➤

METHOD

1. Preheat the oven to 400°F (200°C).

2. In a large deep skillet on medium to high heat, add the vegetable oil. After a minute of the oil getting hot, add the asafoetida and mustard seeds, and wait for 20 seconds for the seeds to splatter. Add the chopped onions and sauté for 3 to 4 minutes until slightly golden brown in color. Reduce the heat to medium to low heat. Add the turmeric, red chili powder, salt, and sugar. Sauté the mixture for about 30 seconds.

3. Next add the bread pieces and sauté the bread in the oil and spice mixture thoroughly for 2 to 3 minutes, such that the bread pieces are coated nicely with the mixture.

4. Spread the bread mixture onto a baking sheet, and bake in the preheated oven for 15 minutes.

5. Remove the baking sheet from the oven.

To Make the Curry Lime Vinaigrette

1. In a small saucepan on medium-low heat, add extra virgin olive oil and heat for a minute.

2. Add the curry leaves. They will start splattering. Wait for the curry leaves to curl slightly, about a minute. Turn off the stove.

3. Add the green chili and let it cook in the hot oil. Remove from the heat and let cool.

4. Next add the honey, lime juice, salt, and pepper and whisk to combine.

To Assemble

1. Add the bread mixture into a large mixing bowl. Add the heirloom tomatoes and peaches.

2. Pour the vinaigrette over the bread mixture, along with the cilantro. Using salad spoons, toss the mixture well to coat uniformly.

3. Plate the Panzanella and garnish with more cilantro. Enjoy!

PRO TIPS

1. Add diced cucumber as well if you wish.

2. The Panzanella is best served fresh.

Chorafali Crackers

Makes 90 to 100 (1½-inch, 4 cm) squares

Chorafali is a Gujarati snack made with chickpea flour and split black gram flour, rolled out thin into long strips that are then deep-fried. Once fried, a sprinkling of red chili powder and salt on the Chorafali gives it that distinct and delicious taste that is unparalleled—a snack you can truly binge on. Chorafali is usually made during Diwali as a snack to serve guests. It is deep fried and stored in containers for up to 2 weeks, if it even lasts that long! It is probably one of my favorite Diwali snacks. Mum always made it in bulk and stored it in these big steel containers that we had, with her name etched on the bottom in the Gujarati language. All the steel ware in India has the owner's name etched at the bottom of the pot or container, so that you always know that it is yours. When I left India to come to the United States, I had my name etched on some of the stainless steel ware as well.

I used the same flours, along with all-purpose flour in this cracker recipe, and they are healthier as you bake them in the oven. The trickiest part is rolling them out as thin as possible. You do not want them to be paper thin, but just thin enough so you can get the cracker crunch from them after they are baked and cooled. The spices, along with the split black gram flour, give these crackers all the flavor and texture, and they do taste just like Chorafali, a wonderful memory of my childhood, and all the goodies that my mum would make during Diwali time. Enjoy them with a soft cheese, like brie or a goat cheese, and pair with the Apricot and Saffron Jam (page 49) for a wonderful spicy addition to your cheese plate.

INGREDIENTS

1 cup (120 g) all-purpose flour, plus extra for rolling out dough

½ cup (52 g) chickpea flour or besan

½ cup (75 g) split black gram flour or urad flour

1½ teaspoons (9 g) table salt

1 teaspoon cracked black pepper

¼ teaspoon baking powder

½ cup (120 g) warm water

3 tablespoons (45 g) vegetable oil

Cooking spray or olive oil spray

1 teaspoon (2 g) red chili powder

¾ teaspoon rock salt

EQUIPMENT

Rolling pin

2-foot ruler

Pastry cutter or pizza cutter

Pastry brush

continued ➞

METHOD

1. In a medium bowl, sift the all-purpose flour, chickpea flour, and split black gram flour to remove any lumps in the flour. Add the salt, pepper, and baking powder, and whisk to combine.

2. Add the vegetable oil to the warm water. Add the warm water to the flour mixture and, using a small rubber spatula, mix it slowly to combine. Clean the sides of the bowl, to get all the dry flour mixture into the middle of the bowl.

3. Get in with your hands and mix the dough to combine. Get all the dry bits from the bowl.

4. Start massaging the dough. Knead the dough on a clean work surface for about 2 to 3 minutes, with the base of the palm of your hand, pushing it out, then folding the dough, and repeating the motion until you get a smooth, soft, pliable dough.

5. Cover it with a damp paper towel in the bowl, and let it rest for 10 to 15 minutes.

6. Preheat the oven to 400°F (200°C).

7. Line two baking sheets with parchment paper.

8. Divide the dough in half. Keep one half of the dough covered with the damp paper towel.

9. On a clean work surface, sprinkle some of the all-purpose flour. Flatten the dough into a rectangular shape on the floured surface. Sprinkle more flour on the top.

10. Using a rolling pin, start rolling the dough to form a rough rectangle. Keep rolling evenly until the dough is about 1/16 inch thick. It should be very thin, not paper thin, but as thin as possible. You can roll it out to approximately 8 by 14 inches (20 by 35 cm).

11. Trim the edges with a pastry cutter to form a neat rectangle.

12. Using a pastry cutter and a ruler, you can measure and cut out 1½-inch (4 cm) strips lengthwise, and then cut out 1½-inch (4 cm) strips widthwise.

13. Lightly spray cooking spray or olive oil spray all over the dough.

14. Sprinkle the red chili powder first evenly all over the dough, then repeat with the rock salt. Place the squares on the parchment paper on one of the baking sheets.

15. Repeat steps 9, 10, 11, 12, 13, 14, and 15 with the second dough.

16. Place one baking sheet at a time on the bottom rack of the oven and bake for approximately 12 minutes, until the crackers are a slight golden brown in color. If you remove it a bit early, the cracker may be soft in the middle and not totally crispy.

17. Remove the first baking sheet from the oven and place the second baking sheet in for 12 minutes. Let the crackers cool for 30 minutes.

18. Store in an airtight container for up to 1 week. Enjoy the crackers with some soft cheese and the Apricot and Saffron Jam (page 49).

 PRO TIP You can replace the rock salt with sea salt, although the crackers taste best with rock salt.

Acknowledgments

This book is a tribute to my dearest mother, Hemlata—who was my best friend and confidante. Every story has a beginning, and mine was by your side, as a 9 year old, in our kitchen in Mumbai. I carry on your lessons to my kids, my family and my loved ones. You put me on a journey of love, food, and perseverance—one I will travel for the rest of my life. But most importantly, you instilled in your children compassion and empathy, raising them as kind human beings. This book would not exist without you. Love for forever, Mum.

To my dear dad, Mahendra. If mom was passion, you were logic. Your cool, thoughtful, and loving approach to life is the perfect balance to the lessons Mum taught me. Without them, I could never be the person I am today. Your lessons of hard work and perseverance drove me, as I completed this cookbook during a very challenging year. Thank you for always lending me your ear, and for showing me encouragement and great advice whenever I needed it the most.

Thank you to my not-so-little brother, Varun, for your support and for listening to me always. I miss spending time with you, especially our late-night talks after Mum and Dad went to sleep! Dude, I could have really used your belly during cookbook testing times! I miss you!

To my dearest family in England, your love and support has been physical, spiritual, and cultural. To my aunts, especially: you've been like surrogate mothers, all these years. I love you all.

Thank you to my mother-in-law, Deepa, and father-in-law, Narain, for your encouragement and support throughout the entire process, as I went on and on about my cookbook.

To my literary agent, Leigh Eisenmann, for believing in my concept and pitching me to publishing companies. You have always been there for me, replying to each and every happy or frustrated email. You have been proactive and held my hand throughout the process, in ways that I had never imagined! A BIG thank-you.

Thank you to my editor, Michael Tizzano at The Countryman Press, for believing in me and my story, and for giving me the opportunity to share it with the world.

Thank you to Adam and Ryan, from the lovely blog, *Husbands That Cook*, and Rebecca from the fun baking blog, *Displaced Housewife*, for your unwavering support and friendship.

A huge thank-you to all my recipe testers: Pinky Jhaveri, Jaimini Shah, Maryanne Welton, Acha Kamath, Varun Dodhia, Anushree Dodhia, Mary-Ann Dwyer, Shivani Sheth, and Roopa Nithyu, for helping out with all the recipe testing and giving constructive feedback.

To Iain Bagwell and Torie Cox: working with you both was daily inspiration in passion for craft and empathy in learning. I challenged you every day, with everything from Mumbai street food to making sure you had the perfect Gujarati daal. You met each challenge with good humor and skill. I will be forever grateful.

To the Instagram community, for always supporting me with my blog and feed. And to many of you, who have believed in my flavor combinations and have asked for a cookbook from me over all these years, thank you from the bottom of my heart!

Leaving the best for last, without whom this cookbook would not exist—my husband, Raj, and my beautiful kids, Anishka and Rishan. To my kids, you both have been my amazing little taste-testers, giving me great feedback throughout the process. What would I have done without such a mature palate from both of you!? Thank you for your utmost patience with me. You bring joy to me with your thoughtfulness, and I hope both of you will cook from this book when you grow older. I love you both to pieces.

Raj, you have been a constant throughout my food journey, encouraging me at every step of the way, right from the Jam Lab–days of owning my jam business, from designing labels to help-ing me shape my photography style, for which I have received many compliments over the years! Thank you for all your advice, for cheering me up with your witty humor, and for your pep talks on days when I doubt whether I am capable of achieving all this: a cookbook, a full-time job, and a family to feed. Thank you for the grocery runs, the infinite dishes that you had to wash, the critiques of my recipes, and the help with all my photo shoots. Thank you for correcting my written English and providing feedback on all the little details in the cookbook. I'm blessed to have a Creative Writer and Photography Art Director in-house! We make a great team. You truly are the best! I love you.

—Amisha

Index